T0318766

Evaluating Social Media Marketing

This book is an innovative attempt to identify and analyse the processes related to social influence in online buying behaviour, with special attention given to the phenomenon of social proof, which is the basis of social media, recommendation marketing, and word-of-mouth (WOM) marketing. It empirically verifies the factors which influence the effectiveness of social proof, and identifies relevant impact factors.

Opening with a literature review of this concept from the perspective of social psychology, sociology, and marketing, this interdisciplinary approach to the issue allows for an in-depth understanding of the mechanisms of the effective use of social proof in contemporary online marketing. Following this, in the context of theoretical considerations, the author analyses the social role and significance of social proof in the buying behaviours of online consumers. The second half of the book presents the results of the author's quantitative and qualitative research into the effectiveness of social proof. The quantitative research verifies the hypotheses concerning the social role and significance of social proof in buying decisions and identifies the level of confidence in the opinions expressed by other web users. The qualitative research focuses on the empirical verification of the effectiveness of social proof mechanisms. Additionally, attention is given to sensitivity to social proof, i.e. the factors that increase the effectiveness of such messages, from both the sender's and the recipient's perspective, as well as the forms and channels of communication.

Written for scholars and researchers interested in the debate on the transparency of activities carried out by companies in the area of online marketing, the book's detailed analysis of influence utilizing both quantitative and qualitative studies may be of interest to a wider group of academics including economists, psychologists, and sociologists.

Katarzyna Sanak-Kosmowska – PhD in Economics, MSc in Psychology, Assistant Professor, Department of Marketing, College of Management Sciences and Quality, Cracow University of Economics, Poland. Her research interests include online marketing communication, the psychology of consumer behaviour, and advertising. She is the author of *Rola Serwisów Społecznościowych w Komunikacji Marketingowej Marki* (*The Role of Social Networking in Brand Marketing Communications*). She is a member of the American Marketing Association, member of the International Association of Researchers and Scientists in Latvia, member of the Polish Scientific Marketing Association, and member of the Spokespersons for Science Association.

Routledge Studies in Marketing

This series welcomes proposals for original research projects that are either single or multi-authored or an edited collection from both established and emerging scholars working on any aspect of marketing theory and practice and provides an outlet for studies dealing with elements of marketing theory, thought, pedagogy and practice.

It aims to reflect the evolving role of marketing and bring together the most innovative work across all aspects of the marketing 'mix' – from product development, consumer behaviour, marketing analysis, branding, and customer relationships, to sustainability, ethics, and the new opportunities and challenges presented by digital and online marketing.

19 **Brand Management in a Co-Creation Perspective**
Communication as Constitutive of Brands
Heidi Hansen

20 **New Consumer Culture in China**
The Flower Market and New Everyday Consumption
Xi Liu

21 **Information Asymmetry in Online Advertising**
Jan W. Wiktor and Katarzyna Sanak-Kosmowska

22 **Evaluating Social Media Marketing**
Social Proof and Online Buyer Behaviour
Katarzyna Sanak-Kosmowska

For more information about this series, please visit: www.routledge.com/Routledge-Studies-in-Marketing/book-series/RMKT

Evaluating Social Media Marketing

Social Proof and Online Buyer
Behaviour

Katarzyna Sanak-Kosmowska

**Reviewed by Prof. dr hab. Henryk Mruk
Translated by Jasper Tilbury and
Mark Aldridge**

Routledge
Taylor & Francis Group

LONDON AND NEW YORK

First published 2022
by Routledge
2 Park Square, Milton Park, Abingdon, Oxon OX14 4RN

and by Routledge
605 Third Avenue, New York, NY 10158

Routledge is an imprint of the Taylor & Francis Group, an informa business

© 2022 Katarzyna Sanak-Kosmowska

British Library Cataloguing-in-Publication Data
A catalogue record for this book is available from the British Library

Library of Congress Cataloging-in-Publication Data
A catalog record has been requested for this book

ISBN: 978-0-367-64652-3 (hbk)
ISBN: 978-0-367-65145-9 (pbk)
ISBN: 978-1-003-12805-2 (ebk)

DOI: 10.4324/9781003128052

Typeset in Times New Roman
by codeMantra

Contents

List of figures   vii
List of tables   ix
Preface   xi
Acknowledgements   xiii

1 Introduction   1

PART I
The phenomenon of social impact in online marketing   5

2 Theoretical framework – online marketing: between
  persuasion and manipulation   7

3 The structure of functions, forms, and organization of
  selected strategies of marketing communication and
  employed tools in the virtual environment   30

4 Social influence and its manifestation in the
  hypermedia computer environment: reasons, definition,
  models, and characteristics   51

5 Social proof as a key factor in social commerce   83

PART II
Social proof in marketing: effectiveness and impact awareness   99

6 Research model, objectives, and hypotheses   101

7 Confidence in social proof and its impact on
  buying decisions   112

8 Characteristics of indicators of social proof based on
  experimental research   136

9 Discussion of findings in a global context   163

10 Summary   170

   Index   173

Figures

2.1 A model of hypermedia communication in the Internet environment 10

2.2 The 'messy middle' interpretation of the purchasing-decision path taken by e-consumers 14

2.3 The evolution of marketing 14

2.4 SM honeycomb model 16

3.1 T-shape marketing concept 31

3.2 Matrix of online marketing tools 33

3.3 Influencers' communication with e-consumers 37

3.4 Communication model of viral marketing 43

3.5 The influence of WOM on consumer loyalty 46

5.1 Categories of online reviews and product ratings 86

5.2 E-commerce 1.0 and social commerce: key differentiating features 92

6.1 The role of comments and reviews in communication between firms and e-consumers 102

6.2 Model of susceptibility to social proof on social media 103

6.3 Assessment of the reliability and frequency of reference to online reviews and susceptibility to social media 106

7.1 Student's t-test for the index of the influence of other Internet users ($p < 0.01$) 116

7.2 The values of the index broken down according to demographic variables 117

7.3 Stages in the data analysis 118

7.4 Graphical illustration of a model of four latent classes 121

7.5 Distribution of participants' gender and age across the four latent classes 123

7.6 Frequency of Internet use across the four latent classes 124

7.7 Frequency of Facebook use across the four latent classes 125

7.8 Frequency of Instagram use across the four latent classes 125

7.9 Use of Internet for professional purposes across the four latent classes 126

7.10 Agreement with the statement 'Internet access makes my work easier' across the four latent classes 127

7.11 Frequency of online shopping across the four latent classes   127
7.12 Agreement with the statement 'Advertising makes it easier to select products and make a purchase' across the four latent classes   128
7.13 Agreement with the statement 'Advertising speeds up the purchasing process' across the four latent classes   129
7.14 Agreement with the statement 'Advertising makes it easier to decide' across the four latent classes   130
7.15 Agreement with the statement 'Advertising is conducive to positive product evaluations' across the four latent classes   130
7.16 Disclosure of personal data when subscribing to newsletters across the four latent classes   131
7.17 Disclosure of personal data when taking part in Internet competitions and promotions across the four latent classes   132
7.18 Disclosure of personal data when creating user accounts in online shops across the four latent classes   132
8.1 Variables manipulated in Experiment I: A – control group; B – experimental group   140
8.2 Variables manipulated in Experiment II: A – control group; B – experimental group   141
8.3 Variables manipulated in Experiment III: A – control group; B – experimental group   142
8.4 Factors influencing e-consumers' purchasing decisions (Experiments I–III)   147
8.5 Purchases made under the influence of online reviews and recommendations (Experiments I–III)   148
8.6 General assessment of products in Experiment I (control group vs experimental group). The assessments are expressed on a scale of 1–5, where 1 is the lowest and 5 is the highest   149
8.7 General assessment of products in Experiment II (control group vs experimental group). The assessments are expressed on a scale of 1–5, where 1 is the lowest and 5 is the highest   150
8.8 General assessment of products in Experiment III (control group vs experimental group). The assessments are expressed on a scale of 1–5, where 1 is the lowest and 5 is the highest   151
8.9 Theoretical model of the role of moderating variables in the relationship between exposure to a message conveying social proof and willingness to share product opinions with other users   153
8.10 Distribution of median scores for the moderating variables (experimental group, Experiment I)   154
8.11 Personality traits versus overall product assessment (experimental group, Experiment I)   156

Tables

2.1	Classification of online marketing tools	9
2.2	A comparison of the traditional process of content publishing with that of the 'new media'	11
2.3	Principles of marketing in the context of the development of ICT (Scott 2009)	12
2.4	Selected models of consumer behaviour	13
2.5	Categories of gratifications offered by SM according to Denis McQuail	18
3.1	Typology of marketing communication strategies and online marketing tools	32
3.2	Selected definitions of the term 'influencer'	35
3.3	Classification criteria and key characteristics of influencers	36
4.1	Primary message types published on websites based on Web 2.0 technology	59
4.2	The personality traits of the Big Five model	69
5.1	Types of social proof-based messages in the digital environment	85
5.2	Selected tools for managing e-consumer reviews and feedback	87
5.3	Selected proposals for the definition of social commerce	91
5.4	The most important features of social commerce	93
7.1	Characteristics of the Polish e-consumers included in the study ($N = 1,004$)	113
7.2	Construction of an index of the influence of other Internet users	116
7.3	Dependent variables referring to social proof	120
7.4	Models (segmentations) of the LCA adapted to the variables referring to social proof	120
7.5	Characteristics of the latent classes	121
7.6	Summary of hypotheses tested in the CAWI survey ($N = 1,004$)	133
8.1	The demographic characteristics of the participants in the experimental research	138

8.2   The manipulated (independent) variables   142
8.3   Measurement of personality constructs based on TIPI
       (Gosling et al. 2003)   144
8.4   Instruments measuring susceptibility to social influence
       (Busch et al. 2013; Kaptein et al. 2012)   145
8.5   Frequency of social media use: distribution of responses   146
8.6   Willingness to share opinions on products or services with
       other Internet users (Experiments I–III)   152
8.7   Spearman's rank correlation coefficient values for the
       variable specifying willingness to recommend products
       to friends   153
8.8   Statistical significance of relationships between personality
       traits and susceptibility to social proof (Kruskal-Wallis test)   155
8.9   Statistical significance of the influence of self-esteem
       on a variable specifying overall evaluation of a product
       (Kruskal-Wallis test)   157
8.10 Spearman's rank correlation coefficient values for three
       dimensions of a relationship between the level of self-
       esteem and overall susceptibility to social influence   157
8.11 Parameters of the linear regression for constructs of
       susceptibility to social influence (Experiment I)   158
8.12 Verification of the hypotheses adopted in the
       experimental research   160
10.1 Determinants of susceptibility to social proof in the online
       environment   172

Preface

Social media, which became widespread at the beginning of the twenty-first century, have introduced an entirely new quality to the marketing communication of firms. The way in which brands communicate with their audiences has become interactive, bi-directional, non-linear, and almost instantaneous, and e-consumers themselves are now equipped with an entirely new set of tools. With the rapid growth of social media, Internet users have become co-creators, reviewers, and sources of opinion for other Internet users. It is also significant that consumers are growing ever more averse to traditional advertisements and that the creators of those advertisements enjoy little public trust (cf. Soh et al. 2009). Due to their specific nature, social media constitute an attractive space for creating and sharing recommendations and for the activities of the 'social proof industry'. Social media also offer an extremely interesting research field. Indeed, there have been many attempts in the literature to interpret susceptibility to social media recommendations (cf. Buettner 2017; Correa 2015; Turcotte et al. 2015) and their actual influence on purchasing decisions (cf. Amblee & Bui 2011; Guo & Johnson 2020; Filieri et al. 2020). Through a review of the subject literature, which is presented in Chapter 2, it was possible to identify important substantive and methodological gaps in the research.

The aim of previous international research attempting to identify factors that differentiate susceptibility to social proof has been to verify the influence of various psychological traits, such as personality, temperament, and sense of control. Interdisciplinary approaches, however, which would make it possible to examine not only individual differences, but also attitudes towards advertising, consumer habits, and the degree of the professionalization of Internet use, have been scarce. The aim of this book is to identify the factors influencing susceptibility to social proof and to investigate the awareness of its manipulative nature. It should be noted, however, that although mechanisms exist for identifying the truth of reviews and opinions, firms – making use of information asymmetry in the process of marketing communication – remain one step ahead of consumers. An example of this informational advantage is the ability to control the order and way in which reviews are displayed and the capacity to quickly personalize the recommendations displayed so that they are tailored to the recipients' demographics. Research (cf. Sanak-Kosmowska & Wiktor 2020) has demonstrated that it is possible in the course of latent class analysis to identify segments of e-consumers with similar levels of awareness of manipulation in online advertising and similar preferences with regard to forms and strategies of Internet advertising. It can be assumed, therefore, that this also applies to using social media recommendations as a source of consumer information: not all Internet users are susceptible to them, and those that are susceptible to this form of social proof do not have full trust in it. The central research objective of this book, therefore, is to attempt to describe the factors that differentiate susceptibility to social proof and to determine how they do so.

References

Amblee, N., & Bui, T. (2011) Harnessing the influence of social proof in online shopping: The effect of electronic word of mouth on sales of digital microproducts. *International Journal of Electronic Commerce, 16*(2), pp. 91–114, doi:10.2753/JEC1086-4415160205

Buettner, R. (2017). Predicting user behavior in electronic markets based on personality-mining in large online social networks. *Electronic Markets, 27*, pp. 247–265.

Correa, T. (2015). Digital skills and social media use: How Internet skills are related to different types of Facebook use among 'digital natives'. *Information, Communication & Society.* doi:10.1080/1369118X.2015.1084023.

Filieri, R., Hofacker, Ch., & Alguezaui, S. (2017). What makes information in online consumer reviews diagnostic over time? The role of review relevancy, factuality, currency, source credibility and ranking score. *Computers in Human Behavior, 80*, doi:10.1016/j.chb.2017.10.039.

Guo, L., & Johnson, B. G. (2020). Third-person effect and hate speech censorship on Facebook, *Social Media + Society.* https://doi.org/10.1177/2056305120923003

Sanak-Kosmowska, K., & Wiktor, J. W. (2020). Empirical identification of latent classes in the assessment of information asymmetry and manipulation in online advertising. *Sustainability, 12*, 8693. https://doi.org/10.3390/su12208693

Soh, H., Reid, L. N., & Whitehill King, K. (2009) Measuring trust in advertising. *Journal of Advertising, 38*(2), pp. 83–104, doi:10.2753/JOA0091-3367380206

Turcotte, J., York, C., Irving, J., Scholl, R. M., & Pingree, R. J. (2015). News recommendations from social media opinion leaders: Effects on media trust and information seeking. *Journal of Computer Mediated Communication, 20*, pp. 520–535. https://doi.org/10.1111/jcc4.12127

Acknowledgements

This book is the result of many years of research into consumer behaviour in the virtual environment conducted at the Cracow University of Economics' Department of Marketing; it would not have seen the light of day had it not been for the tremendous support and assistance provided by numerous people. I wish to take this opportunity to extend my heartfelt thanks to all of them.

Words of gratitude are due to the Head of the Department of Marketing, Professor Jan W. Wiktor. I am extremely grateful for the help and kindness he has shown to me during the writing of this book. I also wish to thank him for our many years of collaboration on research projects, which has greatly contributed to my academic career.

I owe a debt of gratitude to the authorities of the Cracow University of Economics for their organizational and substantive support during my work on the book, and to the National Science Centre for awarding me research grant No 2018/29/B/HS4/00563 (Information asymmetry in online advertising and the manipulation of e-consumer behaviour), which enabled me to fund the research presented herein.

I am no less grateful to my publisher, Routledge (UK), for taking on the project. I am deeply indebted to Guy Loft and Manjusha Mishra, my editors there, for their comprehensive support throughout the editorial process.

I would like to thank Professor Henryk Mruk, who reviewed the manuscript.

I would also like to thank Jasper Tilbury and Mark Aldridge for their excellent translation of this book.

Finally, a special word of thanks goes to my loved ones: my husband, son, and parents. Without their help, daily support, and above all their faith in me and my abilities, this book could never have been written.

Katarzyna Sanak-Kosmowska

1 Introduction

In his novel *The Picture of Dorian Gray*, Oscar Wilde famously stated, 'There is only one thing in the world worse than being talked about, and that is not being talked about'. When he published this work in 1890 he definitely could not have expected that those words would provide such an accurate diagnosis of the direction taken by modern marketing – especially the nature and forms of marketing communication (Mruk 2012). Now, in the twenty-first century, *emo sapiens*, guided by emotions and by likings, and susceptible to social influence, has replaced the paradigm of the rational consumer: *homo oeconomicus* (Ohme 2017). In their attempts to adjust their offers to consumer requirements, modern firms are using ever more advanced marketing research methods and algorithms to implement their marketing communication strategies. One of the tools they use is social influence marketing and the management of online reviews and recommendations.

The aim of this book is to assess the role of that specific form of social influence known as social proof in e-consumers' decision-making processes and to understand what determines susceptibility to it. There are two important reasons for formulating the aim in this way. The first concerns the dynamic advances in the field of technology, which are influencing changes in e-consumers' purchasing models. The virtual environment, and the Internet in particular, has become not only the place to search for information about products and services, but also increasingly the place to purchase them. The second refers to the cognitive processes that underpin e-consumers' purchasing decisions, about which little academic research has been done. The book's specific aims are formulated in three dimensions: cognitive, empirical, and practical.

The objective at the *cognitive level* is to identify the degree to which social proof – as expressed by Internet users in the form of opinions, reviews, and recommendations concerning brand advertising – influences e-consumers' purchasing decisions, and to identify the determinants of their susceptibility to it. Accomplishing the book's central objective involves verifying the influence of e-consumers' behavioural, demographic, and psychographic features. The nature of the message itself – particularly the type of product

DOI: 10.4324/9781003128052-1

or brand, the form of exposure, and the nature of the content based on social proof – is assumed to be a significant determinant of susceptibility.

Formulating the book's central objective involves diagnosing certain premises, two of which are highlighted here.

First, the majority of research in this area has been – and continues to be – conducted in the field of social psychology. Its primary focus is on individual differences and not on the nature of marketing communications containing content based on social proof (cf. Jacquet et al. 2018; Phares 1965; Walters & Parke 1964). For its part, marketing-centred research in most cases limits the measurement of susceptibility to social influence to a particular context, such as the category of products studied or the marketing tool used (cf. Hoffmann & Broekhuizen 2009; Khare & Rakesh 2011).

Second, comparatively little research has produced multi-level and multidimensional analyses of e-consumer behaviour. This book posits that interdisciplinarity in the study of e-consumer behaviour, which is the approach taken by the research presented in Chapters 7 and 8, offers a richer understanding of people's natures (Mruk 2017). The results of that research made it possible to accomplish the empirical and practical objectives set out in this monograph.

At the *empirical level*, the specific objective was to conduct empirical research enabling the formulated hypotheses to be verified. The following research-design assumptions were adopted. First, reflecting the book's title, the scope of the research was narrowed to marketing communications based on social proof and containing Internet users' reviews, recommendations, and evaluations. Second, attention was focused exclusively on social proof in the virtual environment and, in particular, in the social media space. The research model is set out in detail in Chapter 6, while the results are discussed in Chapters 7 and 8.

In addition to their contribution to the science of marketing, the research results and the conclusions that flow from them will also help to achieve the *practical objectives* in two ways. First, for firms, the research results can serve as an important resource for shaping effective online marketing communication strategies – especially where social media are concerned. Second, for Internet users, they can offer a platform for acquiring market knowledge so that they can become familiar with online advertisers' communication mechanisms, educate themselves by acquiring or honing digital and social competences, and develop an awareness that will permit them to detect hidden persuasion and manipulation in advertising messages. Marketing and advertising ethics form an integral part of this study of social proof and online buyer behaviour.

The book is divided into two parts. The first – on the phenomenon of social impact and influence in online marketing – lays out the theoretical framework for the book's subject. It consists of four chapters.

Chapter 1 comprises this introduction. Chapter 2 considers the determinants of the process of the digitization of marketing. Further, it describes the changes under way in marketing communication and presents new models of the way consumers behave when making decisions to purchase online. With the subject of social proof and online buyer behaviour in mind, special attention is paid to the function and importance of online marketing, including social media marketing. A review of the literature devoted to the phenomenon of persuasion and manipulation in online marketing forms an important part of the discussion.

Chapter 3 builds on the themes addressed in Chapter 2 and explores them in greater depth. It begins with a classification of e-marketing tools, with particular emphasis on those whose functioning is based on social influence. They include influencer marketing, electronic word-of-mouth, buzz marketing, viral marketing, celebrity endorsement, and relationship marketing. The chapter presents a detailed description of these tools that is closely linked to the subject of the book.

Chapter 4 sets out a selection of core themes concerning social impact and social influence. Their analysis is prefaced by a specification of the role and importance of social impact and social influence in contemporary advertising. The chapter then presents the history of research into social impact and social influence and looks at selected models of influence drawn from sociology and psychology. Three issues are given particular attention. The first concerns the phenomenon of social influence in the online environment. The second refers to the forms and manifestations of social influence, to possible strategies of influence, and to the social influence principles proposed by Robert Cialdini. The third examines the research into the individual differences – personality traits, self-esteem, self-evaluation – that determine susceptibility to social influence.

In Chapter 5, the theoretical analysis focuses on social proof and online buyer behaviour, in particular the category of social proof in the digital environment, the definition and characteristics of social proof as a concept, types of marketing messages based on social proof, and marketing tools that enable control of reviews and recommendations. Chapter 5 also outlines the problem of fake reviews as one example of unfair practice on the part of firms. The theme of social commerce, which refers to Internet purchases made in the social media environment, is then taken up. The chapter concludes with definitions of social shopping and a description of its most salient features – features that are significant from the point of view of the book's objectives.

Part 2, entitled Social Proof in Marketing: Effectiveness and Impact Awareness (Chapters 6–9), contains an analysis and evaluation of the empirical research carried out. Chapter 6 sets out the assumptions of the author's research model and offers a theoretical justification of the formulated research hypotheses. Chapters 7 and 8 discuss the research results, which were obtained by two methods: quantitative surveys of Polish e-consumers ($N = 1,004$) using computer-assisted web interviewing (CAWI) and three Internet experiments conducted in a Polish and in an international setting.

The following are analysed: (1) the role of social proof in the process by which e-consumers make purchasing decisions and (2) the determinants of susceptibility to social proof.

Chapter 9 summarizes the research results and discusses the limitations of the research. Emphasizing that it is important and necessary to conduct research in an international environment and to include cultural factors in research models, it concludes by suggesting avenues for further research into the role of social proof in modern marketing.

References

Hoffmann, A. O. I., & Broekhuizen, T. L. J. (2009). Susceptibility to and impact of interpersonal influence in an investment context. *Journal of the Academic Marketing Science, 37*, pp. 488–503, https://doi.org/10.1007/s11747-008-0128-7.

Jacquet, P. O., Wyart, V., & Desantis, A. (2018). Human susceptibility to social influence and its neural correlates are related to perceived vulnerability to extrinsic morbidity risks. *Scientific Reports, 8*, pp. 133–147, https://doi.org/10.1038/s41598-018-31619-8.

Khare, A., & Rakesh, S. (2011). Antecedents of online shopping behavior in India: An examination. *Journal of Internet Commerce, 10*(4), pp. 227–244, doi:10.1080/15332861.2011.622691.

Mruk, H. (2012). *Marketing. Satysfakcja klienta i rozwój przedsiębiorstwa.* Warszawa: Wydawnictwo Naukowe PWN.

Mruk, H. (2017). Zachowania konsumentów w świetle ekonomii behawioralnej, *Studia Ekonomiczne. Zeszyty Naukowe Uniwersytetu Ekonomicznego w Katowicach, 317*, pp. 82–95.

Ohme, R. (2017). *Emo Sapiens. Harmonia emocji i rozumu.* Ożarów Mazowiecki: Bukowy Las.

Phares, E. J. (1965). Internal-external control as a determinant of amount of social influence exerted. *Journal of Personality and Social Psychology, 2*(5), pp. 642–647. https://doi.org/10.1037/h0022710.

Walters, R. H., & Parke, R. D. (1964). Social motivation, dependency, and susceptibility to social influence advances in experimental social psychology. *Academic Press, 1*, pp. 231–276.

Wilde, O. (1890). *The picture of Dorian Gray.* London: Lippincott's Monthly Magazine.

Part I

The phenomenon of social impact in online marketing

2 Theoretical framework – online marketing

Between persuasion and manipulation

Introduction

The starting point for considering social influence in online advertising is to attempt to identify and organize the concepts that refer to this phenomenon and that find their expression in the various tools now used by marketing professionals. The forms and tools of advertising that firms use to communicate with the environment are evolving in conjunction with the dynamic development of information and communication technologies (ICT). Traditional communication tools are gradually being replaced by ever newer forms of online marketing that offer cheaper and faster access to target groups and facilitate consumer feedback. A special case is marketing communication on social network sites (SNS), where contemporary brands attract observers and fans to create a special segment of users: a brand community. The personalization and personification of brand-consumer relationships constitute an important space and platform for persuasion and manipulation. The aim of this chapter is to situate the question of social proof and online buyer behaviour within a theoretical framework. It should be stressed that this question, which has been widely addressed in the marketing and management sciences, is very much an interdisciplinary question. Indeed, it has attracted the attention of a number of social science disciplines, but also of technical and engineering ones.

A two-stage literature analysis, closely linked to the book's aims, is performed. First, online marketing and selected associated topics are defined. Particular attention is paid to social media (SM). What defines the content published on SM? How can that content be characterized? Second, a theoretical discussion of the categories of persuasion and manipulation, which relates these ideas to the issue of SM marketing, is presented.

Online marketing: the background to digitization

The first papers to set out the business potential of commerce on the World Wide Web appeared in management science literature when the Internet era began in the early 1990s. Their authors detected its importance and growth

DOI: 10.4324/9781003128052-3

potential primarily in the possibility of expanding distribution channels and increasing firms' organizational effectiveness (Hansen 1995; Westland & Au 1997). In fact, the precursors of academic writing on Internet marketing were already studying consumer perceptions of online shopping in the mid-1990s (Jarvenpaa & Todd 1996). Despite the technological limitations of online stores at that time, consumers and researchers were in agreement as to the advantages and sharp rise in the importance of e-commerce. Primarily, they emphasized 24/7 access to shopping, the partial removal of geographical constraints, and the facilitation and acceleration of customer-firm communication. Apart from serving to refresh historical information, reading the first academic articles devoted to online marketing compels us to reflect on the dynamic growth and development of this field of management. At the beginning of the present century, online marketing was defined – in the narrow sense, referring only to its sales function and direct distribution channels – as 'the use of the Internet as a virtual storefront where products are sold directly to the customer' (Kiang et al. 2000, p. 383). Another more common approach, presented in the literature by, among others, William Pride (Pride & Ferrell 2007), suggested that Internet marketing is a manifestly broader category constituted not only by Internet sales, but also by 'the strategic process of creating, distributing, promoting, and pricing products for targeted customers in the virtual environment of the Internet'. In accordance with this definition, which posits a broad understanding of the concept, many different categories of online commercial activity can find shelter under the umbrella of Internet marketing. Examples include online customer relationship management, e-commerce, technological architecture for online auctions, SM marketing, electronic branding, search engine optimization (SEO), search engine marketing (SEM), marketing automation, electronic word-of-mouth, and online advertising. What is more, it may be assumed given the dynamic advance of ICT that this is not an exhaustive list. For the purposes of this book, it has been assumed, following the work of Steven Dann and Susan Dann (2011), that the term online marketing includes any type of marketing activity that requires the use of any form of interactive technology to accomplish marketing objectives. Nowadays, the term online marketing is often used interchangeably with e-marketing, Internet marketing, and electronic marketing – this approach is also taken here.

With the development of new information technologies, ever newer tools are being created that firms can use in their communication and marketing activities. Here, and especially in the academic literature, there prevails a certain 'pragmatism' derived from practical experience, which is revealed in a lack of in-depth analysis aimed at identifying classification criteria and elaborating uniform tools. It can be stated, then, that there exist two areas in which firms pursue their promotional activities: the 'real world' of offline marketing and the virtual world of online marketing. The former is well documented and researched, including in the academic literature. The second is characterized by lability and a constant need for exploration: existing tools, whose popularity rapidly fades, are superseded by ever newer ones, and stability and predictability are lacking. Let us take one of the most popular tools of online marketing communication – the banner advertisement – as an example. In 1994, the AT&T advertising agency placed the first ever banner advertisement on the World Wide Web (The First Banner Ad 2014). They are still widely used, although now their functionality has been greatly expanded and their appearance and form differ significantly from that of the AT&T prototype. In the space of only a decade, the Internet has become a mass medium, rapidly adapting to individual consumer needs. There is an extensive marketing and management literature that discusses the reasons for these changes and their determinants. The direction of development of online marketing is to be oriented towards users, who express their needs themselves and who expect their preferences to be taken into account. The classification presented in Table 2.1, which is based on the different strategies deployed for communicating with potential recipients, is offered as a systematization of the tools of Internet marketing. A push strategy involves direct action that exerts an influence on potential customers and aims to persuade them to purchase a product or change their perception of the firm. A pull strategy, in turn, is one in which the customers initiate a relationship with the firm (Kumar & Shah 2004). The idea underlying the third group of tools, those that are based on sharing, is to encourage the recipients to initiate a relationship with the firm of their own accord and to share information about it with other Internet users. This group of tools is important from the point of view of the aims of the book and the question of social proof and online buyer behaviour.

This book is devoted to the characteristics, types, and operating mechanisms of 'share'-type interactive tools. The first step in their analysis is to properly define the marketing communication model present in the hypermedia Internet environment. Donna L. Hoffman and Thomas P. Novak (1996) define hypermedia as a 'combination of hypertextual access to information based on logical and non-hierarchical links between messages and a multimedia form of expression and transmission of that information'. Hester Bornman and S.H. von Solms (1993) understand hypertext as a technique for the non-sequential recording of information that makes it possible

Table 2.1 Classification of online marketing tools

Groups of online marketing communication tools	*Examples*
'Push'-type online tools	Graphic advertising, search engine advertising, cost-per-click advertising (CPC), certain electronic public relations tools (EPR)
'Pull'-type online tools	E-mail marketing, mobile marketing, content marketing
'Share'-type interactive tools	Viral marketing, marketing on social network services, recommendation marketing

to connect individual pieces of information by means of paths or links. In practice, this model is implemented through the World Wide Web, which is a system for making documents available on the Internet. The essence of the communication model in a hypermedia computer-mediated environment is displayed in Figure 2.1.

The message in this model is a multimedia message that can take both dynamic forms (sound, film, animation) and static forms (text, drawings, images). The interactions taking place on the World Wide Web are qualitatively new. Both personal and 'machine' (technical) interactions are possible. The medium no longer functions as a channel of communication, but instead creates an entirely new communication environment consisting of two dimensions: a real dimension and a hypermedia dimension. In an online (hypermedia) environment, sellers-cum-senders and buyers enter into a relationship with the medium. These interactions can take a number of forms, including viewing firms' websites and reading the opinions of other customers published online, but also creating websites, publishing offers, and creating databases. Unlike traditional media, the hypermedia environment makes it possible for participants in the communication process to search the Internet independently, to avoid irrelevant information, and hence to retrieve only the information that is useful to them and meets their needs. Because global access to all potential recipients is possible – regardless of country of residence or economic borders – this model is characterized by an extraordinary expansion of the target group. As the costs of communication in the hypermedia computer-mediated environment are lower compared to traditional media, this is of great importance to the economic aspects of marketing communication.

Modelling is extremely important in conceptualizing the question of marketing communication. Its role can be described as follows:

- This process proceeds in a dynamically changing environment exposed to various kinds of noise and interference; it is a dynamic and complex process.

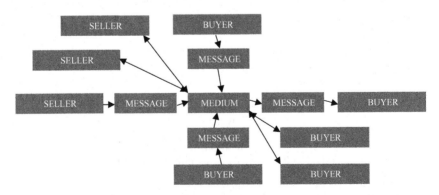

Figure 2.1 A model of hypermedia communication in the Internet environment (Hoffman and Novak, 1996).

- Communication proceeds on various levels and at varying degrees of intensity.
- By its very existence, the process of communication elicits feedback in the form of recipients' direct and indirect responses to senders' communications.

The model of communication in a hypermedia computer-mediated environment described above and the profound changes to communication that have accompanied the development of the Internet have modified the process of media-content publishing too. Table 2.2. compares the traditional process of content publishing with that of 'new media'.

Today's consumers, who have unlimited access to online information, can compare competing offers and shop online for a cheaper deal – even if it originates from another country or continent. In this context, it is worth mentioning David Scott's distinction between the 'old' and 'new' principles of marketing (2009), which makes it possible to identify the core benefits associated with the functionality of new forms of marketing communication, including SNS (Table 2.3).

Unlike with traditional communication, using the Internet requires at least a basic knowledge of computer and Internet technology. The skills of Internet users in this respect, as well as their demographic features, have a significant influence on the way they navigate the Internet and the way they communicate online. This is an area studied by specialists in psychology and IT economics, as well as by software engineers. Research into this field has yielded a number of models specifying the set of features that influence the

Table 2.2 A comparison of the traditional process of content publishing with that of the 'new media'

Traditional content publishing process	'New media' content publishing process
Limited number of content creators, restricted access to text creation (financial and technological barriers), no anonymity	Unlimited number of creators, almost everyone can create and publish their own content, ostensible anonymity
Full control over context, time, and place of publication or broadcast	Restricted control of context of publication or broadcast; changes to content do not require the creator's consent
Content is published only through the media or channels selected by its creator	Content can be published and distributed on multiple channels without the creator's consent
In its final form, the content is consistent with the original intentions of its creator	In its final form, the content does not have to be consistent with the original assumptions – control over the reproduction and modification of content is not straightforward
	The media process begins when the content is published online

Table 2.3 Principles of marketing in the context of the development of ICT
(Scott 2009)

'Old' principles	*'New' principles*
Marketing's primary goal is to increase sales of goods and services	Marketing is about more than merely advertising a product or service
Success depends on reaching as many recipients as possible	Reach is no longer the only measure of successful advertising
Advertisements are often intrusive	Advertisements can be less intrusive and can be displayed at the moment when a decision to purchase is being made
One-way communication according to the business-to-customer (B2C) model	Communication is two-way, so that customer-to-customer (C2C) communication is now just as important as B2C
Firms mostly communicate with customers through press releases published in traditional media	Communication with customers proceeds online; customers can put their questions directly to producers and service providers
Customers seeking additional product knowledge must consult advertisements in traditional media	The communication involved in marketing and public relations is two-way: customers can get information about products online when they want it, or they can seek it from other Internet users

acceptance and use of new technology. The technology acceptance model (TAM), for example, which assumes links between belief and attitudinal constructs and conscious, planned actions, offers a substantial explanation of the acceptance of new technologies (Baron et al. 2006).

The growth of online marketing, including e-commerce, has had a considerable influence on the behaviour of today's consumers. At this juncture it is worth outlining the evolution of marketing models that describe consumer behaviour. The most important examples are presented in Table 2.4.

A new interpretation of consumer behaviour developed by a team of researchers at Google is also worth noting here (Rennie & Protheroe 2020). According to its authors, who analysed the pathways of consumers using the world's most popular search engine, there exists a 'messy middle' in the decision-making process. This is a space abundant with excess information and unlimited choice, which buyers have learned to navigate by employing – sometimes automatically – cognitive shortcuts (Figure 2.2). While Alistair Rennie and his colleagues make express reference to the model of consumer decision-making elaborated by McKinsey (2009) and displayed in Table 2.4, the process of active evaluation they identify is far more cognitively complex. The Google researchers found that active evaluation is in fact composed of two simultaneous mental processes: exploration and evaluation. While exploration is an expansive activity, evaluation is inherently reductive, they argue. When exploring, we add brands, products, and information to the

Table 2.4 Selected models of consumer behaviour

Name of model	Authors	Central assumptions
AIDA model	Elias St. Elmo Lewis (1908)	Hierarchical model positing that consumers pass through four stages when making a purchasing decision: attention, interest, desire, and action
The funnel	William Townsend (1924)	An adaptation of the AIDA model that posits six stages in a customer's journey: awareness, interest, evaluation, decision, re-evaluation, and repurchase
DAGMAR	Russell Colley (1961)	A linear model which proposes that advertising influences consumers in five stages: unawareness, awareness, comprehension, conviction, and action
Moment of truth	Jan Carlzon (1986)	This model proposes that every contact a consumer has with a brand, however fleeting, is a 'moment of truth': either a 'moment of magic' or a 'moment of misery'
ATR-N (awareness, trial, reinforcement, and nudging)	Neil Barnard and Andrew Ehrenberg (1997)	This model assumes that advertising can influence consumers in three areas: building brand awareness, encouraging the first purchase, and reinforcing buying habits. In determining the purchase of a brand, habits are more important than advertising
First and second moments of truth	Alan Lafley and Ram Charan (2008)	A traditional moment-of-truth model that posits the existence of three stages: 1. stimulus, i.e. the moment when consumers first become aware of the existence of a product or service; 2. the first moment of truth in which consumers make a purchasing decision; 3. the second moment of truth, during which consumers begin to use a product and form their first impressions of it
The McKinsey consumer decision journey	McKinsey (2009)	A circular, non-linear model that assumes the existence of what is known as a loyalty loop. According to this model, once aware of the need to buy, consumers actively evaluate the alternatives. They then make a purchase and, depending on the post-purchase evaluation, either repurchase the brand or start the selection process once again
Zero moment of truth	Google (2011)	This moment-of-truth model extends the original versions to include a 'zero moment', in which consumers begin to seek information about a product or service online under the influence of a stimulus. Zero moment of truth (ZMOT) differs from first moment of truth (FMOT) in that verification is performed online rather than directly

mental category of 'consideration sets', and when evaluating we narrow these options down. That these two processes are simultaneous and continuous and that access to online information is almost unlimited is worth emphasizing. The large number of available purchasing options causes consumers to take certain shortcuts in the form of automatisms and cognitive rules that allow for faster and more efficient decision-making. These rules, which are connected with Robert Cialdini's principles of social influence (1984), are discussed in the third chapter of this book.

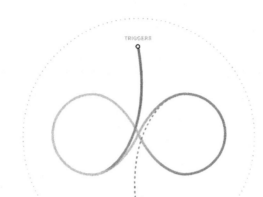

Figure 2.2 The 'messy middle' interpretation of the purchasing-decision path taken by e-consumers (Rennie & Protheroe 2020).

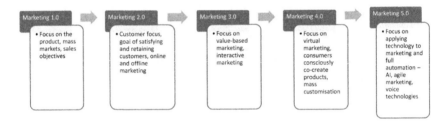

Figure 2.3 The evolution of marketing.

Although it would be impossible to discuss all of today's major trends in online marketing, room must be found for Marketing 5.0 (Kotler et al. 2021), which sees algorithms and artificial intelligence as beginning to play a key role. Consumers and their needs continue to take centre stage, but marketing objectives are not restricted exclusively to increasing sales. Kotler's concept of the evolution of marketing is set out in Figure 2.3. Yet is 'evolution' really the most apt choice of word here? Could it not be argued that the change brought about by digitization involves sudden and radical advances? If so, would not 'revolution' be the more fitting term?

Beginning with Marketing 2.0, and thanks to the development of computerization and the World Wide Web, consumers themselves began to co-create the content available online and share it with other users. And user-generated content (UGC) is precisely that: content produced by Internet users that is available to other Internet users. Thus, Internet users, who create network content but also pursue a variety of online projects that possess their own codes, ideologies, and laws, can be described by the portmanteau word 'produsers' (Bruns 2008). The advent of Web 2.0 has introduced significant changes to patterns of user interaction with the Internet (Lai & To 2015; Yang 2017). Whereas their role in the first generation of the World Wide Web was restricted to passive browsing, Internet users can now communicate and collaborate with each other via UGC (Thomas et al. 2019). The incorporation of UGC has made today's World Wide Web far more social, interactive, and responsive. In particular, it allows users to create, share, and modify their own content (Owusu et al. 2016; Papathanassis & Knolle 2011). In that it offers fertile ground for openness, participation, and sharing, Web 2.0 has prompted significant growth in the creation of UGC (Valcke & Lenaerts 2010). The latter is an important means for individuals, groups, and organizations of all kinds to express themselves and communicate with others online, which they accomplish by sharing videos, text, audio files, and images (YouTube), by blogging (Blogger.com), and by activity on SNS such as Instagram and Facebook (Bakshy et al. 2012; Kim & Lee 2008).

In recent years, firms have begun to make much greater use of UGC in their marketing initiatives (Malthouse et al. 2016; Navarro & Bigné 2017; Thompkins & Rogerson 2012). Modern businesses employ UGC for a variety of purposes, including advertising, promotion, and customer service (Oh et al. 2009). For individuals and consumers, creating their own content helps them to express their identity, interact socially, and collect or disseminate information (Daugherty et al. 2008). According to Pete Blackshaw and Mike Nazzaro (2006), UGC is 'a mixture of fact and opinion, impression and sentiment, founded and unfounded tidbits, experiences, even rumors'. Indeed, this is the view George Akerlof and Robert Shiller (2016) take of online advertising, which in their understanding entails the construction and communication of various stories (2016), including the fairy tales and nonsense served to people by the masters of advertising and marketing, and the stories people tell each other.

UGC offers an important outlet for views and opinions, as well as for communicating with others (Boyd & Ellison 2008). Organizations have adopted it for two-way communication and interaction with current and potential customers (Papathanassis & Knolle 2011). SM have become a very specific locus for this communication. The remainder of this chapter offers an overview of the most important characteristics of SM.

SM marketing in the structure and system of marketing communication Functions and significance

As a form of SM, SNS provide a technological platform that enables their users to connect with each other and to create and share online content (Boyd & Ellison 2008). Their emergence and continued growth has attracted interest from firms, who see considerable potential in this particular form of online marketing to communicate their marketing messages to customers, enter into dialogue with them using word-of-mouth marketing (WOM), and gain a better understanding of them. Consideration of SM cannot begin without a proper definition of the term. In the interdisciplinary literature on the subject, and in the studies of practitioners, there is a lack of precision and uniformity, and even a certain 'terminological chaos'. Hence the category 'social media' is very often used interchangeably with 'social network sites'. That the literature has produced numerous proposals for defining SM may go some way to accounting for this. The definition proposed by Boyd and Ellison (2008), which has more than 20,000 citations on Google Scholar, defines SM as a 'platform to create profiles, make explicit and traverse relationships'. Other definitions of SM state their most important features (Kietzmann et al. 2011). They are exemplified by the honeycomb model, which has been widely adopted in the literature and which is depicted in Figure 2.4. For their part, Kaplan and Haenlein (2010) proposed a taxonomy of six categories for the term SM: blogs, SNS, virtual social worlds, collaborative projects, content communities, and virtual game worlds. This means, therefore, that SNS constitute not a synonym, but merely one of the types of SM, which is the right approach. It is worth recalling that definitions of SM are evolving: a meta-analysis of 132 works devoted to SM published in 1998–2017 found that they are no longer seen as platforms for socializing and spending time with other people (Kapoor et al. 2018). Recent articles have stressed the capacity of SM to aggregate content and to encourage it to be created and shared. The majority of definitions draw on social exchange theory, network theory, and

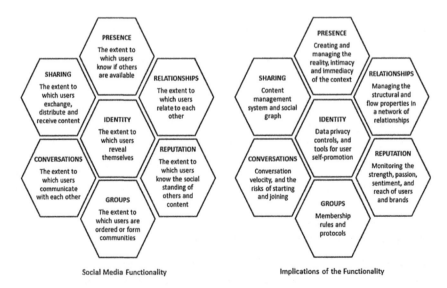

Figure 2.4 SM honeycomb model (Kietzmann et al. 2011).

organization theory. Since 2013, scholars of the SM phenomenon have gradually withdrawn from analysing UGC itself and instead have begun to focus
on examining the 'reviews' (opinions) and recommendations users publish on
SM. It is also worth noting, with respect to the taxonomy proposed by Andreas Kaplan and Michael Haenlein, that most of the articles analysed were
devoted to the social networks Facebook and Twitter.

From the point of view of the aim of this monograph, it is important to
consider uses and gratifications theory when thinking about SM, which
attempts to explain how and why people seek specific media to meet specific needs. It originated in psychosocial communication from within the
behavioural tradition (Katz 1959; Katz et al. 1973; Klapper 1963) and is a
theory of communication that focuses not on the medium itself, but on the
recipients and their individual perspectives. As such, uses and gratifications
theory assumes that people are aware of their needs and oriented towards
achieving specific goals. They do this by active pursuit of media and content that can meet their expectations and, in exchange for using the medium
in question, provide them with appropriate reinforcements, that is, various
types of individual rewards (gratifications). Because people can choose alternative sources to satisfy their needs, the media are in competition and so
must constantly observe and study the reactions of their audiences (Katz
et al. 1973). According to this view, they are primarily intended to satisfy
curiosity (informational, cultural, and utilitarian functions) and to make
time more enjoyable by providing entertainment (entertainment and hedonistic functions). A number of scholars have attempted to classify the benefits
of media within the framework of uses and gratification theory (cf. Finn &
Gorr 1988). They include Denis McQuail (1983), whose taxonomy, although
devised before the development of SM platforms, offers a good description
of the needs that using SM can satisfy. For McQuail, there are four categories of gratifications that users derive from media. They are:

- Entertainment, escape from boredom and problems, attempting to find
  emotional release, and searching for positive stimuli.
- Searching for information, learning about the world, satisfying curiosity, and obtaining information essential to satisfying other needs (e.g.
  shopping).
- Social interaction, seeking the company of others, and satisfying the
  need to belong to a group and feel of use to society.
- Development of personal identity, searching for one's own identity, em-
  ulating or imitating others, confirming one's own worth, and increasing
  self-esteem.

While it is clear that McQuail (1983) drew on other well-known theories
and typologies of communication functions, and on other well-known theories of media reception and influence, he nevertheless made a major creative contribution to advancing the study of social communication and the

social functions of the media. There have been notable attempts by several researchers to adapt uses and gratifications theory to the debate about the Internet and SM (Muntinga et al. 2011; Pletikosa Cvijikj & Michahelles 2013; Ruggiero 2000). In the main, they have taken a simplified approach that treats content published on SM as either useful or entertaining. McQuail's four categories, which are accompanied by exemplifications concerning SM users, are set out in Table 2.5.

Other more advanced approaches to classifying content published on SM can also be found in the literature. However, these go beyond the scope and objectives of this book. Nevertheless, it may be noted that some taxonomies are based on the type and intensity of emotion the content generates (cf. Dolan et al. 2017). Another approach is that of Małgorzata Karpińska-Krakowiak, who proposes a classification of content based on the categories of authenticity and conflict (2018). This stimulating idea, and the empirical research it generated, allowed Karpińska-Krakowiak to create a category matrix consisting of messages grouped according to the criteria under investigation, which she divided in a conventional, yet also distinctly evocative, manner as follows:

– Red messages of low authenticity that are highly conflictual and intended to evoke a powerful emotional reaction.

Table 2.5 Categories of gratifications offered by SM according to Denis McQuail

Functions of media: categories of gratifications offered according to McQuail	*Needs satisfied by SM*
Entertainment and escape from boredom	Option to share content intended to amuse other viewers that is based on powerful emotions, such as joy, feeling moved, and anger or rage
Searching for information	SM are now not only a source of information about the world, but also a means of maintaining human bonds and ties
Social interaction	Social network services make it possible for us to conduct and maintain virtual social relationships with people we know in the real world and with those we meet on the Internet. The extensive functionality of SM makes it possible to pursue many social aims. These range from finding a partner (e.g. Tinder) to searching for people with shared interests or professional profiles (e.g. LinkedIn)
Development of personal identity	Thanks to the option to comment and to receive gratifications ('likes'), SM have become a space for self-creation and for strengthening feelings of social belonging. They also offer immediate feedback in the form of comments or ratings from other users, which are both positive and negative

- Purple messages that are highly conflictual and whose production is characterized by a high level of realism or factual realism.
- Achromatic messages characterized by a high level of fictionality that portrays products per se.
- Blue messages that introduce elements of authenticity and show life as it is without depicting conflict or building tension.

The above discussion concerns advertising content addressed to Internet users and published by brands in SM environments. It is supplemented in the next chapter by an analysis of the function and nature of messages Internet users publish about brands. It cannot commence, however, without a proper definition of the concepts of persuasion and manipulation, which are inseparable from marketing communication. In academic research, the definition of categories is important both in itself and because it determines the area of empirical research. Due to their specificity, SM constitute a field of endless, mutually opposing influences exerted in and through online marketing, in the system of social communication, and in the Internet environment. Much research has been done into these phenomena and multidimensional processes: not only in management science, economics, and marketing, but also in psychology, sociology, cultural studies, media studies, and law. This book concentrates primarily on manifestations of the manipulation of the behaviour of e-consumers and Internet users seeking information online and, potentially, also making online purchases. It should be emphasized, however, that this issue is much more extensive. Here it has received only a cursory treatment as an essential component of the theoretical framework of the book's central question of social proof and online buyer behaviour. The issue of social influence – its models, premises, and examples – will be addressed in Chapter 3.

Persuasion and manipulation in SM

In both the scholarly and popular literature, a variety of sometimes interchangeable terms are associated with exerting influence on human behaviour. These include influencing, impacting, suggesting, inducing, educating, persuasion, persuasive communication, promotion, propaganda, manipulation, latent seduction, mind control, and even brainwashing. A search of the world's largest online book distributor, Amazon, returns more than 7,000 items under the word 'manipulation' (2021). The results are dominated by psychology textbooks that offer tips on how to manipulate other people or a given social group and that promise to lay bare the techniques of 'dark psychology'. Where marketing is concerned, it is striking that of the almost 200 self-help and popular science titles, only a few offer guidance to consumers on how to avoid being manipulated by advertisers. From the point of view of achieving the aim of this monograph, it is important to properly understand the phenomena of persuasion and manipulation.

Therefore, in the next part of the chapter, selected models of persuasion are presented and described: the theory of reasoned action (TRA), the elaboration likelihood model (ELM), and the heuristic-systematic model (HSM).

Persuasion, which involves inducing, urging, convincing, or encouraging other people to behave in a particular way, is the basic form of exerting influence. Shrum et al. (2013) begin their meta-analysis of persuasion in marketing, advertising, and consumer behaviour by examining the TRA (Ajzen & Fishbein 1975), which is described by the following equation:

$$B \sim BI = A_{act}(w1) + SN(w2)$$

where:

B – an action or behaviour (behaviour).

BI – the intention to elicit an action or behaviour (behavioural intentions).

$w1$, $w2$ – empirically derived weights that reflect the influence of each of the factors on the behavioural intention.

A_{act} – attitude to the evocation of an action or behaviour (attitude).

SN – subjective norm concerning the importance of what other people think (subjective norm).

The TRA assumes that people behave rationally and weigh the possible consequences of their behaviour in the context of its usefulness in achieving their goals or satisfying their needs.

Attitudes to behaviour and subjective norms, and to perceived expectations (SN) about behaviours, determine people's behavioural intentions (BI). For their part, intentions are shaped under the influence of subjective norms and individual attitudes with respect to a particular behaviour (A_{act}), while subjective norms result from a special type of beliefs known as normative beliefs (Ajzen & Fishbein 1975). These are the beliefs people have regarding the extent to which those who are significant to them approve or disapprove of a behaviour they plan to undertake. Icek Azjen and Martin Fishbein state that for many behaviours those significant people are our parents, partners, friends, peers, colleagues, neighbours and, in some circumstances, expert professionals such as doctors. The aim of persuasive marketing communication, in this view, is to create new normative beliefs that are to reinforce the decision to purchase a given product or service.

The TRA has had a significant impact on research in marketing, psychology, and sociology. The ability to properly articulate and quantify data allows for relatively simple operationalization of variables and their measurement. It should be stressed, however, that the TRA model can only be applied to volitional behaviour, that is, to behaviour mediated by consciousness, which means that the model does not support the interpretation of spontaneous, impulsive, and unconscious types of behaviour, such as those undertaken under the influence of emotion or mood (cf. Eagly & Chaiken 1993; Fishbein & Middlestadt 1995, 1997; Haugtvedt 1997; Haugtvedt et al. 1997; Schwarz 1997). As the phenomenon of persuasion and consumer-attitude formation can occur as a result of multiple, often parallel, processes (Chaiken & Trope 1999), persuasion researchers have proposed dual-process models of attitude formation and cognitive processing. One of the most important is the ELM, which models the processing of persuasive messages and represents the synthesis of long-term studies conducted by Richard Petty and John Cacioppo (1979, 1986).

They devised the model on the assumption that consumers process information on two levels – superficial and deep – and that they analyse multiple variables associated with engagement, which influence the motivation to process messages, and distractors, which influence the capacity for processing messages. When setting out the principles of the model almost 20 years later, Petty and his colleagues pointed out that the primary task of the ELM is to explain the processes underlying attitude change, the influence of variables inducing central and peripheral processes, and the strength of attitudes resulting from the course of these processes (Petty et al. 2004). This is achieved by carefully analysing the impact of all of the variables involved in the persuasion process on its final outcomes. The central route to persuasion rests on a comparatively extensive and cognitively demanding processing activity aimed at carefully analysing the arguments contained in messages and discovering the major points of the issue being presented. Where situational and individual variables provide high motivation and the ability to think about the message, the likelihood of elaboration will be high and recipients will follow the central route. The peripheral route to persuasion is based on a set of processes that occur during attitude changes which do not require cognitive effort. Where there is low motivation or capacity to process the message, the persuasion process follows the peripheral route, which requires less cognitive effort and is also quantitatively different. The elaboration continuum, which denotes the extent to which individuals process information and develop conclusions, is a core construct in the ELM (Petty & Wegener 1999; Petty et al. 2004). The elaboration continuum hypothesis derives from the claim that it is uneconomical – and impossible from the perspective of environmental adaptation – to invest a significant amount of cognitive effort into considering every item of incoming information and every attitude object. In order to function properly, people must sometimes behave like cognitive misers, because this is more adaptive than being profligate with their cognitive resources. The more people are motivated and able to evaluate the core content of an attitude object, the more likely they are to analyse all of the information associated with it accurately (Petty et al. 2005). This is because analysis requiring cognitive effort is considered the most effective way to truly digest the substance of a message. The connection with the subject of this book – evaluating SM marketing – is that interpreting an advertisement and carefully reading reviews of products or services on several different portals is an example of central-route processing, while quickly selecting the offer Internet users recommend most often – without actually reading any recommendations – is an example of peripheral-route processing.

The second dual-process model of persuasion that merits attention, the HSM, also envisages two modes in which individuals process information when receiving a persuasive message: the systematic mode and the heuristic mode. For Chaiken et al. (1996), the activation of one or the other mode depends on the motivation of the individual person and on the ability to process incoming information. Chen and Chaiken (1999), though, assert that the systematic mode involves a relatively analytical and exhaustive treatment of information relevant to making a judgement. Judgements and opinions formed on the basis of systematic processing correspond to the actual content of the message and convey the correct sense of the matter under analysis. Systematic processing requires that individuals possess both motivation and processing capacity. For this reason, forms of systematic processing in a particular domain of judgement are less likely to occur among addressees who possess little knowledge of that domain or are subject to time constraints. Chaiken et al. (2000) state that opinions and judgements produced by systematic processing are generally more durable than those arising from heuristic processing. In systematic processing, people's attitudes and judgements reflect the content which, based on a broad range of information previously acquired, they have noticed, understood, and cognitively examined. This reading of the concept of systematic processing largely corresponds with the central processing route in the ELM. Heuristic processing is defined as an approach based on the activation and application of a number of simple rules known as heuristics, which are understood as having been learned and stored in memory (Chaiken & Maheswaran 1994; Chen & Chaiken 1999). They cover various aspects of the way individuals function in their environments and take the form of statements concerning, for instance, approval of the message sender ('I tend to agree with people I like'), general agreement ('Consensus opinions are correct'), and the number of arguments and length of the message ('A long message is a valuable message'), etc. People resort to them when motivation is low or processing capacity absent. For Chaiken et al. (1996), heuristic processing focuses on simple decision-making rules that people apply to gauge the accuracy of messages or, more generally, to evaluate the quality or nature of the things being judged. Choosing the hotel with the highest rating on Booking.com without examining any other details of the offer or succumbing to the halo effect and selecting the offer with attractive photographs are two examples of heuristic evaluation. Heuristic processing is not the same as the peripheral processing route in the ELM: its meaning is narrower and arises from recipients' use of heuristics when forming judgements. A key finding of Chen and Chaiken (1999) in relation to the two processing modes is their co-occurrence. Even when individuals are motivated and able to engage in systematic processing, heuristic processing is also likely to occur. When considering the HSM, it is essential to pay attention to the motives held by recipients and to the powerful influence exerted on information processing by types of motivation. The HSM, which is still being developed, distinguishes three types of motivation: accuracy motivation, defence motivation, and impression motivation (Chen et al. 1999). Although each addresses a different aspect of an individual's cognitive functioning in the environment and each has a different effect on message processing, they coalesce in the structure of a single, coherent model. The motivation occurring at any one time and affecting the level of processing is decided by the specific situation and by individual differences (Krok 2006). At this juncture it is worth noting that impression motivation could be a factor of particular significance for the effectiveness of the persuasion process where the results of decisions made in the SM space, such as liking a brand's affiliate page, are available to other users.

Summarizing the above considerations, it can be stated that persuasion is concerned with the routes firms take to get us to say 'yes' and that advertisers take to convince us to buy the products on offer, because the main goal of advertisers is to achieve the highest possible demand for a given product as well as brand preference.

This is an obvious and fundamental goal of marketing and marketing communication.

Communication goals – establishing and developing relationships, creating brand communities and cultivating brand supporters, and forming a strong and powerful image – represent a second, important set of aims. Depending on the situation in which they find themselves, the immediacy of the given problem, individual differences, and the number of distractors, recipients process messages by the central or peripheral route – sometimes having recourse to availability heuristics. The intentions of senders remain obvious – at least to a certain extent – to recipients. If we recall here the 'messy middle' idea (Google 2020), two questions arise: is fully conscious central processing still possible in Marketing 4.0? are the issues in question still about persuasion but no longer about manipulation? It would appear necessary at this point to introduce a terminological distinction between persuasion and manipulation, which are often – and erroneously – used interchangeably in everyday language.

The term 'manipulation' comes from the Latin *manus pellere*, which means 'to hold someone in the palm of your hand' or 'to have somebody in hand'. In the widest sense it means 'to exert influence on a person' or 'to use a person against their will' (Karwat 2019). Perpetrators of manipulation, which is a planned and deliberate action, exert their influence while creating the appearance that they are not directing events. When in receipt of such treatment, people are therefore unaware of any attempt to control them (Hanas 2000). Manipulation is a deliberate form of influence and message recipients do not perceive the intentions of manipulators. The existence of situations in which people do not behave involuntarily, do not precede their behaviour by analysing the situation, do not draw conclusions from it, and do not control their emotions or thoughts makes it possible to employ social engineering.

As the literature shows, manipulation can take a variety of forms. Senders can manipulate information as well as the emotional domain of messages. In terms of information manipulation, the following can be distinguished:

–   Manipulation in the field of linguistic communication.
–   Manipulation in the field of 'physical' messages.
–   Manipulation in the field of the ostensibly 'psychological' backdrop or context of messages.

At the linguistic level, manipulation can involve conveying false information, an excess of unimportant information, or ambiguous information to recipients. Six types of message can be considered to constitute manipulation:

–   False information.
–   Information that is unimportant or that is of little importance and excludes the most important information.
–   Very important information conveyed as if it were of little or no importance.
–   Information that is deliberately fabricated.
–   Information that is ambiguous in order to make it difficult to understand.
–   Information conveyed in excess in order to cause disinformation.

Manipulation in the physical field refers to the medium of the message and also to the form and non-verbal content of the message. Manipulation, which occurs in the emotional realm, often takes the form of sowing anxiety or fear, emotional dislocation, the perpetuation of stereotypes, and rendering a false image of reality. It can also involve the background of a message and thus its context. Combining the information of a message with a specific environment adds expressive power and intensifies impact. It should be noted that – as information overload increases – the background and context of messages are at greater risk of being manipulated. This phenomenon involves the occurrence of psychological discomfort caused by confronting an excess of data. According to Wiesław Babik (2011), it is possible that the reason for overload lies in the rapid expansion in the amount of information generated, the ease with which it can be reproduced and distributed on the Internet, the enlarged capacity of existing message channels, and the increase in the importance of information.
Information overload can result in:

–   The inability to make a decision (there are so many options available to solve a problem that we are inclined to give up or make a sub-optimal choice).
–   A preference for the most up-to-date information rather than information of high value and quality (recency is often wrongly equated with quality).

  – Relinquishing intuition in decision-making processes (the subconscious works best when it can disregard some of the information: creative ideas and decisions are not the result of conscious analysis and the brain cannot access the ones we need most when there are too many of them).

The fundamental difference between persuasion and manipulation is therefore the degree of overtness of the aims of the person or entity attempting to shape behaviour of the other party and so leave them unaware or misinformed. The following are the core features of manipulation as a means of influencing another person, group, or segment of the market: the manipulating entity has hidden aims and intentions, they exploit the other party's incomplete knowledge and unawareness, they conceal the manipulation by distracting attention from the message sender, they use trickery, they parcel information, and they seize the opportunity to take advantage of somebody's weaknesses (Wiktor & Sanak-Kosmowska 2021). We may therefore risk the assertion that for some recipients a particular advertising message, such as a SM advertisement displayed as part of a retargeting campaign, will be purely persuasive (because they are aware of who the sender is and where the ad came from in their news feed), while for others, who have no knowledge or experience in this area, the same message will be purely manipulative. Dynamic pricing strategies and the personalization of advertising content can be similarly interpreted. Chapter 3, which presents a specific kind of online advertising tool – namely, recommendation marketing – attempts to address this question.

References

Ajzen, I., & Fishbein, M. (1975). *Belief, attitude, intention, and behavior: An introduction to theory and research.* Reading, MA: Addison-Wesley.

Akerlof, A. G., & Shiller, R. J. (2016). *Phishing for phools. The economics of manipulation and deception.* Princeton, NJ: Princeton University Press.

Babik, W. (2011). *O manipulowaniu informacją w prywatnej i publicznej przestrzeni informacyjnej* [w:] (Musiał E., Pulak, I., eds.) Człowiek, media, edukacja. Kraków: Uniwersytet Pedagogiczny im. KEN.

Bakshy, E., Rosenn, I., Marlow, C., & Adamic, L. A. (2012). The role of social networks in information diffusion. *ArXiv, abs/1201.4145.*

Barnard, N., & Ehrenberg, A. (1997). Advertising: Strongly persuasive or nudging? *Journal of Advertising Research, 37*(1), 21–31.

Baron, S., Patterson, A., & Harris, K. (2006). Beyond technology acceptance: Understanding consumer practice. *International Journal of Service Industry Management, 17*(2), 111–135. https://ssrn.com/abstract=2003559.

Blackshaw, P., & Nazzaro, M. (2006). *Consumer-generated media (CGM) 101: Word-of-mouth in the age of the web-fortified consumer.* New York: Nielsen.

Bornman, H., & von Solms, S. H. (1993). Hypermedia, multimedia and hypertext: Definitions and overview. *Electronic Library, 4/5*(11), 259–268.

Boyd, D., & Ellison, N. (2008). Social network sites: Definition, history, and scholarship. *Journal of Computer-Mediated Communication, 13*, pp. 210–230.

Bruns, A. (2008). *Blogs, Wikipedia, second life, and beyond: From production to produsage.* New York: Peter Lang.

Cacioppo, J. T., & Petty, R. E. (1979). Effects of message repetition and position on cognitive response, recall and persuasion. *Journal of Personality and Social Psychology, 37*, pp. 97–109.

Carlzon, J. (1986). *Moments of truth.* Pensacola, FL: Ballinger Publishing.

Chaiken, S. L., Gruenfeld, D. H., & Judd, C. M. (2000). Persuasion in negotiations and conflict situations. In M. Deutsch & P. T. Coleman (Eds.), *The handbook of conflict resolution: Theory and practice* (pp. 144–165). San Francisco, CA: Jossey-Bass/Wiley.

Chaiken, S., & Maheswaran, D. (1994). Heuristic processing can bias systematic processing: Effects of source credibility, argument ambiguity, and task importance on attitude judgment. *Journal of Personality and Social Psychology, 66*(3), pp. 460–473.

Chaiken, S., & Trope, Y. (Eds.). (1999). *Dual-process theories in social psychology.* New York: The Guilford Press.

Chaiken, S., Wood, W., & Eagly, A. H. (1996), Principles of persuasion. In E. T. Higgins, & A. W. Kruglanski (Eds.), *Social psychology: Handbook of basic principles* (pp. 702–742). New York: Guilford.

Chen, S., & Chaiken, S. (1999). The heuristic-systematic model in its broader context. In S. Chaiken & Y. Trope (Eds.), *Dual-process theories in social psychology* (pp. 73–96). New York: The Guilford Press.

Chen, S., Duckworth, K., & Chaiken, S. (1999). Motivated heuristic and systematic processing. *Psychological Inquiry, 10*(1), 44–49.

Cialdini, R. (1984). *Influence. The psychology of persuasion.* New York: William Morrow & Company.

Colley, R. H. (1961). *Defining advertising goals for measured advertising results.* New York: Association of National Advertisers.

Dann, S., & Dann, S. (2011). *E-marketing: Theory and application.* New York: Palgrave Macmillan.

Daugherty, T., Li, H., & Biocca, F. (2008). Consumer learning and the effects of virtual experience relative to indirect and direct product experience. *Psychology and Marketing, 25*, pp. 568–586. doi:10.1002/mar.20225.

Dolan, R., Conduit, J., Fahy, J., & Goodman, S. (2017). Social media: Communication strategies, engagement and future research directions. *International Journal of Wine Business Research, 29*(1), pp. 2–19.

E. St Elmo Lewis. (1908). *Financial advertising* (The History of Advertising). Indianapolis, IN: Levey Brothers.

Eagly, A. H., & Chaiken, S. (1993). *The psychology of attitudes.* San Diego, CA: Harcourt Brace Jovanovich College Publishers.

Finn, S., & Gorr, M. B. (1988). Social isolation and social support as correlates of television viewing motivations. *Communication Research, 15*(2), pp. 135–158. https://doi.org/10.1177/009365088015002002.

Fishbein, M., & Middlestadt, S. (1995). Noncognitive effects on attitude formation and change: fact or artifact? *Journal of Consumer Psychology, 4*, pp. 181–202. https://doi.org/10.1207/s15327663jcp0402_05.

Fishbein, M., & Middlestadt, S. (1997). A striking lack of evidence for nonbelief-based attitude formation and change: A response to five commentaries. *Journal of Consumer Psychology, 6*(1), pp. 107–115.

Google. (2011). *Winning the Zero Moment Of Truth* (accessed on: 10.01.2021) https://www.thinkwithgoogle.com/future-of-marketing/emerging-technology/2011-winning-zmot-ebook/.

Google. (2020). *Messy Midde* (accessed on: 10.01.2021), https://www.thinkwithgoogle.com/intl/en-cee/consumer-insights/consumer-journey/navigating-purchase-behavior-and-decision-making/?gclid=CjwKCAiA65iBBhB-EiwAW253W1yW3JB81gLOMqak22COPHzbn9IihUyR3s_5ohJcOHeNR5kcDR_50BoCbzkQAvD_BwE

Hanas, Z. (2000). Różne formy manipulacji człowiekiem. *Communio, 1*(115), 55–67.

Hansen, H. R. (1995). Conceptual-framework and guide-lines for the implementation of mass information-systems. *Information & Management, 28*(2), 125–142. doi:10.1016/0378–7206(95)94021-4.

Haugtvedt, C. P. (1997). Beyond fact or artifact: An assessment of Fishbein and Middlestadt's perspectives on attitude change processes. *Journal of Consumer Psychology, 6*, pp. 99–106. https://doi.org/10.1207/s15327663jcp0601_07.

Haugtvedt, C.P., Herr, P.M., and Kardes, F.R. (2008). *Handbook of consumer psychology*. New York and London: Lawrence Erlbaum Associates.

Hoffman, D., & Novak, T. (1996). Marketing in hypermedia computer-mediated environments: Conceptual foundations. *Journal of Marketing, 60*(3), 50–68. doi:10.2307/1251841.

http://dx.doi.org/10.1111/j.1083-6101.2007.00393.x

Jarvenpaa, S.J., & Todd, P.A. (1996). Consumer reactions to electronic shopping on the World Wide Web. *International Journal of Electronic Commerce, 1*(2), pp. 59–88.

Kaplan, A., & Haenlein, M. (2010). Users of the world, unite! The challenges and opportunities of social media. *Business Horizons, 53*, pp. 59–68.

Kapoor, K. K., Tamilmani, K., & Rana, N. P. (2018). Advances in social media research: Past, present and future. *Information Systems Frontiers, 20*, pp. 531–558. https://doi.org/10.1007/s10796-017-9810-y.

Karpińska-Krakowiak, M. (2018). *Kapitał marki w mediach społecznościowych*. Łódź: Wydawnictwo Uniwersytetu Łodzkiego.

Karwat, M. (2019). *Manipulacja w polityce*. Warsaw: Wydawnictwo Naukowe PWN.

Katz, E. (1959). Mass communications research and the study of popular culture: An editorial note on a possible future for this journal. *Studies in Public Communication, 2*, pp. 1–6.

Katz, E., Gurevitch, M., & Haas, H. (1973). On the use of the mass media for important things. *American Sociological Review, 38*(2), pp. 164–181.

Kiang, M., Santanam, R., Huei, K., & Shang, M. (2000). Marketing on the Internet – Who can benefit from an online marketing approach. *Decision Support Systems, 27*, pp. 383–393. doi:10.1016/S0167–9236(99)00062-7.

Kietzmann, J., Hermkens, K., McCarthy, I., & Silvestre, B. (2011). Social media? Get serious! Understanding the Functional building blocks of social media. *Business Horizons, 54*, pp. 241–251. doi:10.1016/j.bushor.2011.01.005.

Kim, J., & Lee, H. (2008). Consumer product search and purchase behaviour using various retail channels: The role of perceived retail usefulness, *International Journal of Consumer Studies, 32*, pp. 619–627. doi:10.1111/j.1470–6431.2008.00689.x.

Klapper, J. T. (1963). Mass communication research: An old road resurveyed. *Public Opinion Quarterly, 27*(4), pp. 515–527, https://doi.org/10.1086/267201x.

Kotler, P., Kartajaya H., & Setiawan, I., (2021). *Marketing 5.0: Technology for humanity*. Hoboken, NJ: Wiley & Sons.

Krok D. (2015). The role of meaning in life within the relations of religious coping and psychological well-being. *Journal of Religion and Health*, *54*(6), pp. 2292–2308. https://doi.org/10.1007/s10943-014-9983-3

Kumar, V., & Shah, D. (2004). Pushing and pulling on the Internet. *Marketing Research: A Magazine of Management and Applications*, *16*(1), pp. 28–33.

Lai, L., & To, W. M. (2015). Content analysis of social media: A grounded theory approach. *Journal of Electronic Commerce Research, 16*, p. 138.

Malthouse, E., Calder, B., Kim, S. J., & Vandenbosch, M. (2016). Evidence that user generated content that produces engagement increases purchase behaviours. *Journal of Marketing Management*. doi:10.1080/0267257X.2016.1148066.

McKinsey. (2009). (accessed on: 10.01.2021) https://www.mckinsey.com/business-functions/marketing-and-sales/our-insights/the-consumer-decision-journey#.

McQuail, D. (1983). *Mass communication theory: An introduction*. Newbury Park, CA: Sage.

Muntinga, D. G., Moorman, M., & Smit, E. G. (2011). Introducing COBRAs. *International Journal of Advertising*, *30*(1), pp. 13–46, doi:10.2501/IJA-30-1-013-046.

Navarro, J., & Bigné, E. (2017). The value of marketer-generated content on social network sites: Media antecedents and behavioral responses. *Journal of Electronic Commerce Research, 18*, pp. 52–72.

Oh, S. H., Kim, Y. M., Lee, C. W., Shim, G. Y., Park, M. S., and Jung, H. S. (2009). Consumer adoption of virtual stores in Korea: Focusing on the role of trust and playfulness. *Psychology & Marketing, 26*, pp. 652–668. https://doi.org/10.1002/mar.20293.

Owusu, R. A., Mutshinda, C. M., Antai, I., Dadzie, K. Q., Winston, E. M. (2016). Which UGC features drive web purchase intent? A spike-and-slab Bayesian variable selection approach. *Internet Research, 26*(1), pp. 22–37. https://doi.org/10.1108/IntR-06-2014-0166.

Papathanassis, A., & Knolle, F. (2011). Exploring the adoption and processing of online holiday reviews: A grounded theory approach. *Tourism Management, 32*(2), pp. 215–224.

Petty, R. E., & Cacioppo, J. T. (1986). The elaboration likelihood model of persuasion. In *Communication and persuasion*. Springer Series in Social Psychology. New York: Springer. https://doi.org/10.1007/978-1-4612-4964-1_1.

Petty, R. E., & Wegener, D. T. (1999). *The elaboration likelihood model: Current status and controversies*. In S. Chaiken & Y. Trope (Eds.), *Dual-process theories in social psychology* (pp. 37–72). New York: The Guildford Press.

Petty, R. E., Cacioppo, J. T., Strathman, A. J., & Priester, J. R. (2005). To think or not to think: Exploring two routes to persuasion. In T. C. Brock & M. C. Green (Eds.), *Persuasion: Psychological insights and perspectives* (pp. 81–116). Thousand Oaks, CA: Sage Publications, Inc.

Petty, R. E., Rucker, D. D., Gizer, G. Y., & Cacioppo, J. T. (2004). The elaboration likelihood model of persuasion. In J. S. Seiter & R. H. Gass (Eds.), *Perspectives on persuasion, social influence and compliance gaining* (pp. 65–89). Boston, MA: Allyn & Bacon.

Pletikosa Cvijikj, I., & Michahelles, F. (2013). Online engagement factors on Facebook brand pages. *Social Network Analysis and Mining, 3*, pp. 843–861. https://doi.org/10.1007/s13278-013-0098-8.

Pride, W. M., & Ferrell, O. C. (2007). *Foundations of marketing* (2nd ed.). Boston, MA: Houghton Mifflin.

Rennie, A., & Protheroe, J. (2020). How people decide what to buy lies in the "messy middle" of the purchase journey. Google.

Ruggiero, T. E. (2000). Uses and gratifications theory in the 21st century. *Mass Communication and Society, 3*(1), pp. 3–37.

Schwarz, N. (1997). Moods and attitude judgments: A comment on Fishbein and Middlestadt. *Journal of Consumer Psychology, 6*, pp. 93–98.

Scott, D. M. (2009). *The new rules of marketing and PR: How to use social media, Blogs, news releases, online video, and viral marketing to reach. Buyers directly*

Shrum, L. J., Liu, M., Nespoli, M., & Lowrey, T. M. (2013). Persuasion in the marketplace: How theories of persuasion apply to marketing and advertising. In J. P. Dillard & L. Shen (Eds.), *The SAGE handbook of persuasion: Developments in theory and practice* (pp. 314–330). Newbury Park, CA: Sage.

The First Banner Ad. (2014). (accessed on: 10.01.2021) http://thefirstbannerad.com/.

Thomas, M., Wirtz, B., & Weyerer, J. (2019). Determinants of online review credibility and its impact on consumers' purchase intention. *Journal of Electronic Commerce Research, 20*, pp. 1–21.

Thompkins, Y., & Rogerson, M. (2012). Rising to Stardom: An empirical investigation of the diffusion of user-generated content. *Journal of Interactive Marketing, 26*(2), pp. 71–82.

Townsend, C. H. T. (1924). An analysis of insect environments and response. *Ecology, 5*, pp. 14–25. https://doi.org/10.2307/1929161.

Valcke, P., & Lenaerts, M. (2010). Who's author, editor and publisher in user-generated content? Applying traditional media concepts to UGC providers. *International Review of Law. Computers & Technology*, 119–131. doi:10.1080/13600861003644533.

Westland, J. C., & Au, G. (1997). A comparison of shopping experiences across three competing digital retailing interfaces. *International Journal of Electronic Commerce, 2*(2), pp. 57–69.

Wiktor, J. W., & Sanak-Kosmowska (2021). *Information asymmetry in online marketing.* Abingdon: Routledge.

Yang, F. X. (2017). Effects of restaurant satisfaction and knowledge sharing motivation on eWOM intentions: The moderating role of technology acceptance factors. *The Journal of Hospitality & Tourism Research, 41*, pp. 93–127. doi:10. 1177/1096348013515918.

3 The structure of functions, forms, and organization of selected strategies of marketing communication and employed tools in the virtual environment

Introduction

This chapter analyses selected marketing communication strategies and online marketing tools. As mentioned in the previous chapter, the meaning of the term 'online marketing' continues to evolve, as does the catalogue of tools described in the academic literature by e-marketing specialists. While acknowledging the profusion of available online marketing tools, the book takes a deliberately selective approach. Strategies that can be employed in the social media environment and whose form and content are of a distinctly persuasive nature have been selected for discussion. The chapter is divided into two sections. The first, which continues and refines the content of Chapter 1, presents selected proposals for the classification of online marketing strategies and tools, while the second addresses the tools of influence marketing, e-word-of-mouth (eWOM) marketing, and buzz marketing.

A taxonomy of online marketing methods

An analysis of academic papers devoted to online marketing published in 2010–2020 suggests that it remains difficult to draw clear distinctions between e-marketing tools and to classify them definitely. Some authors have proposed to categorize them by degree of complexity (cf. Kieżel & Wiechoczek 2017; Piñeiro-Otero and Martínez-Rolán 2016) or according to similarities and differences (Hajarian et al. 2021). The classic approach is to classify the tools in question as 'push and pull' (cf. Brocato 2010) and 'inbound and outbound' (cf. Dakouan et al. 2019). David Stewart (2009), who studied the strength of marketing tools' influence on firms' success, made an important attempt to systematize the strategies and forms of e-marketing. Taking the Return on Marketing Investment index as a frame of reference, he distinguished three groups of tools: tools for achieving short-term objectives (activating sales and generating profits), tools for achieving long-term objectives (building a firm's value), and tools for achieving alternative objectives (establishing pathways to future growth and development). T-shape marketing, a technique whereby the use of online marketing strategies and

DOI: 10.4324/9781003128052-4

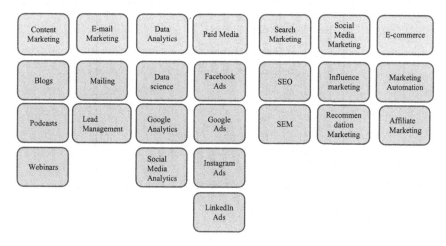

Figure 3.1 T-shape marketing concept.

tactics is alternated, is popular in the literature and also among marketing practitioners. By analysing this model, it is possible to identify the dominant areas of activity of modern e-marketing specialists – this is illustrated in Figure 3.1.

Another relatively common means of classification is to conceive of e-marketing techniques and tools according to the objectives they are employed to achieve. This approach, together with examples of e-marketing tools assigned to each category, is presented in Table 3.1.

For the purposes of this book, a slightly different classification of online marketing tools is proposed. Its typology begins with the assumption that it is difficult to make a clear distinction between marketing strategies designed exclusively to increase sales and those designed exclusively to build or project an image. The majority of advertising campaigns are integrated and global, and the various tools and strategies intertwine. However, it is certainly possible to distinguish them according to the strength of the influence they exert on their recipients, in terms of the persuasiveness of the message, but also the degree of consumer engagement (de Oliveira Santini et al. 2020).

As a consequence of this assumption, an attempt was made to describe various e-marketing tools in two dimensions:

- Low information credibility vs high information credibility according to the assessments of e-consumers (e.g. Harms et al. 2019; Soh et al. 2007).
- Low persuasiveness vs high persuasiveness.

Table 3.1 Typology of marketing communication strategies and online marketing tools

Advertising and promotion	Content marketing and experience marketing	Social marketing and relationship marketing	Commerce and sales	Data	Management
– Mobile marketing	– Mobile applications	– AMB	– Retail marketing	– Marketing analytics	– Budgeting and financial planning
– Display advertising	– E-mail marketing	– Virtual events, webinars	– Marketing channel management (channel, partner, and local marketing)	– Web and mobile analytics	– Workflow
– Search and social advertising (Google ads, FB ads)	– Content marketing	– Call analytics	– Sales automation	– Data visualization	– Agile and lean management
– Native advertising	– Optimization: personalization and testing	– Social media marketing	– Affiliate marketing	– Business intelligence	– Vendor analysis
– Video advertising	– SEO	– Social media monitoring	– E-commerce marketing	– Tag management predictive analytics	
	– DAM and MRM	– Influence marketing	– E-commerce platforms		
	– Marketing automation	– Recommendation marketing			
	– Lead management	– Customer experience			
	– CMS and Web experience optimization	– CRM			

Some indications for the proper assignment of the individual tools to the above categories can be found in a quantitative study of Polish e-consumers, which asked its participants to state their attitudes to particular forms of on-line advertising across a number of categories, such as trust, credibility, and emotional response (Wiktor & Sanak-Kosmowska 2021). As a result of ana-lysing the responses obtained, it was possible to produce a two-dimensional arrangement of the different forms and tools of advertising (Figure 3.2). To clarify the differences between the different types of marketing tools used online, the author then proposed her own original description, which in-volved assigning colours to them.

The matrix in Figure3.2 situates online marketing tools along two axes:

–   E-consumers' perceptions of the credibility of marketing messages.
–   The degree to which marketing messages are persuasive.

The tools to which the colours 'yellow and red' were assigned are charac-terized by high persuasiveness, while those to which the colours 'blue and green' were assigned are characterized by low persuasiveness. The features of each of the colour groups are given below along with examples of the on-line marketing tools assigned to them.

'Red' tools, which e-consumers regard as distinctly persuasive, have a powerful influence on them and arouse their engagement. Internet users trust them, find them credible, and engage with them as recipients. An ex-ample is influence marketing, especially if it involves working with celeb-rities and the 'faces' of a brand. The 'red' tools also include personalized

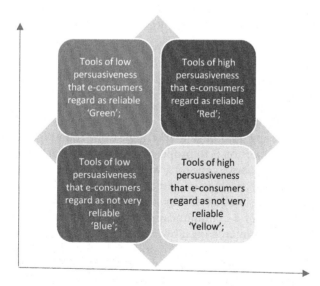

Figure 3.2 Matrix of online marketing tools.

e-mail marketing, which 34% of respondents rated highly or very highly in a study conducted by Jan Wiktor and Katarzyna Sanak-Kosmowska (2021). This category also includes social media marketing – especially if brands employ tools such as viral marketing, real-time marketing, or storytelling.

The 'yellow' tools are also persuasive in nature, but do not have as strong an influence on their recipients and are not considered very credible. They can include native advertising, search engine advertising, advertising displayed on mobile devices, retargeting, advertising displayed on social media, banner advertising, and video advertising. Promotional, sponsored articles published on Internet portals can also be assigned to this category.

The tools in the 'blue' set, which include the highly informational and comparatively neutral material published as part of content marketing campaigns as well as newsletters (also informational), are distinguished by their low persuasiveness and limited influence.

The fourth and final category, 'green', contains high-influence online marketing tools that enjoy high consumer trust and are not purely persuasive in nature. In other words, they inform consumers, but do not necessarily persuade them to make purchases. E-consumers consider the opinions of their friends published on social network sites and the recommendations of other Internet users available on the Internet to be the least manipulative and the most credible. At the same time, 70% of respondents in a study of Polish e-consumers rated recommendations and reviews as being the most trustworthy and having the greatest impact on purchasing decisions (Wiktor & Sanak-Kosmowska 2021). It is for this reason that eWOM marketing, buzz marketing, and recommendation marketing, which involve acquiring knowledge of consumers' behavioural traits and preferences to personalize advertising, belong in the 'green' category (Brown & Hayes 2008). The remainder of this chapter offers a detailed description and analysis of these tools.

Social influence marketing

Social influence marketing is a broad and somewhat indeterminate idea. Indeed, several definitions of the phenomenon and several ways of determining the interrelationships between viral marketing, influencer marketing, eWOM marketing, and buzz marketing can be found in the literature. The purpose of this section is to propose a classification of the features and characteristics of the above concepts, which form an essential part of marketing communication strategy in virtual environments.

As well as being a sine qua non in scholarship, the diverse terminology used in the practice of e-communication – marketing professionals often use the names of tools interchangeably, although they are not synonymous – means that terminological clarity is important in that domain too. It is the view of the author that social influence marketing, which encompasses a wide range of tools and strategies based on the mechanisms of social influence, offers the broadest conceptual category. It should be stressed that this term does not refer to online marketing alone. However, with the purpose and thematic scope of the book in mind, a decision was taken to focus exclusively on marketing in the virtual world.

With the aid of an American social network service for researchers called Academia, an analysis of scholarly papers on social influence marketing published in 2010–2020 was undertaken in order to establish a satisfactory definition of the concept. According to data compiled in January 2021, the platform had by then accumulated 22 million academic papers and was receiving 100 million visits per month (Academia 2021). The initial search returned 500,000 articles that included the phrase 'influence marketing' among their keywords, and 366 articles that included this term in their titles. Of these, 73 were published between 2016 and 2021. The keyword 'celebrity endorsement' returned 14,000 records and 204 articles that used the term in their titles (27 articles were added in 2016–2021). The majority of them concerned influencer marketing in social media with a particular focus on celebrity endorsement and brands' partnerships with influencers. A search on Academia for papers on eWOM marketing returned 100,000 records. In fact, in 2016–2021, as many as 1,771 articles were published with eWOM in their titles. The vast majority, which address specific market sectors, social media channels, or the effectiveness of advertising campaigns, have a very tight thematic reach. By contrast, there are comparatively few reviews or meta-analyses among the papers on eWOM marketing and social influence marketing. The literature does offer, however, a number of proposals for defining the concept of influencers (Kotler et al. 2019; Schaefer & Ruxton 2012; Silva et al. 2019; Wielki 2020), a selection of which is presented in Table 3.2.

Table 3.2 Selected definitions of the term 'influencer'

Author (year of publication)	Definition of 'influencer'
Schaefer (2012)	'(…) Influencers function as a link between the brand and the customer. They try to filter the important information from marketing messages and pass them on to people in their circle'
Kotler et al. (2017)	'Influencers, who have a large group of committed supporters and an audience, are respected in their communities'
Silva et al. (2019)	'Influencers are opinion leaders, mediating in the distribution of information and facilitating its dissemination to their online followers'
Górecka-Butora et al. (2019)	'Influencers are opinion leaders, popular among a wider or higher group of regular recipients, who by acting credibly (increasingly often this takes place on the Internet) inspire the trust and engagement of those they communicate with and convince them to make particular choices, such as those related to shopping, nutrition or worldview'
Wielki (2020)	'A person with the ability to influence potential buyers of a product or service by promoting or recommending it on social media'

Table 3.3 Classification criteria and key characteristics of influencers

Distinguishing criterion	Types of influencers
Number of followers	– Celebrities (more than five million followers) – Mega-influencers (1,000,000–5,000,000), – Top influencers (500,000–100,000) – Macro-influencers (100,000–50,000) – Mid-range influencers (50,000–20,000) – Micro-influencers (fewer than 20,000) – Nano-influencers (10,000–1,000) (Górecka-Butora et al. 2019)
Motivation to share an opinion	The following categories are distinguished: – Idols – Experts – Activists – Artists – Lifestylers (Górecka-Butora et al. 2019)
Type of social media platform employed	Locus of influencer social media activity: – YouTube – Facebook – Instagram – TikTok – Snapchat and others
Dominant mode of operation	– Active influencers employed by firms to promote their products – Passive influencers who are not connected with the firms whose products they promote (Leon & Sanchez-Cartas 2018)

This book adopts a definition of influencers that applies only to their activity in the online environment. Continuing our discussion, it should be noted that influencers are often – and wrongly – treated as a homogeneous group. Indeed, the word itself seems only to evoke associations with promotional activities on Facebook and Instagram. Yet the term in fact subsumes a number of disparate categories of forms and content of communication, which can be classified according to number of followers, motivation to share an opinion, type of social media platform employed, and dominant mode of operation (Wielki 2020). The details of this taxonomy are set out in Table 3.3.

Malcolm Gladwell's stimulating and important typology (2000), which distinguishes three types of influencers, is also worthy of examination:

– Mavens, who accumulate information and actively share it on the social media channels they curate.
– Connectors, who have numerous friends, acquaintances, and relationships (including social media followers) and are popular.
– Salesmen, who specialize in promoting and selling products on the social media channels they curate.

However, Gladwell's typology does not specify variables such as the number of followers or the type of platform used. The key differentiator lies in what motivates the influencer's activity. The distinction he proposes, though, is debatable: after all, many influencers – or connectors, if we employ Gladwell's word – also make use of their extensive networks of contacts for sales purposes.

The impression formed when reviewing the above typologies of influencers and their associated definitions, is that they do not take 'ordinary Internet users', who are the most trusted users, into consideration (Nielsen 2015). Indeed, despite the fact that the opinions they write on Tripadvisor or Amazon guide hundreds of Internet users when making purchasing decisions, the typology set out in Table 3.3 would not even define them as nano-influencers. Bearing in mind the subject matter of this monograph and the need to structure the numerous terms used by marketing scholars and practitioners, a classification of the broad, complex, and heterogeneous category denoted by the term influencers is now proposed. It is set out in Figure 3.3.

Each type of influencer defined in the figure performs different functions and tasks in the marketing communication system. Moreover, each type of influencer possesses a separate set of characteristics.

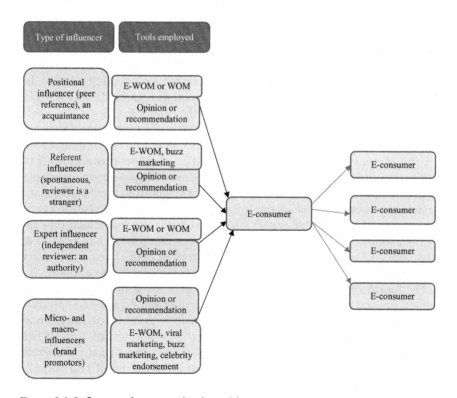

Figure 3.3 Influencers' communication with e-consumers.

The category of positional influencer, which is related to the notion of peer influence, is occupied by our family and friends. These are the people who have the greatest influence on the decisions individuals take (Opoku & Abdul-Muhmin 2017). When searching for information about a product or service, we are guided in many cases by the opinions of people we know. This dependency is not reserved exclusively for relationships in the real world (word-of-mouth (WOM)): it also obtains in the virtual world (eWOM, which is described elsewhere in this chapter). Studies have found that – for e-consumers – reviews and recommendations are particularly convincing: over 80% of the Poles surveyed rated them the most reliable and trustworthy sources of product and purchasing advice. It should be noted here that advances in information and communications technology and the growing popularity of social media have combined to alter – to some degree – the way in which friends are defined. This has not escaped the attention of Dmitry Zinoviev and Vy Duong (2009), who observe that the number of 'online' contacts usually exceeds the number of friends in the real world, and the depth and frequency of interaction is different in each case.

The second category distinguished is that of Sarah Arrow's referent influencers (2013). These are average Internet users (just like you or I) who write online opinions and recommendations. Unlike positional influencers, they are unknown to their audience (recipients). The majority of referent influencers are active Internet users – prosumers – who are willing to share their opinions in a way that benefits other users. To use the language of social media, they might be top fans (Facebook), opinion leaders (Google), or local guides (Google). A study by Paulina Walczyk (2019) found that 68% of Poles trust reviews of this kind, which means that they have a good reputation. In this way, referent influencers can be understood as high-credibility sources of social proof. However, as we have seen in the examples given in the previous chapters of how firms manage reviews and recommendations, they are not always the spontaneous and authentic reviews of average Internet users.

Experts, who appear both in the classification of influencers according to motivation and in Gladwell's typology (2000), are defined as people who specialize in a particular field and whose interests stem from their professions, passions, or hobbies. One example is doctors and nutritionists, for example, who run specialist blogs and affiliate websites through which they offer their followers advice and answer their questions (Sanak-Kosmowska & Śliwińska 2020). Experts inspire trust and, in most cases, even if they enter into a partnership with a firm, they officially inform their fans about it.

The fourth of the categories set out in Figure 3.3 is made up of micro-influencers and macro-influencers, who transmit their experiences, product information, and reviews either spontaneously with no involvement from firms or by publishing sponsored posts with the involvement of firms. When working with macro-influencers and micro-influencers, firms can operate a marketing communications strategy based on social proof and add additional elements to it, such as discounts and special offers promoted by influencers. It is worth mentioning that the United States Federal Trade Commission (FTC), which administers a wide variety of laws and regulations, takes a robust line on the need for Instagrammers to disclose their relationships with brands in the sponsored posts they publish. The FTC has issued guidance on how to comply with the law where sponsored content is concerned. Where a photograph is an advertisement, for example, this must be stated in the first three lines of its caption. Signalling that a photograph is an advertisement can be done, for example, by using the hashtag: #ad #sponsored.

In the United Kingdom, where the advertising industry co-writes the advertising codes via the Committee of Advertising Practice, and where the Advertising Standards Authority is responsible for enforcing them, the latter body requires influencers – as a minimum – to label their sponsored posts by using a suitably prominent reference, such as #ad, #advert, #advertising, or #advertisement. In collaboration with the Competition and Markets Authority, it issued a document entitled 'The labelling of influencer advertising', which informed influencers that in their posts or videos they are obliged to clearly label brand-supplied products as such and to clearly label products they have bought themselves as such. The document also sets general standards for labelling and disclosing influencers' commercial relationships with brands. It is worth mentioning that UK regulations also prohibit celebrities, influencers, and healthcare professionals from promoting medicines in any way (Advertising Standards Authority 2021).

In Poland, concealing an advertising message under the cover of neutral information is perceived as an infringement of the principles of fair competition and is not permitted under a variety of legislation. One regulation is article 16c of the Broadcasting Act of 29 December 1992, which generally prohibits concealed commercial communications. However, marketing communication in the social media environment remains to be regulated under Polish law.

The next section introduces the concept of informal online communication (eWOM), presents the four basic tools used in this form of marketing communication (eWOM, buzz marketing, viral marketing, and celebrity endorsement), and indicates their interrelationships.

Electronic word-of-mouth

Many of the commonly used marketing tools presented in the first part of this chapter are based on the influence of other users' opinions. WOM marketing is defined as a process whereby consumers transmit information about products, services, and brands to other consumers, i.e. it is defined as recommendation in its most classic form. According to Emanual Rosen (2002), WOM can be understood as the sum of statements on a given product, service, or firm in a given time period. Research has demonstrated that eWOM messaging often has a greater influence on e-consumers than advertising or other forms of promotion (Bickart & Schindler 2001; Cotter 2019; Smith Satya & Sivakumar 2005; Trusov et al. 2009; Wangenheim & Bayón 2007). eWOM and WOM should perform two functions as communication tools: persuasive and diffusive (viral). The majority of studies examine the persuasiveness of eWOM/WOM, while analysis of the mechanism of diffusive communication, which is decisive for generating the viral effect so important in marketing, is a slightly less popular research thread (Huang et al. 2011). Specialists have for some time also been using the term consumer review management, which denotes marketing initiatives designed to generate a wave of recommendations for a product or service among consumers. This is accomplished by allowing them to become familiar with a product and by using the appropriate tools to support and diffuse the resulting recommendations. These tools are described in detail in Chapter 5, which is devoted to social commerce. Consumers can gain direct knowledge of products when they are released to some of them before becoming universally available, by receiving time-limited, free-of-charge versions (free trials) or by receiving free samples or testers. Where indirect experience is concerned, firms or brand owners release their products to bloggers or vloggers, who then share their impressions with Internet users. In their meta-analysis, Kristopher Floyd and his colleagues (Floyd et al. 2014) understand recommendation as communication of a non-commercial nature between two or more people in which the form of checking and verification varies. Understood in this way, recommendation can be active and involve the intentional and conscious transmission of information or it can be passive and involve influencing other potential purchasers unintentionally. Blogger recommendations are of both kinds. In addition, they reach a relatively wide range of people and so achieve high virality in providing consumers with reasons for making purchasing decisions (Floyd et al. 2014).

It can be stated with reference to the 'messy middle' model presented in the previous chapter that in addition to exploring and evaluating purchase information on the Internet, contemporary e-consumers are also researchers and reviewers. In the former capacity they discover new content, locate alternative products, and read other peoples' opinions, while in the latter they perform the role of reviewers and by doing so generate and share opinions themselves.

Several types of reviews are encountered when browsing the recommendations of other Internet users. They may be interpreted by identifying the nature of the relationship with the sender and by analysing their content. With reference to the subject literature, six types of review can be distinguished:

- Active (intentional) and passive (unintentional) reviews.
- Sponsored reviews (where sponsors are named), hidden reviews (constituting product placement and not compliant with the rules of some social media platforms), autonomous reviews (without the participation or knowledge of the brand).

- Positive, neutral, and negative reviews.
- Reviews with known or unknown senders; a known sender is an influencer, celebrity, or friend on social media, and an unknown sender is someone who is on social media but is not a friend or is an unknown Internet user.
- Genuine or fake reviews.
- Spontaneous reviews that e-consumers publish on their own initiative or that are elicited by offers of additional discounts or participation in loyalty programmes.

A large number of studies have been undertaken by scholars of marketing and psychology to investigate the cognitively demanding task of verifying e-consumers' recommendations that accompanies exploration and evaluation (Google 2020). The approaches they take can be classified as follows:

- The development and testing of algorithms that detect fake reviews based on semantic analysis of review content (text mining, opinion mining; e.g. Chen et al. 2019).
- Modelling of pathways for analysing the content of reviews and the detection by consumers of fake reviews (e.g. Munzel 2016).
- Analysis of the factors that contribute to greater susceptibility to fake reviews (e.g. Wagenheim & Bayón 2007).

From the perspective of the aims of this monograph, interesting conclusions can be drawn from the results of a study conducted by Andreas Munzel (2016), which includes two experiments that are particularly demonstrative of the power of social proof. In line with attribution theory (Kelley & Michela 1980; Weiner 2000), he found that the consistency of the researched reviews with the overall ratings given by the online community helped the study participants to assess the reviews as credible. However, when reviews were clearly more positive or negative than others, experimental participants were more likely to suspect their authors of manipulation. Similar results were obtained by Dina Mayzlin et al. (2014). The question of reviews and recommendations from the perspective of the firm is explored in Chapter 5.

Buzz marketing (a form of WOM marketing)

Buzz marketing plays a significant role in the analysis of tools based on social influence (Figure 3.3). To explore and interpret this idea it is necessary to establish two important analytical premises. First, it is essential to clearly distinguish buzz marketing from eWOM. Second, because many firms do not integrate buzz marketing into their marketing communication correctly, it is necessary to set out the challenges firms face when doing this (Karr 2015).

The definition of WOM marketing refers to the activities firms undertake to elicit positive recommendations about products, brands, or services from their customers (Taufique & Shahriar 2011). As stated above, buzz marketing is often and erroneously treated as a synonym of eWOM marketing in the popular literature. That there is in fact an important distinction to be made between them has been pointed out by the Word-of-Mouth Marketing Association (WOMMA). In its classical sense, WOM has always existed: people have always talked to each other about products, issues, and events that are important in their lives (Oosterwijk & Loeffen 2005). Yet there is a clear difference between WOM arising from everyday human interactions and WOM arising as a result of a specific campaign to create or encourage it (Riegner 2007; WOMMA 2005). Where WOM marketing is organic, e-consumers share their opinions about products spontaneously. Yet if these opinions are shared as a result of the actions of firms, we are confronted with a different phenomenon known as amplified WOM. From this point of view, buzz marketing consists of a message in amplified form that is the outcome of organized efforts by firms to induce or encourage people to talk about a product or brand with other people. What this means, therefore, is that buzz marketing, rather than being entirely synonymous with WOM communication, is in fact one of the forms that WOM communication takes. It may therefore share those characteristics that describe the mechanism of persuasion and manipulation, whereby supposedly independent users may in fact be acting covertly on behalf of a firm or employees may be impersonating ordinary users. It is worth noting at this juncture that many firms regard buzz marketing as an aggressive form of marketing communication whose sole aim is to increase sales. What is more, some of the content it generates takes the form of spam.

Viral marketing

The second tool used by influencers to communicate with the environment – to communicate with e-consumers – is viral marketing. Just as in the case of buzz marketing, the definitional boundaries are blurred: 'viral marketing' is often used in the literature to describe WOM marketing initiatives.

Viral marketing, which entails initiating situations in which potential customers themselves begin spreading information about a brand, service, or product, is a kind of WOM marketing (Figure 3.4). The principle of viral marketing lies in its very name and, if it is to be successful, the information conveyed must be attractive enough to prompt Internet users to share it with one another. Viral marketing is defined in the literature as a set of marketing instruments that are used to target certain groups of recipients in a way that induces them to spread information and thereby raise brand awareness and boost sales (Touba et al. 2011).

In viral marketing, information is sent from one network user to the next, so that its diffusion resembles a two-stage and multi-stage marketing communication model (Hoffman & Novak, 1996). If they find the information or video they receive sufficiently interesting, Internet users can share them

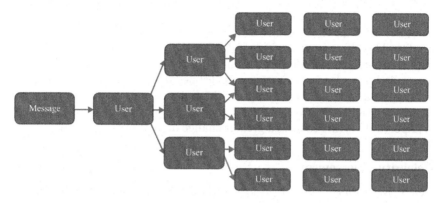

Figure 3.4 Communication model of viral marketing.

with their personal network via, for example, social network sites, e-mail, etc. The literature often refers to information diffusion occurring on the World Wide Web as the snowball effect, whereby the ball gathers size and pace as one user tells another about the content they have received and that person tells other people, who do the same, and so on (Finne & Grönroos 2017).

The crucial point is that viral marketing is based on the voluntary behaviour of users who decide that a given piece of information is worth sharing. The role of the marketing specialist is to supply the target group with content that is attractive enough to make them want to pass it on. Most viral marketing messages are sent online or by SMS because these methods allow information to be transmitted swiftly and at low cost. The term viral marketing was coined by Professor Jeffrey Rayport in 1996 and popularized in 1997 through the Hotmail free e-mail account campaign (Rayport 1996). One of the first examples of viral marketing was the Evian Roller Babies commercial (Edwards 2013), which received over 100 million views in 2009 alone and was recorded in the Guinness Book of Records as the most viewed online advertisement of all time. It should be stressed that it owed its popularity to the involvement of Internet users who, in a manner consistent with the model of marketing communication in hypermedia computer-mediated environments (Hoffman & Novak 1996), invited other users to see a marketing message that they had found attractive. The popularity of the spot, and the number of viewers it reached as a consequence, had wide-ranging consequences: brand awareness increased, brand image improved, and sales objectives were met (Edwards 2013).

Angela Dobele and her team, who investigated the influence of viral messages conveying the six primary emotions (surprise, joy, sadness, anger, fear, and disgust) on the emotional responses of the recipients of viral marketing campaigns and their subsequent readiness to forward the content, reached a number of important and interesting conclusions on viral marketing (2007). It was found that viral messages cannot be effective without an element of surprise, but that they need to combine it with other emotions to be successful. The effectiveness of viral messages is also moderated by gender, with campaigns based on disgust and fear, for example, more likely to be forwarded by male recipients than female ones. To ensure that they continue to be spread, messages must capture the imagination of recipients and be clearly targeted. Moreover, matching the campaign to the emotions featured is important, as this ensures a greater chance of diffusion.

Celebrity endorsement

Celebrity endorsement, which arose as advertising tools and techniques developed and marketing messages began to use famous faces to extol the virtues of products and stimulate their purchase, is the third online marketing tool to be examined. It is not, however, reserved exclusively for online marketing: the use of celebrities in advertising is widespread in almost all channels of marketing communication.

After Grant McCracken (1989), celebrity endorsement can be understood as the strategy of using the images of famous people for promotional activities in the broad sense. A celebrity's support for a given product can be expressed directly by means of:

- The statement 'This is the product for me' (explicit mode).
- Implication through the use of a given product (implicit mode).
- The co-presence of the celebrity and the product (co-presence).

For their part, Irving Rein, Philip Kotler, and Martin Stoller (1997) proposed a slightly different classification of this tool, which takes account of the symbolic connection between the celebrity's field of activity and the nature of the product:

- Tools of the trade, meaning endorsement of products closely related to the celebrity's activities.
- Endorsement of unrelated products.
- Taking advantage of the celebrity's image and appearance to attract attention.

Though the above approaches were conceived in the era of traditional marketing, they also apply to the world of online marketing.

An interesting comparison between celebrity endorsements and influencer endorsements was made in research published by Alexander Schouten and his team (2020), who established through a series of experiments that influencers are considered more trustworthy than celebrities, and that people feel more similar to, and identify more with, influencers than celebrities. These processes, in turn, influence the effectiveness of advertising and the achievement of its sales and image goals. Schouten and his colleagues also established the importance of studying the processes underlying effective product recommendation. They identified wishful identification, similarity to the influencer, and trustworthiness as among the explanations for the greater effectiveness of marketing communication conducted with influencers in a virtual environment compared to that conducted with celebrities. The underlying processes that explain advertising effectiveness may depend on specific combinations of products and recommendations. In particular, for influencer recommendations to be more effective than celebrity recommendations, the promoted product must be able to reinforce the impression of similarity between the influencer and the e-consumer in terms of the needs or desires that such a relationship satisfies (Schouten et al. 2020). When promoting products, it is important that influencers are seen as similar to their audience, and identification with them must be based on genuine aspirations, not just on wishful thinking of the 'I wish I could be like him or her' type.

Relationship marketing: the role of eWOM in building customer relationships

It is important when reflecting on the role of social influence, and of opinions and recommendations, to indicate the importance to firms of simply listening to the needs and desires of consumers. Indeed, to listen in this way – made possible by market research into consumer preferences and the ways in which they search for purchasing information – lies at the heart of modern marketing. Rapid advances in information and communication technologies (ICT) mean that firms have at their disposal ever more data, including the opinions, reviews, and recommendations e-consumers publish online – their digital footprints – which are particularly important.

Recommendations and reviews serve not only as inspiration for other Internet users seeking product information, but also as important feedback, which signals their expectations, needs, and attitudes in respect of brands. Listening to consumers is part of an approach known as relationship marketing, whereby – rather than giving priority to finalizing transactions – building relationships with customers is taken to be marketing's most important objective. Based on the results obtained in selected studies, the cost of retaining a customer – depending on the product or service – may be several to ten times lower than that of acquiring a new customer (Dziedzic & Szymańska 2011), which means that the customer is in the centre of interest. Research has found that firms employing eWOM communications often use them to play a mediating role between relationship marketing and consumer loyalty (e.g. Akbari et al. 2016; Ngoma et al. 2019). This is illustrated in Figure 3.5.

Positive reviews, published through eWOM initiatives, can serve as powerful marketing tools for building customer loyalty (Ferguson et al. 2006). In this way, upbeat eWOM is likely to strengthen customer confidence in organizations and their services and, in turn, have a positive impact on customer loyalty. Firms make skilful use of this mechanism when offering customers

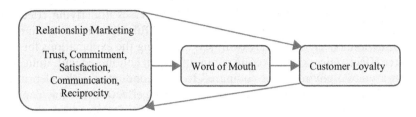

Figure 3.5 The influence of WOM on consumer loyalty.

membership in loyalty programmes or participation in closed consumer groups on Facebook. The reciprocity of this relationship merits emphasis: satisfied customers who feel they are part of a community organized around a brand are more likely to share their opinions with other Internet users and thereby encourage them to take up the firm's offer.

Summary

This chapter identifies and characterizes selected online marketing communication tools and proposes a classification of the strategies used to implement them. The typology devised here draws distinctions between social influence marketing, eWOM, buzz marketing, and celebrity endorsement. This is an important systematization because the academic, popular, and practitioner literature use different terms, with different and inexact definitions, which makes precise analysis more difficult and the communication within and between environments less accurate. Special attention is paid in this monograph to the online marketing tools that consumers trust and that have a very powerful influence on them: opinions and reviews shared by other Internet users. Just as models adopted in academic research involve a certain degree of simplification, so too, of course, does this approach. Research findings have clearly demonstrated the enormous and still growing role of eWOM in purchasing decisions (Katona et al. 2011; Keller 2007; Pingdom 2011; Qualman 2009). There are several aspects of this phenomenon that are worth noting. First, eWOM marketing messages which take the form of user feedback and recommendations do not always need to be initiated by firms. A great proportion of them arise spontaneously without their involvement. Second, influencers do not constitute a homogeneous group. Aside from the opinions of celebrities and mega-influencers, influence is now also exerted by the recommendations of experts, niche influencers and, above all, by ordinary, average Internet users. They may not have several thousand followers, but thousands of e-consumers seeking product information read their opinions every day.

It is difficult to clearly define the boundaries between the concepts discussed in this chapter. The tools of online marketing communication discussed above are intertwined, so the best results are achieved by campaigns that combine and integrate the various tools of e-marketing. Although much has been written in academic and popular literature about marketing communication, the impression remains that no sound and authoritative attempt has yet been made to classify these tools. This chapter has paid particular attention to social influence marketing, that is, to the influencing of the process of searching for information about products and services and of the purchasing decisions of Internet users. Generally speaking, this influence can be stimulated by firms (buzz marketing, influencer marketing, celebrity endorsement) or be spontaneous, bottom-up, and initiated by Internet users. This chapter has presented the concept of influencers and proposed a typology of them. It has described eWOM and given an introductory account of buzz marketing and celebrity endorsement. The connection between eWOM and relationship marketing has been sketched. These are important elements that concretize the findings of Chapter 2 and preface the material to be considered in Chapter 4.

That chapter, which now follows, turns to the theoretical aspects of social influence and to the identification and analysis of the processes that underlie the phenomenon of social influence in online shopping behaviour. Particular emphasis is placed on the categories, processes, and determinants of social proof.

References

Academia. (2021). (accessed online on: 10.01.2021) https://www.academia.edu/about.

Advertising Standards Authority. (2021). (accessed online on: 10.01.2021) https://www.asa.org.uk/.

Akbari, M., Kazemi, R., & Haddadi, M. (2016). Relationship marketing and word-of-mouth communications: Examining the mediating role of customer loyalty. *Marketing and Branding Research, 3*, pp. 63–74. doi:10.19237/MBR.2016.01.06.

Arrow, S. (2013). *Types of influencers in your social media sphere* (accessed online on: 10.01.2021). https://tinyurl.com/n3lcz99s.

Bickart, B., and Schindler, R. M. (2001). Internet forums as influential sources of consumer information. *The Journal of Interactive Marketing, 15*, pp. 31–40. https://doi.org/10.1002/dir.1014.

Brocato, D. (2010). Push and pull marketing strategies. In J. Sheth and N. Malhotra (Ed.), *Wiley International Encyclopedia of Marketing* (pp. 71–72). Oxford: Wiley-Blackwell.

Brown, D., & Hayes, N. (2008). *Influencer marketing. Who really influences your customers?* Amsterdam: Elsevier.

Chen, L., Li, W., Chen, H., & Geng, S. (2019). Detection of fake reviews: Analysis of sellers' manipulation behavior. *Sustainability, 11*(17), pp. 1–13.

Cotter, K. (2019). Playing the visibility game: How digital influencers and algorithms negotiate influence on Instagram. *New Media Society, 21*, pp. 895–913.

Dakouan, C., Benabdelouahed, R., & Anabir, H. (2019). Inbound marketing vs. outbound marketing: Independent or complementary strategies. *Expert Journal of Marketing, 7*(1), pp. 1–6.

de Oliveira Santini, F., Ladeira, W.J., Pinto, D., et al. (2020). Customer engagement in social media: A framework and meta-analysis. *Journal of the Academic Marketing Science, 48*, pp. 1211–1228. https://doi.org/10.1007/s11747-020-00731-5.

Dobele, A., Lindgreen, A., Beverland, M., Vanhamme, J., & Wijk, R. (2007). Why pass on viral messages? Because they connect emotionally. *Business Horizons, 50*, pp. 291–304. doi:10.1016/j.bushor.2007.01.004.

Dziedzic, D., & Szymańska, A. I. (2011). Marketing transakcji a marketing relacji. *Zeszyty Naukowe WSE, 7*, pp. 205–214.

Edwards, J. (2013). Evian's babies, the most successful viral ad campaign of all time, roll again (accessed online on: 10.01.2021) https://www.businessinsider.com/evians-babies-the-most-successful-viral-ad-campaign-of-all-time-roll-again-2013-4?IR=T.

Ferguson, R. F., Paulin, M., & Leiriao E. (2006). Loyalty and positive word-of-mouth. *Health Marketing Quarterly, 23*(3), pp. 59–77, doi:10.1080/07359680802086174

Finne, Å., & Grönroos, C. (2017). Communication-in-use: Customer-integrated marketing communication. *Journal of Marketing, 51*(3), pp. 445–463.

Floyd, K., Freling, R., Alhoqail, S., Cho, H. Y., & Freling, T. (2014). How online product reviews affect retail sales: A meta-analysis. *Journal of Retailing, 90*(2), pp. 217–232.

Gladwell, M. (2000). *The tipping point: How little things can make a big difference.* Boston, MA: Little, Brown and Company.

Google. (2020). *Messy Middle* (accessed online on: 10.01.2021) https://www.thinkwithgoogle.com/intl/en-cee/consumer-insights/consumer-journey/navigating-purchase-behavior-and-decision-making/.

Górecka-Butora, P., Strykowski, P., & Biegun, K. (2019). *Influencer marketing Od A Do Z* (pp. 11–53).Bielsko-Biała: WhitePress.

Hajarian, M., Camilleri, M., Díaz, P., Aedo, I. (2021). A taxonomy of online marketing methods. In M. A. Camilleri (Ed.), *Strategic corporate communication in the digital age* (pp. 235–250). Bingley: Emerald. doi:10.1108/978-1-80071-264-520211014.

Harms, B., Bijmolt, T. H. A., & Hoekstra, J. C. (2019). You don't fool me! Consumer perceptions of digital native advertising and banner advertising, *Journal of Media Business Studies, 16*(4), pp. 275–294. doi:10.1080/16522354.2019.1640517.

Hoffman, D., & Novak, T. (1996). Marketing in hypermedia computer-mediated environments: Conceptual foundations. *Journal of Marketing, 60*(3), pp. 50–68. doi:10.2307/1251841.

Huang, M., Cai, F., Tsang, A. S. L., & Zhou, N. (2011). Making your online voice loud: The critical role of WOM information. *European Journal of Marketing, 45*(7/8), 1277. doi:10.1108/03090561111137714.

Karr, D., (2015). Buzz, viral or word of mouth marketing: What's the difference? Martech Zone (accessed online on: 10.01.2021) https://martech.zone/whats-the-difference-buzz-viral-word-of-mouth-marketing/.

Katona, Z., Zubcsek, P. P., & Sarvary, M. (2011). Network effects and personal influences: The diffusion of an online social network. *Journal of Marketing Research, 48*, pp. 425–443.

Keller, E. (2007). Unleashing the power of word of mouth: Creating brand advocacy to drive growth. *Journal of Advertising Research, 47*, pp. 448–452.

Kelley, H. H., & Michela, J. L. (1980). Attribution theory and research. *Annual Review of Psychology, 31*(1), pp. 457–501.

Kieżel, M., & Wiechoczek, J. (2017). Narzędzia e-marketingu w procesie kreowania wartości dla klienta. *Zeszyty Naukowe Politechniki Śląskiej, 114*, pp. 203–220.

Kotler, P., Kartajaya, H., & Setiawan, I. (2017). *Marketing 4.0: Moving from traditional to digital.* New York: Wiley.

Kotler, P., Lane Keller, K., Brady, M., Goodman, M., & Hansen, T. (2019). *Marketing management* (4th ed.) Harlow: Pearson Education.

Leon, G., & Sanchez-Cartas, J. (2018). On "influencers" and their impact on the diffusion of digital platforms. In J. Bajo, J. M. Corchado, E. Navarro, E. Osaba Icedo, P. Mathieu, P. Hoffa-Dabrowska, E. Del Val, S. Giroux, A.J.M. Castro, N. Sánchez-Pi, et al. (eds.), *Highlights of practical applications of agents, multi-agent systems, and complexity: The PAAMS collection. PAAMS 2018* (pp. 210–222). Communications in Computer and Information Science. Cham: Springer.

Martin Schaefer, H., & Ruxton, G. D. (2012). By-product information can stabilize the reliability of communication. *Journal of Evolutionary Biology, 25,* pp. 2412–2421.

Mayzlin, D., Yaniv D., & Chevalier, J. (2014). Promotional reviews: An empirical investigation of online review manipulation. *American Economic Review, 104*(8), pp. 2421–2455.

McCracken, G. (1989). Who is the celebrity endorser? Cultural foundations of the endorsement process. *Journal of Consumer Research, 16*(3), pp. 310–321.

Munzel, A. (2016). Assisting consumers in detecting fake reviews: The role of identity information disclosure and consensus. *Journal of Retailing and Consumer Services, 32,* pp. 96–108.

Ngoma, M., Dithan Ntale, P., & Wright, L. T. (2019). Word of mouth communication: A mediator of relationship marketing and customer loyalty. *Cogent Business & Management, 6*(1). doi:10.1080/23311975.2019.1580123.

Nielsen. (2015). *Global trust in advertising* (accessed online on: 10.01.2021) https://www.nielsen.com/eu/en/insights/report/2015/global-trust-in-advertising-2015/

Opoku, R. A., & Abdul-Muhmin, A. G. (2017). Peer group influence and products purchase decisions of young Saudi adult males. In C. L. Campbell (Eds.), *The customer is not always right? Marketing orientations in a dynamic business world.* Developments in Marketing Science: Proceedings of the Academy of Marketing Science. Cham: Springer. https://doi.org/10.1007/978-3-319-50008-9_203.

Oosterwijk, L., & Loeffen, A. (2005). *How to use buzz marketing effectively: A new marketing phenomenon explained and made practical.* Unpublished master's thesis, Mälardalen University, Eskilstuna, Sweden.

Piñeiro-Otero, T., & Martínez-Rolán, X. (2016). *Understanding digital marketing—basics and actions.* Berlin: Springer.

Pingdom, A. B. (2011). Internet 2010 in numbers (accessed online on: 10.01.2021) http://royal.pingdom.com/2011/01/12/internet-2010-in-numbers.

Qualman, E. (2009). *Socialnomics: How social media transforms the way we live and do business.* Hoboken, NJ: John Wiley & Sons.

Rayport, J. F. (1996, December). *The virus of marketing. Fast Company, 6,* p. 68.

Rein, I., Kotler, P., & Stoller, M. (1997). *High visibility: The making and marketing of professionals into celebrities* (2nd ed.). New York: NTC/Contemporary Publishing Company.

Riegner, C. (2007). Word of mouth on the Web: The impact of web 2.0 on consumer purchase decisions. *Journal of Advertising Research, 47*(4), 436–447. doi:10.2501/S0021849907070456.

Rosen, E. 2002. *The anatomy of buzz: How to create word-of-mouth marketing.* New York: Doubleday/Currency.

Sanak-Kosmowska, K., & Śliwińska, I. (2020). The sources of knowledge and their impact on consumers' decisions concerning proper nutrition. *Organization & Management: Scientific Quarterly*, nr *3*(51), s. 89–100.

Schaefer, M. (2012). *Return On Influence: The Revolutionary Power of Klout, Social Scoring, and Influence Marketing*. New York: McGraw-Hill.

Schouten, A. P., Janssen, L., & Verspaget, M. (2020). Celebrity vs. influencer endorsements in advertising: The role of identification, credibility, and Product-Endorser fit. *International Journal of Advertising*, *39*(2), 258–281. https://doi.org/10.1080/02650487.2019.1634898.

Silva, M. J. D. B., De Farias, S. A., Grigg, M. K., Barbosa, M. D. L. D. A. (2019). Online engagement and the role of digital influencers in product endorsement on Instagram. *Journal of Relationship Marketing*, *19*, 133–163.

Smith, D., Satya, M., & Sivakumar, K. (2005). Online peer and editorial recommendations, trust, and choice in virtual markets. *Journal of Interactive Marketing, 19*(3), 15–37.

Soh, H., Reid, L. N., & King, K. W. (2007). Trust in different advertising media. *Journalism & Mass Communication Quarterly*, *84*(3), pp. 455–476. https://doi.org/10.1177/107769900708400304.

Stewart, D. W. (2009). Marketing accountability: Linking marketing actions to financial results. *Journal of Business Research*, 62, pp. 636–643.

Taufique, K., & Shahriar, F. (2011). Online social media as a driver of buzz marketing: Who's riding?. *International Journal of Marketing, 1*, pp. 57–67. doi:10.4018/ijom.2011040104.

Touba, O., Stephen A., & Freud, A. (2011). Viral marketing: A large-scale-field experiment. *Economics, Management, and Financial Markets, 6*(3), pp. 43–65.

Trusov, M., Bucklin, R. E., & Pauwels, K. (2009). Effects of word-of-mouth versus traditional marketing: Findings from an Internet social networking site. *Journal of Marketing, 73*, pp. 90–102. doi:10.1509/jmkg.73.5.90.

Walczyk, P. (2019) Przez opinie klientów do serca… klientów! – Jak recenzje online zwiększają wartość biznesu? Brand 24 (accessed online on: 10.01.2021) https://brand24.pl/blog/przez-opinie-klientow-do-serca-klientow/.

Wangenheim, F., & Bayón, T. (2007). The chain from customer satisfaction via word-of-mouth referrals to new customer acquisition. *Journal of the Academy of Marketing Science, 35*, pp. 233–249. doi:10.1007/s11747-007-0037-1.

Weiner, B. (2000). Attributional thoughts about consumer behavior. *Journal of Consumer Research*, *27*(3), pp. 382–387. https://doi.org/10.1086/317592.

Wielki, J. (2020). Analysis of the role of digital influencers and their impact on the functioning of the contemporary on-line promotional system and its sustainable development. *Sustainability*, *12*, 7138.

Wiktor, J. W., & Sanak-Kosmowska, K. (2021). *Information asymmetry in online advertising*. London: Routledge. Word-of-mouth Marketing Association (Womma). (2005). *Word-of-mouth 101, an introduction to word- of mouth marketing* (accessed online on: 10.01.2021) http://www. womma.org/wom101/.

Zinoviev, D., & Duong, V. (2009). Toward understanding friendship in online social networks. *The International Journal of Technology, Knowledge, and Society: Annual Review*. 5. doi:10.18848/1832–3669/CGP/v05i02/55977.

4 Social influence and its manifestation in the hypermedia computer environment

Reasons, definition, models, and characteristics

Introduction

Interpretation of the question this book addresses, which is the phenomenon of social proof with respect to social media marketing, should properly begin with a presentation of the basic, classical models of social influence developed within the disciplines of sociology and psychology. In much the same spirit – as a means of addressing a question – basic models are adopted and applied in other fields of social science, such as economics and management. There exists a substantial research literature on social influence. Anthony Pratkanis (2007) identifies six key areas in the history of research on public space: (1) mass communication (including Richard Petty and John Cacioppo of the Ohio State School); (2) questions of cognitive dissonance (Leon Festinger); (3) theories and mechanisms of governance and the exercise of authority (Tom R. Tyler, among others); (4) methods for researching social influence (Jonathan Freedman and Scott Fraser, among others); (5) the power of the social situation (including conformism – Muzafer Sherif and Solomon Asch); and (6) rules of social influence (Robert Cialdini and others). Social psychology, for its part, is dominated by three main functional models: Social Influence Theory (SIT; Latané 1981; Latané & Wolf 1981), the Other-Total Ratio (OTR) model (Mullen 1983), and the Social Influence Model (SIM) by Sarah Tanford and Steven Penrod (1984). This chapter will discuss their basic assumptions where these are relevant to the book's objectives and will examine how they can be implemented in marketing – especially marketing communication and advertising. Attention will also be paid to Robert Cialdini's principles of social influence. The considerations in this chapter are based on an in-depth review of research reports and other academic literature on social proof.

The importance of social influence in contemporary advertising

Understanding how people influence others and are themselves influenced by the social environment is an important area of research in many disciplines, including psychology, sociology, ethics, political science, economics,

DOI: 10.4324/9781003128052-5

management, and marketing. Social influence is one of the ways of explaining the phenomena, processes, and mechanisms occurring in the life of society – very often in situations where logic and rationality might suggest alternative accounts. This general statement applies essentially to all areas of social relations and public life. However, to analyse them extensively would be neither possible nor advisable. Instead, the considerations to follow are distinctly selective and relate to marketing as an area in which social relations take shape.

Examples of how the significance of social influence in marketing is interpreted can be seen in its role in consumer decision-making (Katz & Lazarsfeld 1955), in the process of technology diffusion and adaptation (Rogers 1962), and in engagement in health-protective behaviour (Centola 2010). Social influence takes many forms and, depending on the mechanism explained, we call it conformity (Asch 1956), attitude change (e.g. McGuire 1989; Sherif et al. 1965), persuasion (Petty & Cacioppo 1986), obedience to authority (Milgram 1974), submissiveness (Cialdini & Goldstein 2004), or power (French & Raven 1959). As Gordon Williard All port put it, social psychology is 'the attempt to understand ... how the thoughts, feelings, and behaviour of individuals depend on the real, imagined, or indirect presence of others' (1968, p. 3).

It should be stressed that the debate on social influence has been under way in the social sciences for several decades, but it has been thoroughly reframed by the rapid advances in information and communications technologies (ICT). The development of the online environment and the virtualization of life means that social influence is now often mediated by technology. This phenomenon can be described as online social influence. It takes place, with the assistance of technological devices such as smartphones, computers, and tablets, in a virtual environment. The Web 2.0 environment and its subsequent versions – up to and including Web 5.0 – provide, by their very nature and specificity, entirely new conditions for the development of new manifestations of social influence (Walther et al. 2012). While the Internet's earliest iteration (Web 1.0) offered limited contact with other Internet users and no content sharing, virtual communities began emerging at an unprecedented rate when Web 2.0 appeared.

The behaviour of Internet users, including their thoughts, interactions, and initiatives, became visible to others due to user-generated content and the digital traces users leave behind online. This can be intentionally created and shared content, such as blog entries, reviews, and ratings, as well as content displayed automatically, such as information about visits to a website or interactions on social network sites. The content users provide serves as a source of information about consumers which, once it has been qualitatively and quantitatively analysed, makes it possible to predict the needs and expectations of Internet users successfully. This means that each item of content published by Internet users in the social media environment can influence the behaviour of other network users and, at the same time, constitute a source of marketing data for use by firms in campaigns based on social influence. In this way, contemporary technologies influence all aspects of the communication process. We shall now turn to a synthesis of the social influence research conducted in the second half of the twentieth century, which forms the basis for further discussion.

An outline of the history of social influence research

Consideration of social influence should properly begin with Solomon Asch (1951, 1956), a social psychologist and one of the pioneers of research into the role and importance of the presence of other people in the decision-making process. Asch's work placed particular emphasis on studying the influence of other people on the objective judgements made by research participants. He did so by asking his volunteers to look as closely as possible at a standard line and decide which one of three comparison lines it resembled most. Eighteen trials were conducted and the volunteers achieved 99% accuracy when they performed the task alone. The situation changed when the task was carried out in groups and when seven fake volunteers, who were in fact Asch's assistants, joined the experiment. Under these conditions only 63.2% gave correct answers. The study found considerable individual variation: approximately 5% of participants always conformed with the group's opinion, while approximately 25% of them stuck to their own judgements in each case. The remaining participants – experiencing the interaction of two opposing forces: 'the evidence of their senses and the unanimous opinion of a group of peers' (Asch 1951, p. 32) – were influenced by other participants in at least some of the trials. Follow-up research conducted in the form of interviews revealed that some participants had accepted the wrong answer as true because they treated it as the consensus. Other participants confirmed that they had had doubts about the correctness of the answer they chose, but had nevertheless made the decision suggested by others. Changes in behaviour due to the real or imagined influence of other people is referred to in social psychology as conformity.

Morton Deutsch and Harold Gerard (1955) continued this work in the form of several modifications of the experimental situation devised by Asch. They included an anonymous situation (in which the subjects were invisible to each other) and, exactly as in Asch's experiment, a face-to-face situation. The way in which other people's opinions were presented, that is, before the judgement was made, while it was being made, and based on visual cues (pressing a button that lit a bulb; the participants were separated from each other by partitions), was also a modification of Asch's work. Deutsch and Gerard found that social influence is weaker in anonymous situations without the physical presence of the other participants. This effect was also weaker when the false cues were presented visually. Deutsch and Gerard distinguished two types of social influence. The first is informational in nature. When observing other people's behaviour or listening to their judgements, we treat them as sources of information about reality. Individuals who react in the same way that others react do so to be right or to have a plausible, social justification for their decisions or behaviour. In the case of Solomon Asch's experiment, informational influence would mean participants succumbing to the influence of the experimenter's accomplices because of visual difficulties and the inability to compare the lines presented. The opinions of other participants would therefore be a source of information they would draw upon if they were unable to make a decision independently.

The second type of influence is distinctly social. Asch's experiment revealed a special case of conformity: one motivated primarily by a fear of rejection by the group or a desire to be accepted by it. Deutsch and Gerard (1955) refer to this as normative conformity, whereby people who imitate others' actions are behaving according to the norm of not being different from other group members, of becoming like them. On this understanding, conformity is a means of maintaining or forging a bond with a group, of gaining acceptance from other people, and of securing membership in a social group based on convergent opinions or values, or at least avoiding disapproval or being labelled a crank. The results of numerous studies have demonstrated that people who disagree with a group have difficulties in gaining its acceptance and that most people are well aware of this principle (cf. Campbell & Fairey 1989). The typology proposed by Deutsch and Gerard, despite having been created over half a century ago, still represents 'a cornerstone of dual motive approaches to social influence' (Prislin & Crano 2012, p. 328).

Leon Festinger's experiment (1953) had a significant impact on the social influence debate, while Festinger himself went down in the history of social psychology as the author of the theory of cognitive dissonance. This concept described a situation in which two cognitive elements contradict each other simultaneously. In his research, though, Festinger concentrated on public conformity and private acceptance. He sought in this way to explain the different motives underlying conformist behaviour. For example, it can be said that when individuals behave consistently with others and with their own attitudes there is public conformity and private acceptance, whereas when individuals behave consistently with others without accepting this within themselves there is public conformity without private acceptance. In conclusion, it is worth emphasizing that these ideas remain relevant today. In terms of the aims of this monograph, it is essential to clarify the nature of social influence in the social media environment. Referring to the characteristics of influencer marketing set out in the previous chapter, it can be assumed that the social influence that influencers exert on website users can be both informational and normative.

Jennifer Campbell and Patricia Fairey's (1989) original work on the influence of groups on individuals' decisions marked an important advance in the study of social influence. It is to them that we owe our knowledge of the importance of group size for social influence, which turns out to be meaningful when the normative need is higher than the informational need. Indeed, their finding that acceptance of social influence does not always have to mean uncritical adaptation to others is permanently inscribed in the development of the discipline. Other social psychologists (Cialdini & Goldstein 2004; Cialdini & Trost 1998; Wood 2000) took up this line of research and, based on a series of experiments, concluded that accepting social influence can also be a way to achieve individual goals, such as maintaining appropriate social relationships (goal of affiliation) or behaving correctly (goal of accuracy). Moreover, it has also been found that people analyse each other's behaviour in the cognitive process of finding the correct solution to a problematic situation, such as the need to make a choice. This has been called the principle of social proof (Cialdini 2001) or the principle of social validation (Rhoads & Cialdini 2002). Scholars of this theme found that when individuals are looking for a suitable solution to a problem, the tendency to follow others and be guided by the opinions of others increases in uncertain or unclear situations. When, however, the objective is to maintain a sense of belonging, susceptibility to influence depends on whether the setting is public or private (Asch 1951; Deutsch & Gerard 1955) or on cultural factors, such as collectivism versus individualism (Bond & Smith 1996). Given that they offer almost unlimited choice of seller, product features, and product variants, it can be assumed that online purchases foster a sense of uncertainty and ambiguity, which reviews and opinions written by other consumers and available to everyone can mitigate – thereby helping fellow consumers to make purchase decisions.

Models of social influence

The literature offers numerous examples of attempts to develop general models describing social influence, to explain its essential nature, and to show how it functions (Latané & Wolf 1981; Mullen 1983; Tanford & Penrod 1984).

Bibb Latané's proposition (1981), which is known as Social Impact Theory, provides a good starting point from which to explore this issue. It built on the earlier achievements of physicists and biologists in describing how large groups operate. The approaches taken by physics (spin glass theory, Anderson 1988; Fisher & Hertz 1991) or by biology (swarm theory, Beni & Wang 1990) assume that extremely complex structures do not require an overarching mechanism to govern them, and that self-organization is sufficient for them to function (Camazine et al. 2003). Scientists have demonstrated clearly that flocks of birds or the chaotic structures of magnetic states order themselves because the interactions between their elements are very simple (Conevey & Highfield 2007; Wooldridge 2002). Latané suggested in his seminal work (1981) that complex human societies function no differently: a few simple laws describing the mutual influence of individuals are sufficient to convey and predict the full complexity of a complicated web of social phenomena. Thus began a new method of interpreting change within whole communities, rather than only in dyads as before. In Latané's proposition, the magnitude of the social influence exerted on individuals by their social environments is defined as a multiplicative function of the number, immediacy, and strength of sources of influence. It increases in direct proportion to the square root of the number of people involved, in proportion to the power those people possess (social status and credibility, for example), and in inverse proportion to the square of an individual's distance from those people. The influence of individuals is thus cumulative, and the individuals closest to a target of influence and with the greatest power have the greatest impact.

By creating a simple numerical algorithm called the Other-Total Ratio, Brian Mullen (1983) devised an important model to explain social influence. It was based on a model of self-regulation (Carver et al. 1979; Carver & Scheier 1981), which assumes that the more other people's attention is focused on an individual, the more that individual will be inclined to conform to behaviours the individual perceives as (behavioural) norms. The perceived attention focused on an individual depends greatly on the relative number of people in the group to which an individual belongs that support a given viewpoint. Group structure therefore determines the degree of conformity or agreement.

Sarah Tanford and Steven Penrod (1984) developed the widely used SIM. When constructing it they drew on a computer model of jury decisions known as DICE (Penrod & Hastie 1979), which simulated differences in jury size and in the number of jurors who deliberately decided that a suspect was not guilty (even though he was). Tanford and Penrod criticized Latané's approach for its lack of precision in prediction and its inability to account for the data obtained in Asch's experiments. The SIM's most noteworthy advance is its inclusion of significant factors of social influence not considered in previous models, such as task type, group type, and individual variations in resistance to the influence under investigation. Like Latané, Tanford and Penrod believed that social influence is highly dependent on the number of information sources in a particular group. Unlike Latané, however, they described this relationship as cubic. In their view, it is not the case that each additional element increases the level of compliance. Instead, they argue, there is a critical point at which the effect evens out.

Summing up the discussion of the above models of social influence, it should be noted that none can fully predict an individual's susceptibility to social influence. They do not take account of the abilities of those who are subject to social influence and those who exert it, which are important variables. The abilities that determine changes in behaviour in situations of social exposure have been the subject of much research. An analysis of these variables, which are relevant to social proof and buyer behaviour in social media marketing, is presented later in this chapter.

Social influence online

The dynamic development of information and communication technologies and the extremely rapid growth of the World Wide Web mean that social influence is no longer thought of solely in terms of physical human interaction. Based on a review of essential research into online social influence, it may be stated that the role of communication media has been redefined: face-to-face communication and physical co-presence are no longer necessary to create a context conducive to the occurrence of social influence. This change, however, has been a gradual one. Where Web 1.0 was a unidirectional, sender-receiver information channel, Web 2.0 provides a medium for interpersonal communication based on the many-to-many model (Hoffman & Novak 1996). Web 3.0, in turn, is a network that supports relationships between people (Fuchs et al. 2010), while Web 4.0 offers a mobile version of Web 2.0 by connecting different devices in real time (Fleerackers & Meyvis 2018). One example of Web 4.0 technology is provided by websites that identify users and are thus able to personalize the information they offer. The definition of Web 5.0 continues to be debated. It is anticipated that it will be based on emotional, neurotechnology-based interaction between people and their devices (Fleerackers & Meyvis 2019; Kotler et al. 2021).

Over the period of its emergence as the primary channel of communication infrastructure, which allows its users to communicate with each other using computers connected to the World Wide Web, the Internet's role in human relations has become an area of research for specialists in management, psychology, and sociology. In the era of Web 1.0, computer-mediated communication was narrowly defined and usually meant communication via e-mail. As new communication tools emerged, however, the possibilities offered by Web 1.0 gradually expanded (Walther & Parks 2002). For Gary Marx (2001), the seeming anonymity of computer-mediated communication clearly distinguished it from face-to-face communication. Anonymity was generally believed to be highest when callers' identities and locations were unknown. What is more, the investigations Marx conducted in the early 2000s demonstrated that social cues resulting in, among other things, social influence were far weaker in the computer-mediated environment than in face-to-face interactions. From today's perspective, this statement would probably strike us as incorrect. What it does convey, however, is just how rapidly the World Wide Web has changed and just how far reaching its technological transformations have been. According to pioneering research conducted in the 1970s (Short et al. 1976), the absence in computer-mediated communication of signals such as physical presence, social cues, non-verbal cues, and contextual cues, which are important for communication and social interaction, resulted in a reduced sense of social presence. Subsequent studies that attempted to verify this hypothesis obtained inconclusive results. Vitaly Dubrovsky et al. (1991), for example, found that the relative influence of high- and low-status members on group decisions was more balanced in groups where computer-mediated communication was used than in face-to-face groups. By contrast, Suzanne Weisband et al. (1995), and then Andrea Hollingshead (1996), found that – where status differences were known to all group members and regardless of the communication medium – high-status members generally had more influence on group decisions than low-status members. A number of other studies have, on the other hand, detected effects in the computer environment that correspond to the category of social influence (Spears & Lea 1992; Postmes et al. 1998, 2000, 2001).

Experiments testing the social identity model of deindividuation effects proved to be an interesting and important line of research. The researchers that performed them demonstrated that, under conditions of deindividuation and where shared group identity is highly salient, interpersonal influence, social attraction, and stereotyping were more pronounced in groups communicating in a computer-mediated environment. This was so because, unable to individualize signals (as is possible in face-to-face communication), participants instead employed whatever social cues were available, even subtle ones, to form impressions of other people. Yet when shared identity was not important to their members, interpersonal influence, social attraction, and stereotyping were less pronounced in the groups communicating in a computer-mediated environment than in groups communicating face to face. For Joseph Walther (1992), this was evidence that people have such a strong need to engage in social interaction that, over time, they adapt to the communication medium used and find ways to convey social-emotional messages through it. Communication of this kind is exemplified by emoticons used in text messages and by users' near-instantaneous reactions to notifications that they have received a new message by e-mail, via Messenger, or from a social network site.

Advances in ICT and in software (Web 2.0) saw user-generated content begin to play a fundamental role in websites. Within the Web 2.0 environment, websites changed the paradigm of interaction between their owners and their users, who now became co-creators of content. Although the issue of social media is addressed in earlier chapters, it is worth restating their distinctly social nature, which is captured in the term 'social web'. The goal of Web 2.0-based platform developers is for the World Wide Web to provide users with as many options as possible to interact and integrate and to place pages that can be personalized at the disposal of Internet users the world over. The centre of gravity of webpages has shifted towards users. Developers and designers may build websites, but it is users who form the core that enables those websites to function. Users provide content (photographs, videos, links to interesting websites) and create dynamic communities that take on a life of their own. In this way, Web 2.0 supports individual participation in content creation and collaboration, whereas the early Web only enabled webmasters to create and manage content (Cormode & Krishnamurthy 2008; O'Reilly 2005). The specific conditions of Web 2.0, though, entail changes to all aspects of human-to-human communication. This insight is intrinsic to the purpose of this monograph. And three points related to it deserve to be highlighted.

First, because Web 2.0 explicitly promotes social connections and inter-actions between new and existing relationships, potential sources of social influence are not limited only to friends, family members, or opinion leaders we can meet face to face. Nor are they limited to anonymous strangers we only meet online (this is connected with the early era of computer-mediated communication). Instead, Web 2.0 makes it simple and straightforward for all types of senders – whether close acquaintances, anonymous strangers, or experts – to create and share content, and hence to increase the number and variety of sources of social influence. Depending on their credibility and the strength of their relationship with the recipient, these sources may generate different levels of social influence. Establishing online credibility is an ex-tremely complex process that is influenced by many factors (Metzger et al. 2010). What is important, though, is that social networks make it possible to interact with senders by following their activities, subscribing to their blogs or 'friending' them, that is, making their acquaintance or, even, forming a close friendship on Facebook and other social media. Second, not all messages gen-erated online that can influence recipients are purposefully crafted by sources and reach them directly. Messages can also be understood as traces of the digital activity of people being observed or followed, which are registered and aggregated at the level of the website. These can include likes, comments, rec-ommendations, shares, and check-ins. The four basic types of messages pub-lished on Web 2.0 sites are shown in Table 4.1 (Walther & Jang 2012).

Table 4.1 Primary message types published on websites based on Web 2.0 technology

Message type	Description	Example of message
Content belongs to website owner	A message created and displayed by the main content provider or owner of a website that remains on that site	A blogpost, an article on a webpage, a post on a managed social media profile
User-generated content	News, posts, messages, comments, and reviews added to the owner's content	Comments, likes, and reviews posted on social media, blogs, or news sites
Deliberate aggregation of user data	Computer-generated descriptive statistics displayed on webpages that describe site-related behaviour	The aggregated value of ratings and comments provided by users, such as those on Booking.com
Random aggregation of user data	Data generated by the system not originally intended as indicators for users	Numbers of views of multimedia on sites such as YouTube or Vimeo; the number of friends a user has

Third, different levels of social influence can be associated with the channels of communication operative on Web 2.0-based websites. On social networks such as Facebook and Twitter, the social connections of users who generate content are public. In this way, the user is distinguishable as the sender and the group of recipients is clearly listed.

Recipients play an important role in the process of social influence taking place on the 'social web'. In this connection it is particularly important to note that recipients interact with senders by providing public feedback in the form of likes, comments, and shares. What is more, recipients can easily criticize senders, for instance, by writing negative reviews about firms.

The focus of contemporary research into social influence in the virtual environment is on ways to assess the credibility of senders and message content, the effectiveness of social influence-based marketing activities, and the impact of information on the behaviour and well-being of network users.

Attempts to identify ways of assessing online leaders' credibility as message senders (influencers) represent one interesting line of research (cf. Huffaker 2010). The reach of influencers, who are described in detail in the previous chapter, can be measured in different ways, including by the number of followers and number of retweets (Cha et al. 2010), by using existing algorithms such as PageRank (Kwak et al. 2010), and through a cascade approach (Bakshy et al. 2011). The impact of information generated by influencers' peers in the virtual environment has also attracted the interest of researchers. The willingness to follow others also depends on how strongly we associate with the source or sender (Brown & Reingen 1987). Research has shown that, much as they do in the case of social influence in the real world, social ties on social networks and online communities influence users' purchasing behaviour (Iyengar et al. 2009) and content creation (Shriver et al. 2013).

Analysis of the influence of particular forms of marketing messages on purchasing decisions represents an important strand of research. Studies in this field have shown that users also pay attention to anonymous posts when considering purchases (Mayzlin 2004, cited in Godes & Mayzlin 2004). Furthermore, the results of laboratory experiments suggest that recommendation systems have a greater impact than the guidance of experts or other consumers (Chen 2008; Senecal & Nantel 2004). Moreover, researchers have also found that disloyal and dissatisfied customers exert a greater impact on consumers' awareness of new products – especially those that have appeared on the market relatively recently (Godes & Mayzlin 2009). In contrast, Zeinab Abbassi et al. (2012) reported that recommendations from an anonymous 'crowd' have a greater impact on the probability of making a purchase than recommendations from friends. More specifically, whereas one additional star increases the probability by 17%, one additional friend recommendation increases the probability by 22%. Sinan Aral and Dylan Walker (2011) showed that the influence of a friend's review is greater than that of an anonymous person, but due to the relatively small number of messages written by friends, the influence of reviews written by strangers is just as strong. A detailed analysis of the ways in which modern enterprises manage reviews and recommendations is presented in the next chapter.

As the frequency of human interaction in virtual environments increases, so too does the number and variety of potential sources of influence. While in the real world sources of influence were limited to face-to-face contact, they are almost unlimited in the social web environment. Now, at the threshold of the twenty-first century's second decade, we are confronted with the 'mass personalization' of the influence exerted on individuals – a process that is itself supported by artificial intelligence algorithms used on social network sites, which further amplify this effect. Social influence on social network sites applies not only to consumer behaviour, but also, and perhaps especially, to global social issues such as the polarization and radicalization of social media users' political views (cf. Greenberg 2016; Thompson 2012), to voting (Di Grazia et al. 2013), and to the mental health and self-esteem of Internet users (De Choudhury et al. 2012; Wylie 2020). It should not be forgotten, however, that although the forms and ways in which it is mediated change, the mechanisms underlying social influence remain the same – despite the massive strides forward taken by information and communication technologies. One of the most prominent scholars to have set out the basic principles of social influence is Robert Cialdini.

Robert Cialdini's principles of social influence

Robert Cialdini (1984) concluded from his examination of phenomena related to the field of social influence that most situations in which people agree to comply with the requests, suggestions, or commands of others are related to at least one of the following mechanisms: reciprocity, commitment and consistency, social proof, liking, scarcity, and authority. Known as the principles of social influence, they are of universal significance. They can be applied in all areas of social life and they shape social and business relationships, where they permeate all functions of marketing, including advertising. Moreover, they have come to form an important element of research into the mechanisms of social influence, including manipulation. It is for this reason that they form part of the analysis and narrative presented in this chapter.

Robert Cialdini identified the following six principles for exerting social influence to shape social reality and the relationships that comprise it:

1   *The principle of reciprocity.* Reciprocity is one of the strongest and most hallowed principles governing social interactions. According to it, when we receive goods, we wish to give something back in return. It is a norm that organizes the life of individuals, social groups, and whole societies. Thanks to this principle, social ties, trust, and lasting coalitions can be established (Uehara 1995, pp. 483–502; Yamagishi & Kiyonari 2000,

pp. 116–132). Adherence to it signals the importance – for shaping human behaviour, for changing opinions and attitudes, and for cultivating goodwill – of reciprocating a received benefit or reward. The creation of obligations generates a sense of duty to respond appropriately, which may take different forms and be more strongly or less strongly felt. Of course, this duty can be extended to apply to the 'mixed', institutional-personal relationships typical of the business-to-consumer (B2C) market, and to the incentives to buy promoted products and offers of unique values typical of advertising. The norm of mutual concessions is a special variant of the principle of reciprocity. It underpins a technique of social influence known as door-in-the-face. The idea is that in order to get someone to fulfil a rather difficult request, it is advantageous to preface it with a request that is even more difficult to fulfil. The first request will probably be rejected, but the refusal will make the person more likely to meet the second, easier request (Doliński 2011). The rule of reciprocity is one of the most important principles governing social life. Those who do not adhere to it risk being ostracized or even excluded from the community altogether (Gouldner 1960).

2   *The principle of commitment and consistency.* Many factors determine the mechanism of commitment and consistency. One is to increase the mental availability of a given behaviour. Just imagining a course of action or thinking about it increases the chances of it happening. This is linked to the way every human being's knowledge functions: an increase in the mental availability of a way of behaving increases the likelihood of our actually behaving in that way. For example, a study by Larry Gregory et al. (1982) found that people who were led to imagine themselves as cable TV users were more likely than others to become cable TV subscribers. Another process that determines commitment is the justification of effort or other resources, such as time or money, that have already been invested. If we have already put some of our resources into achieving an effect, then the only way to avoid wasting them is to continue the project in question (Doliński 2011).

Two factors are important in exerting influence on another person. First, the information recipient's 'commitment to the cause' and, second, consistency in maintaining this. Exerting influence and inducing particular behaviour begins by arousing and sustaining psychological tension in recipients of advertising messages and then guiding their motivation. This is possible by showing the particular value of taking an action, adopting a particular opinion, or suggesting a particular behaviour. When recipients acknowledge them as their own and internalize them, the grounds are created for consistency of action and continuity of influence. Consistency refers to important features of people's personalities and attitudes: accepting a given opinion, norm, or standpoint 'forces' the information recipient into a particular type of behaviour that accords with the already accepted standpoint of the sender. Social psychology and sociology (including social engineering) offer many detailed methods for implementing this rule, including the well-known 'foot-in-the-door', 'low-ball', and 'door-in-the-face' techniques. It has been shown in studies of the foot-in-the-door technique, for example (Freedman & Fraser 1966), that a person's compliance with an easy request, such as signing a petition in favour of greater road safety, subsequently makes that person more likely to comply with a much more difficult request of a similar nature, such as agreeing to erect a sign on one's own property that asks drivers to drive carefully. Analogous effects can be brought about even by arousing the intention to fulfil the initial request (Doliński 2000). The wish to preserve one's public image is another important factor that strengthens commitment. If we wish to present ourselves to other people as consistent, we feel obliged to continue the actions we have started. This rule is also relevant to advertising as a form of exerting influence on recipients. The strength and attractiveness of the unique value of the message, the originality of the advertising, and continuous, multichannel communication are important conditions for arousing recipients' interest and involvement in the communication process.

3   *The principle of liking and sympathy.* This is an important and socially accepted form of exerting influence on other people. We are more willing to comply with the requests and wishes of those who arouse sympathy in us or who we know and like. We prefer people who are polite, but also those with views similar to ours. The relationship between similarity and liking is not, however, limited to the views we express. Robert Cialdini (1984) showed that insurance policy salespeople are more likely to succeed when they are of a similar age to their potential customers. Physical attractiveness has an influence on liking (Hatfield & Sprecher 1986), while performing an action with another person or working together to achieve a goal also has a significant effect on mutual attraction (cf. Duck & Sants 1983).

The principle of liking and sympathy can be employed in many specific techniques for exerting social influence and shaping interpersonal relationships that aim to sway interlocutors and persuade them to behave in a particular way. Advertising offers myriad opportunities to exploit this principle. In advertising spots, this means the deliberate use of people who are known, liked, and who arouse affection with the intention of exerting a particular influence on the recipients of a message. Consumers have a considerable propensity to succumb to such character traits in advertising.

4   *The principle of authority.* Authority is an important means of influencing the behaviour of other people by respecting them, taking them seriously, valuing them and recognizing their knowledge, skills, and social position. The same applies to institutions that possess authority.

Authority – both formal and real – is a form of legitimization of a given individual's power and the degree of internalization by a social group of their values, beliefs, and outlooks, including knowledge, skills, and objectivity. In the context of influencing another person, the issues of an authority's influence and submission to their views are also important in the realm of advertising and marketing communication. Creative advertising strategies that involve selecting a character – an authority or expert – that matches the value system and expectations of the target market are based on the principle of authority. The work done on the subject within the field of psychology offers a stimulating complement to this discussion of authority. In an experiment conducted in the mid-1970s, Stanley Milgram (1974) demonstrated that most people complied when prompted by an authority figure to inflict pain on another person. The reasons why people comply with commands are many and varied, as are the commands themselves (cf. Blass 2000; Doliński 2000). One of the most important is that those to whom the commands are directed find themselves in positions of subordination and dependency. This pattern of behaviour is formed in early childhood when we receive instant positive reinforcement for complying with instructions immediately and without reflection.

5   *The principle of scarcity.* Reactance theory, which was formulated by Jack Brehm (1966), states that if an object or opportunity to act is taken away from us, or the possibility of its removal arises, its subjective value increases. Sellers and service providers often take advantage of the fact that a product's limited availability makes it more desirable in the eyes of customers (Cialdini 1984; Doliński 1998). Suggestions or information to the effect that a product might be unavailable spur people to act in particular ways. To highlight the essence of this rule, it is of secondary importance whether a product's scarcity is real (the model or series is no longer being made) or merely suggested (to increase demand). In response to scarcity, or to news of scarcity, everyone reacts strongly and activates the appropriate homeostasis mechanism. Therein lies the power and significance of the principle of scarcity. The availability of a product is a factor that lowers subjective impressions of its value – and also its price. This is illustrated by the supply and demand curve. In turn, there is a marked increase in the utility function of goods that are beginning to be scarce. The principle of scarcity is familiar both in social life and in marketing. We need only think of advertisements referring to limited editions, special offers, promotions rapidly nearing their end, products available while stocks last, and prices that apply only for limited periods. Advertisements of this kind have a powerful influence on demand by creating incentives for consumers and thereby increasing sales of the brands promoted in this way.

The sixth principle, the principle of social proof, which is the focus of the research presented in this book, is discussed in detail below.

Cialdini's principles serve as a platform for the formulation of various techniques for influencing other people in all of their social roles – including that of consumer. Their properties are relevant to all situations in which influence is sought. However, it is important to note that not all consumers are equally susceptible to them. The discussion turns now to the traits or abilities that determine susceptibility to social influence.

Strategies of social influence

According to Mehdi Moussaïd and his colleagues (2013, p. 1), social influence refers to 'the process by which individuals adapt their opinions, revise their beliefs, or change their behaviour as a result of social interactions with other people'. As mentioned earlier, there are two basic types of social influence: informational and normative (Deutsch & Gerard 1955). Informational social influence involves accepting information obtained from other people as a valuable source of knowledge about the surrounding reality. Normative social influence involves conforming to the positive expectations of other people (Deutsch & Gerard 1955; Wood 2000). The subject literature, though, expands the informational-normative paradigm to offer a more detailed understanding of social influence in terms of strategies. Kiemute Oyibo and Julita Vassileva (2019) have proposed three theoretical constructs reflecting possible social influence strategies. These are:

*   Social learning.
*   Social proof.
*   Social comparison.

Social learning entails the acquisition of new behaviours by observing and imitating others (Oinas-kukkonen & Harjumaa 2008; Stibe & Oinas-Kukkonen 2014). The mechanism of this strategy is based on Albert Bandura's theory of social learning (1971), which assumes that, in a process of social cognition, people learn by observing the behaviour of others and its consequences. Bandura referred to social learning as a self-regulatory process in which learning and regulation of one's own behaviour occurs through the observation of reinforcement and punishment. It is important to note, though, that social learning may or may not lead to a desired change in attitude and behaviour. This is instead largely dependent on an individual's susceptibility to social influence. In empirical (self-report) research, social learning is a subjective measure of the extent to which an individual will change their behaviour as a result of observing the behaviour of others (Oyibo et al. 2017).

Social proof involves accepting the behaviour of others as a way of conforming to perceived correct norms of behaviour or making a choice of correct behaviour in a situation of uncertainty or ambiguity. A detailed account of social proof appears later in this chapter. It is worth noting that in empirical research, susceptibility to social proof is assumed to be a subjective measure of the extent to which a person assumes that the actions of others are the correct behaviours to imitate (Deutsch & Gerard 1955). In the persuasion susceptibility scale constructed by Maurits Kaptein and his team (2012), susceptibility to social proof is expressed in the construct 'When I am in a new situation, I look to others to see what I should do'.

Social comparison is the tendency to self-evaluate by comparing ourselves to people we are similar to (Festinger 1954). It includes comparing our opinions and abilities with those of other people and is motivated by the desire to mitigate uncertainty (Garcia et al. 2013). A propensity for social comparison is therefore a subjective measure of susceptibility to the tendency to compare oneself with others.

Social proof as a special case of social influence

Social influence, understood as a change in the behaviour, attitudes, or emotions experienced by an individual as a result of the actions of others, can take many forms. After Morton Deutsch and Harold Gerard (1955), the literature analysis presented in the first part of this chapter outlines the two most important types of social influence: informational and normative. Robert Cialdini (1984), in turn, identified a number of ways of exerting influence, which are known as the principles of social influence and which are sketched above. The sixth of these is the principle of social proof.

When we are unsure of how to behave in a given situation, we tend to observe the behaviour of others and take it as a cue for the action appropriate for us to take (Sherif 1936; Wooten & Reed 1998). Cialdini (2001) defined social proof as a strategy that influences people to perceive certain actions as 'correct in a given situation to the extent that we see others perform it'. Social proof strategies influence their addressees' normative beliefs about behaviour and encourage them to conform to the behaviour of others (Cialdini 2001; Cialdini et al. 1999). This principle, also known as 'the wisdom of the crowd', is one of the fundamental rules governing human behaviour. In one of his books, Cialdini (2014) presented a simple experiment illustrating the mechanism of social proof. In a busy and crowded subway station in New York City, his assistants counted how many subway passengers were giving money to buskers. Very few were. After some time had passed, a small modification was made that had an immediate and impressive effect. Before an unsuspecting passer-by drew near to the busker, one of Cialdini's assistants would toss a few coins into the hat in full view of the passer-by. As a result, there was an eightfold increase in the number of subway passengers who chose to leave the busker some money. The principle of social proof induces changes in behaviour in a variety of contexts, such as the influence of other people's laughter on the perception of humorous content (Fuller & Sheehy-Skeffington 1974; Nosanchuk & Lightstone 1974) or the level of pain and fear experienced by people when tolerance or intolerance of it is socially validated beforehand (Craig & Parkachin 1978; O'Conner 1972).

The principle of social proof rests on the theory of social comparison devised by Leon Festinger (1954). Because the desire to make the right choices is strong, there is an equally powerful and widespread tendency to follow the 'crowd'. This is accompanied, in Festinger's view, by a desire for accurate self-evaluation. People assess their own opinions and abilities through constant social comparison with others to whom they relate. In this way they reduce their uncertainty and confirm the validity of their behaviour. Social comparison theory contends that the perceived normative behaviour of similar people influences the decision-making of the target audience.

The principle of social proof, whose mechanisms have been described by Cialdini and his followers, has been employed in advertising and direct selling for decades. Nowadays, the principle of social proof provides the platform for the effective operation of some Internet marketing tools. Buzz marketing on Internet forums, celebrity endorsement, and influence marketing are all based on the mechanism of recommendations. Social media platforms – the general ones, used primarily to keep in touch with friends and exchange messages, photos and news, such as Facebook and Instagram, as well as specialist services dedicated to tourism, such as Tripadvisor, or to professional life, such as LinkedIn – present a special case of platforms on which Internet users exchange opinions and recommendations. (It should be emphasized that the exchange of opinions and mutual recommendations lies at the operational core of these services.) The phenomenon of social proof in the digital environment is examined in the next chapter.

Abilities that determine behaviour in situations of social exposure

Extensive research has been done on social influence and its significance for consumer attitudes and behaviour. Yet there have been far fewer reports on the role of individual differences in determining susceptibility to social influence. This section seeks to describe the abilities that determine behaviour in situations of social exposure and pays particular attention to the under-researched role of individual differences in determining susceptibility to social influence.

Much research on social influence focuses on why individuals choose to be influenced by others (Cialdini et al. 1991). Some scholars, however, including Wendy Wood and her colleagues (1994), have attempted to identify the reasons why some people are able to resist social influence. Jack Brehm (1966) referred to this phenomenon as 'psychological reactance'.

That people become motivationally aroused by a threat to, or by elimination of, a behavioural freedom is the central assumption of psychological reactance theory. The threats often include 'attempts at interpersonal influence' (Clee & Wicklund 1980), such as persuasion from political activists and advertisers. What is more, threats can also be self-imposed – quite independently of external hazards such as social influence and product availability. As we progress through a decision-making process, we reach a point beyond which the freedom to decide is undesirably restricted, which can be caused, for example, by the need to process too much information (Clee & Wicklund 1980). The degree of reactance varies according to the proportion or importance of the freedom to behave as we wish that is lost or threatened. Reactance may be reduced where there are grounds for believing that a threat is temporary or unavoidable. As Brehm (1966) argues, as the pressure to follow rules imposed by other people increases, so does the pressure not to follow them, and the resulting impact on the individual's ultimate response is difficult to predict. The reason why 25% of the participants in Asch's (1951) experiments did not succumb to the influence of the majority may have been that their residual reactance was greater than the social influence, or that the pressure to conform to the majority actually increased the amount of reactance.

From a psychological perspective, the motivation for using social networks such as Facebook and Instagram is to satisfy a variety of social needs, including the need for belonging and affiliation, and to take advantage of the opportunity for self-expression and self-presentation (Back et al. 2010; Gosling et al. 2011; Toubia & Stephen 2013). Psychological factors, including individual differences, are therefore an important part of explaining the social influence that occurs in the Web 2.0 environment. This chapter has set out selected psychological constructs whose relationship to susceptibility to social influence has been reported in the psychology, sociology, and management literature. Two of these – personality and self-esteem – are elements of the research model presented in this book.

The e-consumer personality and susceptibility to social influence

Personality traits are among the most fundamental variables in the description of personality (cf. Goldberg 1992; McAdams & Pals 2006; McCrae & Costa 1999). They refer to a relatively enduring predisposition to respond in a certain way, including the tendency to exhibit both certain behaviours and certain emotional reactions. Traits do not reveal themselves directly, but their existence can be inferred from observable behaviour and emotional responses. With the development of research in the psychology of individual differences, a variety of personality models have emerged. One of the most frequently used is the Big Five model (Goldberg 1992), in which the basic structure of personality traits consists of extroversion, agreeableness, conscientiousness, emotional stability (or its reverse – neuroticism), and the factor of intellect or imagination, which is also referred to – in the psychometric tradition (McCrae & Costa 1999) – as openness to experience. These dimensions of personality are set out in detail in Table 4.2 (Topolewska et al. 2014).

Table 4.2 The personality traits of the Big Five model

Personality dimension	Description
Extroversion	Level of activeness, energy, and sociability. Low scores describe people who are untalkative, socially inhibited, and reserved, while high scores describe people who are active, sociable, assertive, and talkative
Agreeableness	Positive versus negative attitude to people. A low score describes people who are distrustful, impolite, and emotionally cold, while a high score describes people who are trusting, polite, and cordial in their relationships with others
Conscientiousness	Level of organization and consistency in action and goal achievement and propensity for order. A low score describes people who are unsystematic, careless, and noncommittal, while a high score describes people who are thorough, precise, and dutiful
Emotional stability (versus neuroticism)	Level of excitability and emotional balance, and tolerance of frustration. A low score describes people who are neurotic, who are anxious and nervous, and who are prone to worry. A high score describes people who are balanced and emotionally stable
Intellect or openness to experience (sensation seeking)	Intellectual openness, imagination, and creativity. Those of a low intellect are non-abstract, mundane, and not particularly creative. Those of a high intellect are cognitively open, reflective, and have a rich imagination

Personality traits determine all of these human behaviours and, therefore, all of those connected with purchasing decisions too. The literature records many cases in which knowledge of personality categories made it possible to predict consumer behaviour in specific situations. According to Todd A. Mooradian and K. Scott Swan (2006), knowledge of someone's personality makes it possible to predict their emotional response to advertisements. Kurt Matzler et al. (2006), who focused their attention on hedonistic products, found that openness to experience and extroversion correlated positively with brand affect. Researchers have also addressed the phenomenon of brand loyalty, with agreeableness and intellect proving to be statistically significant in this case (Lin 2010).

Teresa Correa et al. (2010) produced one of many studies of social networks that have shown a relationship between personality and Internet user behaviour in a social context. For their part, Tel Amiel and Stephanie Lee Sargent (2004) examined the relationship between personality and the motives for Internet use. They found that people who scored high on the neuroticism scale were more likely to use the Internet for information and a sense of belonging. What is more, they found that people who score high on the extroversion scale are more likely to reject the social benefits of the Internet – that is, to reject its use as a substitute for real human interaction – and to use the World Wide Web in a goal-oriented manner. Stefan Wehrli's (2008) investigation of the influence of personality traits on behaviour on social network sites produced some interesting findings. He determined that users with high levels of neuroticism use social network sites more often and have more friends. Kelly Moore and James McElroy (2012) examined the influence of personality on Facebook use. They found that users with high levels of extroversion use Facebook more rarely, while those with low levels of conscientiousness are more likely to post pictures about themselves and others on their Facebook profiles. Moreover, Yair Amichai-Hamburger and Gideon Vinitzky (2010), who conducted a similar study, found that people with high levels of neuroticism also post photos of themselves on Facebook more often. Neurotics are also foremost among those who spend the most time on Facebook (Orr et al. 2009; Ryan & Xenos 2011), while extroverts are most active in brand communities (Aspendropf & Wilpers 1998). Małgorzata Karpińska-Krakowiak (2018) and Marco Nitzschner and his colleagues (2015) have written stimulating research reports on the relationship between personality traits and the response to content in advertising messages.

The findings of Vikanda Pornsakulvanich (2017), who examined the relationship between personality and satisfaction with online social support, are also pertinent to the research objectives of this book. She found that the higher a participant scores on the agreeableness and openness scales, the more likely they are to be satisfied with the social support provided by other Internet users online.

In the literature we can find numerous methods for measuring the intensity of personality traits. Two of the most widely known grew out of the psychometric conceptualization of personality traits: Paul Costa and Robert McCrae's Revised NEO Personality Inventory (NEO-PI-R 1992) and NEO Five-Factor Inventory (NEO-FFI 2004), both of which have Polish adaptations (Siuta 2006; Zawadzki et al. 1998). The NEO-PI-R Inventory consists of 240 items, and in addition to the five general scales, the results also provide information on six specific characteristics within each of the five major dimensions. The NEO-FFI is a more concise tool. It consists of 60 statements and makes it possible to determine the intensity of the five main personality traits without specifying the six detailed characteristics within each of the dimensions. The Big Five Inventory devised by Oliver John et al. (1991), which consists of 44 sentences that reflect the characteristics most typical of each dimension, is another frequently used method from the lexical tradition. The Structured Interview for the Five-Factor Model of Personality (SIFFM), developed by Thomas Widiger and Timothy Trull (1997), is an interesting tool used mainly in the diagnosis of personality disorders (Klinkosz & Sękowski 2008).

The questionnaires that the above tools rest on take a long time to complete and require a high degree of involvement from researcher and participant alike.

Yet this does not present a problem for psychological diagnosis and clinical research. It should be noted, however, that personality trait measurement frequently forms a part of research undertaken in social psychology, sociology, and marketing. Researchers in these disciplines often decide to use a shortened version of the test, such as the TIPI (Ten-Item Personality Measure) scale, which contains ten questionnaire indicators. That scale, which is employed in the research presented here, is described in detail in the chapter on research methodology.

Susceptibility to social influence and self-esteem

According to Rosenberg's definition (1965), self-esteem implies an awareness of one's value system and one's emotional evaluation of one's self-worth. For Philip Zimbardo (1999), though, it is a generalized evaluative attitude about oneself that affects both mood and personal and social behaviour. Stanley Coopersmith (1967) takes the view that self-esteem is the evaluation we make and customarily maintain with regard to ourselves. Self-esteem expresses an attitude of approval or disapproval of ourselves, also in our dealings with other people, and is a measure of how we perceive our abilities, importance, chances of success, and worth.

Self-esteem is measured using standardized psychological tools. The primary one – which is also used in this book – is the Morris Rosenberg Self-Assessment Scale, which consists of ten sentences eliciting responses on a four-point scale. It is simple, easily understood and interpreted, and stable over time, but it is not without its flaws (Anastasi & Urbina 1999). Self-esteem measurement techniques based on narrowly defined constructs, such as 'me at work' or 'me at school', are also used in psychological diagnosis. Harrison Gough and Alfred Heilbrun's Adjective Check List (ACL), which contains a list of 300 adjectives that can be freely chosen by the person under investigation, is a further measurement tool worthy of consideration.

Self-esteem has been studied extensively within the disciplines of psychology and sociology. Its dominant research strand involves the relationship of self-esteem to mental health and well-being, but important work is also being done on the relationship between self-esteem and susceptibility to social influence. The results obtained by Arthur Cohen (1959) indicate that people with high self-esteem actually exert more influence on others, and perceive that they do so, than people with low self-esteem. Individuals with high self-esteem are, moreover, better able to protect themselves from an unfavourable evaluation by not responding to expectations communicated by their group when unfavourable comparison with others would be likely. Individuals with high self-esteem, who seem less sensitive to external influences, also have a preference for ego defences that help them suppress, deny, or ignore difficult and conflicting impulses. Individuals with lower self-esteem, who are more open, or exposed, to external influences, prefer more pronounced defence mechanisms, such as projection or regression, and may be more affected by situations and events.

Evidence for the important role of self-esteem in susceptibility to social influence was also provided by Gregory Pool et al. (1998), who reported that opinions expressed by important social groups can significantly impair self-esteem. The participants in their study who wanted to join a majority group, but who learned that it took a position that conflicted with their own, experienced a reduction in self-esteem. However, group attitudes did not affect the self-esteem of participants who were indifferent to joining the majority group.

Much of the research into self-esteem has addressed the social media environment. The researchers rightly suspected that such intense exposure to interpersonal relationships might have important implications for self-esteem. Erin Vogel and her team (2014) examined the effect on self-esteem of chronic exposure to social comparisons with others on social media. Their results confirmed that participants who use Facebook are most likely to have lower self-esteem, and this was mediated by greater exposure to positive social comparisons on social media. They also revealed that participants' self-esteem was lower when the profile of the person they were comparing themselves to contained upward comparison information, such as a large number of friends, appealing photographs, and healthy habits, than when the profile of the person they were comparing themselves to contained downward comparison information, such as a small number of friends, unappealing photographs, and unhealthy habits. Elisa Bergagna and Stefano Tartaglia (2018) examined whether the tendency to make social comparisons plays a mediating role in the relationship between time spent on Facebook and levels of self-esteem. The results revealed the role of orientation to social comparison in mediating the relationship between low self-esteem and some indicators of Facebook use, i.e. the times of the day when Facebook activity takes place and the total number of hours a person is active on the site. For women, using Facebook to engage in social interactions was directly related to high levels of self-esteem. Women also showed a stronger tendency towards social comparison than men.

An important line of research in terms of the objectives of this monograph is the measurement of the relationship between self-esteem and the perception of, and susceptibility to, advertising. In his landmark article on consumer self-esteem, Jeffrey Durgee (1986) hypothesized that advertising that has a positive effect on consumers' attitudes towards themselves also has a positive effect on their attitudes towards the brands advertised. Durgee also formulated the idea of self-esteem advertising, which is understood as a specific type of advertising that aims to change attitudes and behaviour towards products by making consumers feel positive about themselves. In their study of the impact of advertising beauty images on female preadolescents and adolescents, Mary Martin and Patricia Kennedy (1993) established that women with lower self-esteem were more likely to compare their appearance with models presenting products in advertisements.

Ways of measuring susceptibility to social influence

As indicated earlier, measuring individual differences that determine susceptibility to social influence is possible using standardized psychological inventories. Such tools possess a number of advantages: standardized measurements deliver reliable results, most scales have well established sten scores, and linguistic adaptations allow for research to be conducted in international conditions. Nevertheless, there are a number of factors that constrain the use of psychological tests. First, most inventories consist of dozens of questionnaire items and thus take a long time to complete. Second, controlled experiments under appropriate conditions, which are managed by teams of psychologists and for which the participants are properly prepared, are required. Finally, studies that use psychological measurement tools should not be repeated: participants 'learn' the answers, so the reliability of results obtained with repeated measurement may be limited.

A number of research tools for measuring social influence can be found in the literature. Using them makes it possible to reduce the time needed to carry out research while ensuring that the results are highly reliable. The Persuadability Inventory, which was devised by Marc Busch et al. (2013) and which can be used to gauge susceptibility to persuasion techniques based on content personalization, is one of them. It measures constructs such as susceptibility to social comparison, social learning, preference for persuasive content, and trust in persuasive content.

The Susceptibility to Persuasive Strategies scale, which was elaborated by Maurits Kaptein and his colleagues (2012) and measures susceptibility to Cialdini's six principles of social influence, is another interesting tool. Its value lies in its capacity for reliable assessment of susceptibility to, and of preferences for, particular influence strategies – including susceptibility to social proof.

David Modic et al. (2018) proposed a slightly different questionnaire, which is known as Susceptibility to Persuasion-II. It contains 54 items relating to over a dozen constructs, including sensation seeking, self-control, susceptibility to the opinions of others, the need to fit in with the behaviour of others, attitudes towards advertising, and the need for originality. The tool measures overall susceptibility to persuasion techniques. The authors of the questionnaire report a number of options for using it in practice, including for investigating the susceptibility to persuasion of IT security officers and for screening victims of cybercrime.

The experimental studies presented in Chapter 8 demonstrate how particular research constructs can be used to measure the determinants of susceptibility to social proof.

The next chapter of the book is devoted to the role of social proof in the process of social commerce, which denotes online purchases made in the social media environment. It should be emphasized that deploying marketing messages that use social proof on social network sites significantly increases sales. It can thus be said, after Jaron Lanier, that 'what might once have been called advertising must now be understood as continuous behaviour modification on a titanic scale' (2018).

References

Abbassi, Z., Aperjis, C., & Huberman, B. (2012). Swayed by friends or by the crowd? In K. Aberer, A. Flache, W. Jager, L. Liu, J. Tang & C. Gueret (Eds.), *Proceedings of the 4th international conference on social informatics* (pp. 365–378). doi:10.1007/978-3-642-35386-4_27

Allport, G. W. (1968). *The person in psychology: Selected essays.* Boston, MA: Beacon Press.

Amichai-Hamburger, Y., & Vinitzky, G. (2010). Social network use and personality. *Computers in Human Behavior, 26*(6), 1289–1295. https://doi.org/10.1016/j.chb.2010.03.018

Amiel, T., & Sargent, S. L. (2004). Individual differences in Internet usage motives. *Computers in Human Behavior, 20*(6), pp. 711–726.

Anastasi, A., & Urbina, S. (1999). *Psychological testing.* New York: Pearson.

Anderson, J. A. (1988). Cognitive Styles and Multicultural Populations. *Journal of Teacher Education, 39*(1), pp. 2–9. https://doi.org/10.1177/002248718803900102

Aral, S., & Walker, D. (2011). *Identifying social influence in networks using randomized experiments.* IEEE Intelligent Systems, Forthcoming, Available at SSRN: https://ssrn.com/abstract=1907785.

Asch, S. E. (1951). Effects of group pressure upon the modification and distortion of judgment. In H. Guetzkow (Ed.), *Groups, leadership and men.* Pittsburgh, PA: Carnegie Press.

Asch, S. E. (1956). Studies of independence and conformity: I. A minority of one against a unanimous majority. *Psychological monographs: General and applied, 70*(9), pp. 1–70.

Asendorpf, J., & Wilpers, S. (1998). Personality effects on social relationships. *Journal of Personality and Social Psychology, 74*, pp. 1531–1544. doi:10.1037/0022-3514.74.6.1531.

Back, M. D., Stopfer, J. M., Vazire, S., Gaddis, S., Schmukle, S. C., Egloff, B., & Gosling, S. D. (2010). Facebook profiles reflect actual personality, not self-idealization. *Psychological Science, 21*(3), pp. 372–374. https://doi.org/10.1177/0956797609360756

Bakshy, E., Hofman, J. M., Mason, W. A., & Watts, D. J. (2011). Everyone's an influencer: Quantifying influence on Twitter. In *Proceedings of the 4th ACM international conference on web search and data mining* (pp. 65–74). doi:10.1145/1935826.1935845.

Bandura, A. (1971). *Social learning theory.* New York: General Learning Press.

Beni, G., & Wang, J. (1990). *Self-Organizing Sensory Systems," in "Highly Redundant Sensing in Robotic Systems.* In:J. T. Tou, &J. G. Balchen (Eds.), *Proceedings of NATO advanced workshop on highly redundant sensing in robotic systems* (pp. 251–262). Berlin: Springer-Verlag.

Bergagna, E., & Tartaglia, S. (2018). Self-esteem, social comparison, and Facebook use. *Europe's Journal of Psychology, 14*(4), pp. 831–845. https://doi.org/10.5964/ejop.v14i4.1592.

Blass, T. (Ed.). (2000). *Obedience to authority: Current perspectives on the Milgram paradigm.* New York: Lawrence Erlbaum Associates Publishers.

Bond, R., & Smith, P. B. (1996). Culture and conformity: A meta-analysis of studies using Asch's (1952b, 1956) line judgment task. *Psychological Bulletin; Psychological Bulletin, 119*, pp. 111–137. doi:10.1037/0033–2909.119.1.111.

Brehm, J. W. (1966). *A theory of psychological reactance.* Cambridge, MA: Academic Press.

Brown, J. J., & Reingen, P. H. (1987). Social ties and word-of-mouth referral behavior. *Journal of Consumer Research, 14*, pp. 350–362. doi:10.1086/20911

Busch, M., Schrammel, J., & Tscheligi, M. (2013). Personalized persuasive technology – Development and validation of scales for measuring persuadability. In *International conference on persuasive technology*(pp. 33–38). Berlin: Springer.

Camazine, S., Deneubourg, J., Franks, N. R., Sneyd, J., Theraula, G., & Bonabeau, E. (2003). *Self-organization in biological systems.* Princeton, NJ: Princeton University Press.

Campbell, J. D., & Fairey, P. J. (1989). Informational and normative routes to conformity: The effect of faction size as a function of norm extremity and attention to the stimulus. *Journal of Personality and Social Psychology, 57*(3), pp. 457–468. https://doi.org/10.1037/0022-3514.57.3.457.

Carver, C. S., Blaney, P. H., & Scheier, M. F. (1979). Reassertion and giving up: The interactive role of self-directed attention and outcome expectancy. Journal of Personality and Social Psychology, 37(10), 1859–1870. https://doi.org/10.1037/0022-3514.37.10.1859

Carver, C. S., & Scheier, M. F. (1981). Attention and Self-Regulation: A Control Theory Approach to Human Behavior. New York: Springer.

Centola, D. (2010). The spread of behavior in an online social network experiment. *Science, 329*, pp. 1194–1197. doi:10.1126/science.1185231

Cha, M., Haddadi, H., Benevenuto, F., & Gummadi, K. P. (2010). Measuring user influence in Twitter: The million follower fallacy. In *Proceedings of the 4th international AAAI conference on Weblogs and Social Media* (pp. 10–17). Retrieved from https://www.aaai.org/ocs/index.php/ICWSM/ICWSM10/paper/view/1538

Chen, M.-J. (2008). Reconceptualizing the competition—cooperation relationship: A transparadox perspective. *Journal of Management Inquiry, 17*(4), pp. 288–304. https://doi.org/10.1177/1056492607312577

Choudhury, M. D., Counts, S., & Gamon, M. (2012). Not all moods are created equal! Exploring human emotional states in social media. In J. G. Breslin, N. B. Ellison, J. G. Shanahan, & Z. Tufekci (Eds.), *ICWSM*. Menlo Park, CA: The AAAI Press.

Cialdini, R. (2001). *Influence, science and practice.* Boston, MA: Allyn & Bacon.

Cialdini, R. (2014). *Mała wielka zmiana*, Sopot: GWP.

Cialdini, R. B. (1984). *Influence: The psychology of persuasion.* New York: William Morrow.

Cialdini, R. B., & Goldstein, N. H. (2004). Social influence: Compliance and conformity. *Annual Review of Psychology, 55*(1), pp. 591–621.

Cialdini, R., Kallgren C. A., & Reno, R. (1991). A focus theory of normative conduct: A theoretical refinement and reevaluation of the role of norms in human behavior. In M. P. Zanna (Ed.), *Advances in experimental social psychology* (vol. 24, pp. 201–234). San Diego, CA: Academic Press.

Cialdini, R. B., & Trost, M. R. (1998). Social influence: Social norms, conformity and compliance. In D. T. Gilbert, S. T. Fiske, & G. Lindzey (Eds.), *The handbook of social psychology* (pp. 151–192). New York: McGraw-Hill.

Clee, M. A., & Wicklund, R. A. (1980). Consumer behavior and psychological reactance. *Journal of Consumer Research, 6*(4), pp. 389–405. https://doi.org/10.1086/208782

Cohen, A. R. (1959). *Some implications of self-esteem for social influence.* In C. I. Hovland & I. L. Janis (Eds.), *Personality and persuasibility.* Yale: Yale University Press.

Conevey, P., & Highfield, R. (2007). *Granice złożoności. Poszukiwania porządku w chaotycznym świecie.* Warszawa: Prószyński i s-ka.

Coopersmith, S. (1967). *The antecedents of self-esteem.* San Francisco: Freeman.

Cormode, G., & Krishnamurthy, B. (2008). Key differences between Web 1.0 and Web 2.0. *First Monday, 13*(6). doi:10.5210/fm.v13i6.2125

Correa, T., Hinsley, A. W., & de Zúñiga, H. G. (2010). Who interacts on the Web? The intersection of users' personality and social media use. *Computers in Human Behavior, 26*(2), pp. 247–253. https://doi.org/10.1016/j.chb.2009.09.003

Craig, K. D., & Parkachin, K. M. (1978). Social modeling influences on sensory decision theory and psychophysiological indexes of pain. *Journal of Personality and Social Psychology, 36*, pp. 805–815.

Deutsch, M., & Gerard, H. B. (1955), A study of normative and informational social influences upon individual judgment. *Journal of Abnormal and Social Psychology, 51*(3), pp. 629–636. http://doi.org/10.1037/h0046408.

Doliński D. (1998). To control or not to control. In M. Kofta, G. Weary, & G. Sędek (Eds.), *Personal control in action. Cognitive and motivational mechanisms* (pp. 319–340). New York: Plenum Press.

Doliński, D. (2000). *Psychologia wpływu społecznego.* Wroclaw: Towarzystwo Przyjaciół Ossolineum.

Doliński, D. (2011). A rock or a hard place: The foot-in-the-face technique for inducing compliance without pressure. *Journal of Applied Social Psychology, 41*, pp. 1514–1537.

Dubrovsky, V. J., Kiesler, S., & Sethna, B. N. (1991). The equalization phenomenon: Status effects in computer-mediated and face-to-face decision-making groups. *Human–Computer Interaction, 6*(2), pp. 119–146. doi:10.1207/s15327051hci0602_2

Duck, S., & Sants, H. (1983). On the origin of the specious: Are personal relationships really interpersonal states? *Journal of Social and Clinical Psychology, 1*(1), pp. 27–41. https://doi.org/10.1521/jscp.1983.1.1.27

Durgee, J. F. (1986). Self-esteem advertising. *Journal of Advertising, 15*(4), pp. 21–42. doi:10.1080/00913367.1986.10673034

Festinger, L. (1953). An analysis of compliant behavior. In M. Sherif & M. O. Wilson (Eds.). *Group relations at the crossroads* (pp. 232–256). New York: Harper.

Festinger, L. (1954). A theory of social comparison. *Human Relations, 7*, pp. 117–140.

Fischer, K. H., & Hertz, J. A. (1991). *Spin glosses.* New York: Cambridge University Press.

Fleerackers, T., & Meyvis, M. (2018). Digital evolution. Past, present and future outlook of digital technology. *Flat World Blog.* (accessed on: 01.02.2021) https:// flatworldbusiness.wordpress.com/digital-evolution/.

Fleerackers, T., & Meyvis, M. (2019). Web 1.0 vs Web 2.0 vs Web 3.0 vs Web 4.0 vs Web 5.0 – A bird's eye on the evolution and definition. *Flat World Blog* (accessed on: 01.02.2021) http://bit.ly/2X87Iiz.

Freedman, J. L., & Fraser, S. C. (1966). Compliance without pressure: The foot-in-the-door technique. *Journal of Personality and Social Psychology, 4*(2), pp. 195–202. https://doi.org/10.1037/h0023552

French, J. R. P., Jr., & Raven, B. (1959). *The bases of social power.* In D. Cartwright (Ed.), *Studies in social power* (pp. 150–167). Michigan: University of Michigan.

Fuchs, C., Hofkirchner, W., Schafranek, M., Raffl, C., Sandoval, M., & Bichler, R. (2010). Theoretical foundations of the web: Cognition, communication, and co-operation. Towards an understanding of Web 1.0, 2.0, 3.0. *Future Internet, 2*(1), pp. 41–59. https://doi.org/10.3390/fi2010041.

Fuller, R. G., & Sheehy-Skeffington, A. (1974). Effects of group laughter on responses to humorous material: A replication and extension. *Psychological Reports, 35*(1, Pt 2), pp. 531–534. https://doi.org/10.2466/pr0.1974.35.1.531

Garcia, S. M., Tor, A., & Schiff, T. (2013). The psychology of competition: A social comparison perspective. *Perspectives on Psychological Science, 8*(6), pp. 634–650.

Godes, D., & Mayzlin, D. (2004). Using online conversations to study Word-of-Mouth Communication. *Marketing Science, 23*(4), pp. 545–560. https://doi.org/10.1287/mksc.1040.0071

Godes, D., & Mayzlin, D. (2009). Firm-created word-of-mouth communication: Evidence from a field test. *Marketing Science, 28*(4), pp. 721–739. https://doi.org/10.1287/mksc.1080.0444

Goldberg, L. R. (1992). The development of markers for the Big-Five factor structure. *Psychological Assessment, 4*(1), pp. 26–42. https://doi.org/10.1037/1040-3590.4.1.26.

Gosling, S. D., Augustine, A. A., Vazire, S., Holtzman, N., & Gaddis, S. (2011). Manifestations of personality in Online Social Networks: Self-reported Facebook-related behaviors and observable profile information. *Cyberpsychology, Behavior and Social Networking, 14*(9), pp. 483–488. https://doi.org/10.1089/cyber.2010.0087

Gouldner, A. W. (1960). The norm of reciprocity: A preliminary statement. *American Sociological Review, 25*, pp. 161–178.

Greenberg, K. J. (2016). Counter-radicalization via the Internet. *The ANNALS of the American Academy of Political and Social Science, 668*(1), pp. 165–179. https://doi.org/10.1177/0002716216672635.

Gregory, W. L., Cialdini, R. B., & Carpenter, K. M. (1982). Self-relevant scenarios as mediators of likelihood estimates and compliance: Does imagining make it so? *Journal of Personality and Social Psychology, 43*(1), pp. 89–99. https://doi.org/10.1037/0022-3514.43.1.89

Hatfield, E., & Sprecher, S. (1986). Measuring passionate love in intimate relationships. *Journal of Adolescence, 9*(4), 383–410. https://doi.org/10.1016/S0140-1971(86)80043-4

Hoffman, D., & Novak, T. (1996). Marketing in hypermedia computer-mediated environments: Conceptual foundations. *Journal of Marketing, 60*(3), pp. 50–68. https://doi.org/10.2307/1251841

Hollingshead, A. B. (1996). Information suppression and status persistence in group decision making the effects of communication media. *Human Communication Research*, *23*, pp. 193–219. https://doi.org/10.1111/j.1468-2958.1996.tb00392.x

Huffaker, D. A. (2010). Dimensions of leadership and social influence in online communities. *Human Communication Research*, *36*, pp. 593–617. doi: 10.1111/j.1468–2958.2010.01390.x

Iyengar, R., Han, S., & Gupta, S. (2009). *Do friends influence purchases in a social network?* (pp. 09–123). Marketing Unit Working Papers. Cambridge, MA: Harvard Business School.

John, O. P., Donahue, E. M., & Kentle, R. L. (1991). *The big five inventory – Versions 4a and 54*. Berkley: University of California, Berkeley, Institute of Personality and Social Research.

Kaptein, M., De Ruyter, B., Markopoulos, P., & Aarts, E. (2012). Adaptive persuasive systems: A study of tailored persuasive text messages to reduce snacking. *ACM Transactions on Interactive Intelligent Systems*, *2*(2), pp. 1–25. http://doi.org/10.1145/2209310.2209313.

Karpińska-Krakowiak. (2018). *Kapitał marki w mediach społecznościowych*, Łódź: Wydanictwo Uniwersytetu Łódzkiego.

Katz, E., & Lazarsfeld, P. F. (1955). *Personal influence*. New York: The Free Press.

Klinkosz, W., & Sękowski, A. (2008). Pięcioczynnikowy model osobowości a narzędzia pomiaru Wielkiej Piątki. Głos w dyskusji w obronie modelu Big Five. *Roczniki Psychologiczne*, *11*(1), pp. 142–151.

Kotler, P., Kartajaya, H., & Setiawan, I. (2021). *Marketing 5.0: Technology for humanity*. Hoboken: John Wiley & Sons.

Kwak, H., Lee, C., Park, H., & Moon, S. (2010). What is Twitter, a social network or a news media? In *Proceedings of the 19th International Conference on World Wide Web* (pp. 591–600). doi:10.1145/1772690.1772751

Lanier, J. (2018). *Ten arguments for deleting your social media accounts right now.* New York: Henry Holt and Co.

Latané, B. (1981). The psychology of social impact. *American Psychologist*, *36*, pp. 343–356. doi:10.1037/0003–066X.36.4.343

Latané, B., & Wolf, S. (1981). The social impact of majorities and minorities. *Psychological Review*, *88*, pp. 438–453. doi:10.1037/0033–295X.88.5.438

Lin, L. (2010). The relationship of consumer personality trait, brand personality and brand loyalty: An empirical study of toys and video games buyers. *Journal of Product & Brand Management*, *19*, pp. 4–17. doi:10.1108/10610421011018347.

Martin, M. C., & Kennedy, P. F. (1993). Advertising and social comparison: Consequences for female preadolescents and adolescents. *Psychology & Marketing*, *10*, pp. 513–530. https://doi.org/10.1002/mar.4220100605

Marx, G. T. (2001). Murky conceptual waters: The public and the private. *Ethics and Information Technology*, *3*, pp. 157–169. https://doi.org/10.1023/A:1012456832336

Matzler, K., Bidmon, S., & Grabner-Kräuter, S. (2006). Individual determinants of brand affect: The role of the personality traits of extraversion and openness to experience. *Journal of Product and Band Management*, *15*, pp. 427–494. doi:10.1108/10610420610712801.

McAdams, D. P., & Pals, J. L. (2006). A new Big Five: Fundamental principles for an integrative science of personality. *American Psychologist*, *61*(3), pp. 204–217. https://doi.org/10.1037/0003-066X.61.3.204

McCrae, R. R., & Costa, P. T., Jr. (1999). A five-factor theory of personality. In L. A. Pervin & O. P. John (Eds.), *Handbook of personality: Theory and research* (pp. 139–153). New York: Guilford Press.

McGuire, W. J. (1989). A mediational theory of susceptibility to social influence. In: V. A. Gheorghiu, P. Netter, H. J. Eysenck, & R. Rosenthal (Eds.), *Suggestion and suggestibility*. Berlin: Springer. https://link.springer.com/chapter/10.1007%2F978-3-642-73875-3_24

Metzger, M. J., Flanagin, A. J., & Medders, R. B. (2010). Social and heuristic approaches to credibility evaluation online. *Journal of Communication, 60,* pp. 413–439. https://doi.org/10.1111/j.1460-2466.2010.01488.x

Milgram, S. (1974). *Obedience to authority; An experimental view*. New York: Harpercollins.

Modic, D., Anderson, R., & Palomäki, J. (2018). We will make you like our research: The development of a susceptibility-to-persuasion scale. *PLoS ONE, 13*(3). https://doi.org/10.1371/journal.pone.0194119

Moore, K., & McElroy, J. C. (2012). The influence of personality on Facebook usage, wall postings, and regret. *Computers in Human Behavior, 28*(1), 267–274. https://doi.org/10.1016/j.chb.2011.09.009

Moussaïd, M., Schinazi, V. R., Kapadia, M., & Thrash, T. (2018). Virtual sensing and virtual reality: how new technologies can boost research on crowd dynamics. *Front Robot AI, 5*(July), p. 82. https://doi.org/10.3389/frobt.2018.00082

Mullen, B. (1983). Operationalizing the effect of the group on the individual: A self-attention perspective. *Journal of Experimental Social Psychology, 19*(4), pp. 295–322. doi:10.1016/0022–1031(83)90025-2

Nitzschner, M., Nagler, U., Rauthmann, J., Steger, A., & Furtner, M. (2015). The role of personality in advertising perception: An eye-tracking study. *Psychology of Everyday Activity, 8*(1), pp. 10–17.

Nosanchuk, T. A., & Lightstone, J. (1974). Canned laughter and public and private conformity. *Journal of Personality and Social Psychology, 29*(1), pp. 153–156. https://doi.org/10.1037/h0035737

O'Reilly, T. (2005). *What is Web 2.0: Design patterns and business models for the next generation of software* www.oreillynet.com/pub/a/oreilly/tim/ news/2005/09/30/what-is-web-20.html.

Oinas-Kukkonen, H., & Harjumaa, M. (2008). A systematic framework for designing and evaluating persuasive systems. In H. Oinas-Kukkonen, P. Hasle, M. Harjumaa, K. Segerståhl, & P. Øhrstrøm (Eds.), *Persuasive technology. PERSUASIVE 2008. Lecture notes in computer science, vol. 5033.* Berlin: Springer. https://doi.org/10.1007/978-3-540-68504-3_15.

Orr, E., Sisic, M, Ross, C., Simmering, M., Arseneault, J. & Orr, R. (2009). The influence of shyness on the use of Facebook in an undergraduate sample. *Cyberpsychology & Behavior: The Impact of the Internet, multimedia and virtual reality on behavior and society, 12,* pp. 337–340. doi:10.1089/cpb.2008.0214.

Oyibo, K., & Vassileva, J. (2019). The relationship between personality traits and susceptibility to social influence. *Computers in Human Behavior, 98,* pp. 174–188.

Oyibo, K., Orji, R., & Vassileva, J. (2017). Effects of personality on Cialdini's persuasive strategies. In *Adjunct Proceedings of the 12th International Conference on Persuasive Technology.* Amsterdam: Springer Nature Scientific Publishing Services.

Penrod, S., & Hastie, R. (1979). Models of jury decision making: A critical review. *Psychological Bulletin, 86*(3), pp. 462–492. https://doi.org/10.1037/0033-2909.86.3.462

Petty, R. E., & Cacioppo, J. T. (1986). *Communication and persuasion: Central and peripheral routes to attitude change.* New York: Springer/Verlag.

Pool, G. J., Wood, W., & Leck, K. (1998). The self-esteem motive in social influence: Agreement with valued majorities and disagreement with derogated minorities. *Journal of Personality and Social Psychology, 75*(4), pp. 967–975. https://doi.org/10.1037/0022-3514.75.4.967

Pornsakulvanich, V. (2017). Personality, attitudes, social influences, and social networking site usage predicting online social support. *Computers in Human Behavior, 76,* 255–262. https://doi.org/10.1016/j.chb.2017.07.021

Postmes, T., Spears, R., & Cihangir, S. (2001). Quality of decision making and group norms. *Journal of Personality and Social Psychology, 80*(6), pp. 918–930. https://doi.org/10.1037/0022-3514.80.6.918

Postmes, T., Spears, R., & Lea, M. (2000). The formation of group norms in computer-mediated communication. *Human Communication Research, 26,* 341–371. https://doi.org/10.1111/j.1468-2958.2000.tb00761.x

Pratkanis, A. R. (Ed.). (2007). *Frontiers of social psychology. The science of social influence: Advances and future progress.* London: Psychology Press.

Prislin, R., & Crano, W. D. (2012), *A history of social influence research. In A. W. Kruglanski & W. Stroebe (Eds.). Handbook of the history of social psychology* (pp. 321–339). New York: Psychology Press.

Rhoads, K. V. L., & Cialdini, R. B. (2002). The business of influence: Principles that lead to success in commercial settings. In J. P. Dillard & M. Pfau (Eds.). *The persuasion hand-book: Developments in theory and practice* (pp. 513–542). Thousand Oaks, CA: Sage.

Rogers, E. M. (1962). *Diffusion of innovations.* New York: Free Press.

Rosenberg, M. (1985). *Society and the adolescence.* Princeton, NJ: Princeton University Press.

Ryan, T., & Xenos, S. (2011). Who uses Facebook? An investigation into the relationship between the Big Five, shyness, narcissism, loneliness, and Facebook usage. *Computers in Human Behavior, 27*(5), pp. 1658–1664. https://doi.org/10.1016/j.chb.2011.02.004.

Senecal, S., & Nantel, J. (2004) The influence of online product recommendations on consumers' online choices. *Journal of Retailing, 80,* 159–169. http://dx.doi.org/10.1016/j.jretai.2004.04.001

Sherif, C. W., Sherif, M. S., & Nebergall, R. E. (1965). *Attitude and attitude change.* Philadelphia, PA: W.B. Saunders Company.

Sherif, M. (1936). *The psychology of social norms.* New York: Harper.

Short, J., Williams, E., & Christie, B. (1976). *The social psychology of telecommunications.* New York: John Wiley & Sons.

Shriver, S. K., Nair, H. S., & Hofstetter, R. (2013). Social ties and user-generated content: Evidence from an online social network. *Management Science, 59,* pp. 1425–1443. doi:10.1287/mnsc.1110.1648

Siuta, J. (2006). *Inwentarz osobowości NEO-PI-R.* Warszawa: Pracownia Testów Psy-chologicznych Polskiego Towarzystwa Psychologicznego.

Stibe, A., & Oinas-Kukkonen, H. (2014). Designing persuasive systems for user engagement in collaborative interaction. In *Proceedings of the European conference on information systems* (pp. 1–17). Berlin: Springer.

Tanford, S., & Penrod, S. (1984). Social influence model: A formal integration of research on majority and minority influence processes. *Psychological Bulletin, 95*(2), pp. 189–225. doi:10.1037/0033–2909.95.2.189

Thompson, R. L. (2012). Radicalization and the use of social media. *Journal of Strategic Security, 4*(4), pp. 167–190.

Topolewska, E., Skimina, E., Strus, W., Cieciuch, J., & Rowiński, T. (2014). Krótki kwestionariusz do pomiaru Wielkiej Piątki. *Roczniki psychologiczne, 17*(2), pp. 365–382.

Toubia, A., & Stephen, A. T. (2013), Intrinsic vs. image-related utility in social media: Why do people contribute content to Twitter? *Marketing Science, 32*(3), pp. 368–392. https://doi.org/10.1287/mksc.2013.0773

Uehara, E. S. (1995). Reciprocity reconsidered: Gouldner's 'moral norm of reciprocity' and social support, *Journal of Social and Personal Relationship, 12*, pp. 483–502.

Vogel, E., Rose, J., Roberts, L., & Eckles, K. (2014). Social comparison, social media, and self-esteem. *Psychology of Popular Media Culture, 3*, pp. 206–222. doi:10.1037/ppm0000047.

Walther, J. B. (1992). Interpersonal effects in computer-mediated interaction: A relational perspective. *Communication Research, 19*(1), pp. 52–90. https://doi.org/10.1177/009365092019001003

Walther, J. B., & Jang, J. (2012). Communication processes in participatory websites. *Journal of Computer-Mediated Communication, 18*, pp. 2–15. doi:10.1111/j.1083–6101.2012.01592.x

Walther, J. B., & Parks, M. R. (2002). Cues filtered out, cues filtered in: Computer-mediated communication and relationships. In M. L. Knapp & J. A. Daly (Eds.), *Handbook of interpersonal communication* (pp. 529–563). Thousand Oaks, CA: Sage.

Walther, J. B., Liang, Y., Ganster, T., Wohn, D. Y., & Emington, J. (2012). Online reviews, helpfulness ratings, and consumer attitudes: An extension of congruity theory to multiple sources in Web 2.0. *Journal of Computer-Mediated Communication, 18*, pp. 97–112. doi:10.1111/j.1083–6101.2012.01595.x

Wehrli, S. (2008). Personality on social network sites: An application of the five factor model, ETH. *Zurich Sociology Working Papers, 7*, ETH Zurich, Chair of Sociology.

Weisband, S. P., Schneider, S. K., & Connolly, T. (1995). Computer-mediated communication and social information: Status salience and status differences. *Academy of Management Journal, 38*, pp. 1124–1151. https://doi.org/10.5465/256623

Widiger, T. A., & Trull, T. J. (1997). Assessment of the five-factor model of personality. *Journal of Personality Assessment, 68*(2), 228–250. https://doi.org/10.1207/s15327752jpa6802_2

Wood, W. (2000). Attitude change: Persuasion and social influence. *Annual Review of Psychology, 51*(1), pp. 539–570. http://doi.org/10.1146/annurev.psych.51.1.539.

Wood, W., Lundgren, S., Ouellette, J., Busceme, S., & Blackstone, T. (1994). Minority influence: A meta-analytic review of social influence processes. *Psychological Bulletin, 115*, pp. 323–345.

Wooldridge, J. M. (2002). *Econometric analysis of cross section and panel data.* Cambridge, MA: The MIT Press.

Wooten, D. B., & Reed, A. II. (1998). Informational influence and the ambiguity of product experience: Order effects on the weighting of evidence. *Journal of Consumer Psychology, 7*(1), pp. 79–99. https://doi.org/10.1207/s15327663jcp0701_04

Wylie, Ch. (2020). *Mindf*ck. Cambridge Aanlytyca, czyli jak popsuć demokrację.* Kraków: Insignis.

Yamagishi, T., & Kiyonari, T. (2000). The group as the container of generalized reciprocity. *Social Psychology Quarterly, 63*, pp. 116–132.

Zawadzki, B., Strelau, J., Szczepaniak, P., & Śliwińska M. (1998). *Inwentarz osobow-ości NEO-FFI Costy i McCrae. Adaptacja polska*, Warszawa: Pracownia Testów Psychologicznych Polskiego Towarzystwa Psychologicznego.

Zimbardo, P. G. (1999). *Psychologia i życie.* Warszawa: PWN.

5 Social proof as a key factor in social commerce

Introduction

On the threshold of the twenty-first century's second decade, modern social media are not only places where people can connect with friends and loved ones, they are also the most important communication and sales platforms for firms, allowing them to reach potential customers and target groups. Because in most cases the use of social media is free of charge, user data and information have become the source of monetization. This means not only the demographic and geographical data provided when registering on sites, but also, first and foremost, information about site usage and interaction: pages followed, links opened, and likes and comments. It is on these data, which are processed by learning algorithms, that marketing initiatives are based. This chapter consists of two complementary sections.

The first addresses ways of using social proof in the digital environment and pays particular attention to ways of integrating communication based on social proof into firms' marketing strategies as well as methods for exploiting the potential of reviews and the phenomenon of fake reviews.

Before illustrating its development using data, the second defines, describes, and examines social commerce, which is e-commerce conducted via social media. Special attention is paid to the role played in social commerce by reviews and recommendations written by other users (social proof). The chapter is complemented by a review of research into the role and importance of social proof and on contemporary trends in recommendation management.

Social proof in the digital environment

Robert Schnuerch and Henning Gibbons (2015) define social proof as the psychological phenomenon whereby people copy the actions of others because they assume this action is acceptable when others are doing it. As we have seen above, social proof is one of the fundamental principles governing human behaviour. The principle of social proof in the context of digital communities (Weinberg & Pehlivan 2011) is of particular relevance to this

DOI: 10.4324/9781003128052-6

monograph's central research objective. Numbers of followers, likes, impressions, and even comments play an important role in the perception process not only of other users but also of brands and organizations present on social media platforms. Mutual evaluation plays a role in relationships with other people just as it does in the interactions taking place on websites enabled by Web 2.0 technology, which possess an inherent potential for evaluation. First, these services have become an important space for self-presentation and, second, the option to follow the activity of other users is somehow conducive to automatic evaluation. Moreover, social media offer users a number of tools allowing them to quickly express their opinions and leave comments. Examples of such tools include the ability to leave opinions, reviews, comments, or ratings on the affiliate websites of brands present on social media platforms. Services that place strong emphasis on aggregating the opinions of Internet users and of which the exchange of opinions and mutual recommendations is a core feature are also popular. On Tripadvisor, a website that helps Internet users choose hotels, restaurants, and tourist attractions, what is written about a tourist product depends on other Internet users. A firm creates a subpage on the website, which features basic information and professional photographs, but the remaining data, which can include ratings (expressed on a scale of one to five), descriptions, pictures, and videos, come from the users themselves. The position in the popularity ranking of products in a given location depends on the opinions of other Internet users, and the ratings themselves are considered to be objective and reliable. It is similar in the case of affiliate pages on Facebook. There, Internet users can express their opinions by leaving a comment or review, or by making a virtual assessment of the brand (also on a scale of one to five). It is important to note here that Facebook's algorithm automatically displays information about which of your friends likes a particular brand, has visited a place (if they have performed a Facebook check-in), or left a review.

Table 5.1 displays the most common types of social proof content published online. It should be stressed, though, that this is not an exhaustive list: marketing specialists continue to create new tools that allow users to both share their opinions and learn about the recommendations of other Internet users.

It should be noted that the forms of social proof we have mentioned constitute a diverse set of messages, which differ from each other in both form and content. To distinguish them in terms of their form, place of publication, and the way they are controlled by firms is, however, the decisive issue. In the case of users' opinions published on websites (testimonials) or success stories (case studies), we are dealing with content inspired and intentionally made available by firms, whereas reviews, ratings, and user-generated content are created spontaneously and initiated by the users themselves. Firms cannot exercise full control over the latter forms of content and, where network monitoring is absent, are sometimes unaware that they exist.

Chapter 3 of this book gives an account of the concept of influence marketing and celebrity endorsement. According to the accepted definition of

Table 5.1 Types of social proof-based messages in the digital environment

Type of social proof	Description	Example
Testimonials	Firm selects customer reviews that extol the product's virtues	Feedback published on the website or social media profiles managed by the firm
User reviews	Users' opinions published spontaneously on websites, both those controlled by the firm, such as websites and Facebook fan pages, and other sites, such as review sites	Reviews published on Tripadvisor, price comparison sites, etc.
Influencer endorsements	Firm-initiated product or service recommendations made by influencers	Sponsored posts on Facebook or Instagram
Client case studies	Case studies published by firms with the permission of customers	Posts on a firm's blog or on LinkedIn
Product ratings	Aggregated product and service ratings given by users according to a standard scale	Ratings of products purchased on Amazon
Number of product users	Number of products sold	Number of people currently viewing a product or offer
Number of e-mail subscribers	Number of newsletter subscribers	Information encouraging people to join a list of newsletter subscribers
User-generated content	Encouraging users to generate content related to the brand, product, or service offered	Creating a unique hashtag, with which users can describe the brand-associated content they have created (on Facebook or Instagram, for example)
Social media shares	Publishing the number of shares using social share buttons	Including a social share button alongside content published on the firm's website
Number of social media followers	Building brand awareness on social media by inviting users to like or follow your page	Publishing the number of followers or fans

social proof, reviews and recommendations produced by influencers on behalf of firms also fit a broad definition of this concept. The present chapter, however, limits its analysis to reviews and opinions spontaneously created by Internet users or to reviews written by Internet users impersonating real users on behalf of firms.

Data released by Amazon, the world's largest e-commerce platform, indicate that in 2020, 82% of American adults shopping online had read reviews beforehand (Dobrilova 2020). More than half (58.1%) paid attention to reviews found on the site when making a purchasing decision, and only 4.1% did not believe reviews at all. These data also apply to residents of other countries, where, just as in the United States, the opinions of other Internet users are important to e-consumers as a source of information when making purchasing decisions online. It is for this reason that firms are looking for ways to optimize and manage user reviews. Figure 5.1 depicts the main categories of online consumer reviews. Because social proof expressed in user reviews and comments is such an important determinant of purchasing decisions, firms do all they can to acquire and maintain a good online image. The following section will present the tools for managing online reviews and the ways in which firms can attract greater numbers of positive reviews.

There are many benefits to incorporating online review and recommendation management into marketing strategies, including:

– The positive impact of consumer reviews and opinions on raising brand awareness.
– The importance of reviews and recommendations to purchasing decisions made by e-consumers.
– The management of brand image and reputation.
– Monitoring levels of consumer satisfaction.
– Acquisition of analytical data and knowledge about e-consumers.
– The ability to gather information on what competitors are doing.

The process by which firms monitor and control recommendations can take many forms (Ripley 2017), but the primary tool of online feedback management is review moderation, which requires an official representative of a firm – a profile administrator – to add responses or comments. The majority

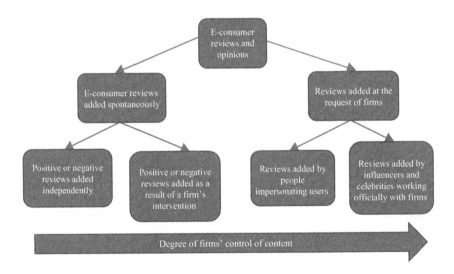

Figure 5.1 Categories of online reviews and product ratings.

of platforms that aggregate consumer reviews allow users to add responses and notify administrators automatically when a review is received. However, some of the content that constitutes social proof is published on informal sites, forums, and Internet user groups, to which firms are not automatically alerted and of which they are therefore unaware. Tools for monitoring online content, such as Hootsuite, Brandwatch, Reputology, and Brand24, which not only notify firms when brands or products are mentioned online, but also analyse the activity of competitors, offer a remedy for this problem. Passive tools, such as those above, have no influence on the reviews and opinions added spontaneously by e-consumers because they seek to manage them after they have been published.

Firms that have a virtual presence can also benefit from tools that allow them to not only analyse existing comments, but also acquire new reviews from users who have previously made purchases. Table 5.2 presents an overview of selected tools that can be used in the review management process (Proofly, ProveSource, UseProof, Barilliance 2021).

Of the many ways in which e-consumers can be encouraged to leave feedback, e-mail requests to leave a review sent following the purchase of a product or service from a firm are the most common. In exchange for leaving a review, or for a recommendation sent to friends, some firms offer discounts or extra points in a loyalty programme. Some firms, though, go a step further by also choosing to have fake reviews published. In 2018, fakespot.com

Table 5.2 Selected tools for managing e-consumer reviews and feedback

Name of tool	Description
Proofly	A tool that makes it possible to add social proof widgets to websites. These include instant messaging and chat rooms, information about the number of people now viewing the site, the number of people who have bought a given product, and the number of people who have viewed an offer; also tools for collecting reviews from existing customers
ProveSource	A plugin for websites or e-commerce platforms that allows information about the number of users and buyers at a given time and the most valuable opinions and reviews from various sources (including Google, consumer tests, and price comparison sites) to be displayed. It also has a visitor counter that shows the number of people who have visited the site or made a purchase in a given period
UseProof	A tool that – based on data made available by Internet users – personalizes web pages according to the characteristics of its users. Web content can be adjusted to previously visited websites, interests, or e-mail address. Reviews and opinions about products displayed on the website can also be personalized
Barilliance	This system makes it possible to monitor the opinions of Internet users and to manage them automatically. The opinions displayed to Internet users are tailored to their profiles and personalized. The platform also supports A/B tests for experimenting with the effectiveness of opinions and recommendations

analysed reviews published on Amazon and found that fake reviews outnumbered real ones in some product categories. For example, 61% of all reviews of electronics were fake and created at the request of firms, while the proportion of fake reviews of cosmetics and supplements was approximately 63–64%. These percentages demonstrate just how big a problem fake reviews represent and reveal that opinions found on the Internet can be thoroughly manipulative. The analysis now turns to the question of fake reviews.

Fake reviews as unfair business practice

In an article published by the International Conference on Data Mining, Nitin Jindal and Bing Liu (2007) proposed a three-pronged classification of false opinions:

1   Positive or negative fake reviews written to promote sales or discredit the reputation of a firm or brand whose authors have no actual experience of using the product or service.
2   Brand-only reviews that address emotional relationships with brands but not the actual experience of using the products or services.
3   Advertisements or irrelevant reviews, which look like reviews but do not contain actual user feedback.

Fake reviews are deliberately created by mimicking real consumer opinions, which makes them much more difficult to identify than content that falls into the other categories. The two most relevant strands of the research devoted to detecting fake reviews are the following:

–   Research focused on technologies that enable the automatic detection of fake reviews, including those based on textual analysis or machine learning (cf. Li & Fu 2014; Wang et al. 2017; Zhao et al. 2013).
–   Consumer-centric research focused on the individual strategies and methods e-consumers use to identify fake reviews (cf. Lee 2013; Maslowska et al. 2017).

As stated above, fake reviews come in many varieties. Nevertheless, the vast majority are created at the request of firms with the main objective of promoting products or services (by adding fake positive reviews) or discrediting competitors' offers (by adding fake negative reviews). Employees can add fake reviews themselves, or they can outsource this task to freelancers or to firms that specialize in word-of-mouth marketing. Plenty of proposals for cooperation in this area can be found on websites such as freelancer.com (2021). Administrators of social media platforms try to combat this pathological phenomenon by blocking reviews added by bots. The struggle is less straightforward, though, in the case of reviews that have been commissioned.

In practice, the largest review-aggregation sites use algorithms to filter fake reviews, whose detection depends on analysing two key elements: the content of the review and the characteristics of the author. As stated earlier, most methods for detecting fake reviews involve machine learning, the aim of which is to classify reviews as either fake or genuine. The specific review characteristics addressed include number of characters, rating given, sentiment (emotional colouring), subjectivity, and writing style (Mukherjee and Bala 2017). Xiaolong Deng and Runyu Chen (2014) proposed 11 types of content that are indicative of a fake review, which they placed into three categories: frequency of keywords, richness of the information contained in the review, and the reliability of the information. Another approach to detecting fake reviews is based on reviewer behaviour. It entails recording the average number of comments posted by reviewers each day, the time interval between a reviewer's first and last comment, first reviews of products as a proportion of all comments posted by a reviewer, and the number of votes obtained as part of review evaluation in response, for example, to the question, 'Was this review helpful?' (Kamerer 2014; Mukherjee et al. 2013b). By combining information derived from review texts and from reviewers' behaviour, Dongsong Zhang and his team (2016) were able to achieve good results in identifying fake reviews.

It is difficult for e-consumers to distinguish between real and fake reviews. As a result of an investigation by a team of journalists from the *Financial Times* (Lee 2020), which uncovered evidence that users were adding thousands of positive reviews at the request of firms in exchange for financial rewards, Amazon removed over 20,000 fake reviews from its service in September 2020. Drawing on investigations conducted in May 2020, a group of analysts from fakespot.com suggested that as many as 58% of the products offered on Amazon have fake reviews and opinions.

The struggle against opinion spamming presents a challenge not only for administrators of websites that allow review posting, but also for legislators. Regulations that afforded adequate protection to the weaker parties in commercial relationships in pre-digital times have turned out to be insufficient, and institutions have not kept pace with the rapidly developing e-commerce market and the new technologies associated with it. For the European Union (EU), taking action against fake reviews is part of a broader drive to modernize consumer protection rules, whose aim is to adapt regulation to the increasing digitalization of trade and to changes in consumer shopping habits. Directive (EU) 2019/2161 of the European Parliament and of the Council as regards the better enforcement and modernization of Union consumer protection rules, whose implementation is expected in November 2021, includes new regulation of free services for which we actually 'pay' with our personal data, regulation in the area of dual product quality, new requirements for the transparency of search results (European Parliament 2019), and specific provisions for false product reviews. The EU's New Deal for Consumers, as it is known, entails two main sets of measures.

First, where traders provide access to consumer reviews of products, the directive requires that information be published on whether the reviews originate from consumers who have actually used or purchased the product.

Furthermore, not including such information, or not communicating it clearly, can amount to a misleading omission. Operators of shops or platforms whose products are accompanied by buyer reviews will therefore have to state – in a comprehensible manner – whether they screen the reviews for their veracity and, if so, what actions they take to accomplish this.

Of course, this provision will not in itself ensure that sellers screen product reviews: a truthful indication that they do not do so will not constitute an infringement. Having said that, traders may find that review screening is a desirable feature that attracts buyers. Importantly, the recitals of the directive further state that when informing consumers about the procedures in place to ensure that reviews are written by genuine consumers, traders should also say how the reviews are processed: Are all opinions, including negative ones, published? Are the reviews sponsored? Are the reviews influenced by contractual relationships with the trader? The last two questions prompt an interesting further question: If the reviews are sponsored, or if they are influenced by a contractual relationship with a trader, how can this be reconciled with the requirement for reviews to come from consumers who have bought or used the product? Unfortunately, it cannot be ruled out that traders will see a loophole here that will allow them to publish reviews by 'co-operating consumers' and to treat them as genuine and as positively verified.

Second, the directive adds two cases concerning fake reviews to the catalogue of practices that are unfair in all circumstances. To claim that product reviews have been posted by consumers who have actually used or purchased the product without taking reasonable and proportionate steps to verify that the reviews originate from such consumers is to be prohibited. This is clearly linked to the information requirement described above. Misleading consumers about the use of review mechanisms will always be considered an unfair market practice. However, it should be noted that the trader is only obliged to take 'reasonable and proportionate steps', while the example the directive gives of such steps is asking reviewers to confirm that they have indeed purchased the product. Hence the posting of fake reviews is not effectively prevented and there is no guarantee that reviews will not in fact come from sellers themselves. The EU also plans to prohibit submitting or commissioning another legal or natural person to submit false consumer reviews or endorsements, or misrepresenting consumer reviews or social endorsements, in order to promote products. Theoretically, this ban could be the most powerful weapon in the fight against fake and misleading product reviews. Indeed, it is reasonable to conclude from a proper interpretation of the provisions that sellers would be allowed to publish sponsored reviews, or reviews resulting from a contractual relationship, only if they were clearly disclosed. However, it cannot be ruled out that traders will deny that reviews are fake by claiming that they commissioned somebody else to write them but had no influence whatsoever over their content.

So far, the prohibition of unfair market practices has not been particularly effective in Poland because it requires individual consumers to bear the costs and risks of taking traders to court, which they are unwilling to do.

The president of the Office of Competition and Consumer Protection (UOKiK) has only been able to punish firms involved in unfair market practices where such practices infringe the collective interests of consumers. This is despite the fact that EU rules already required Member States to introduce effective, proportionate, and dissuasive sanctions. It will remain in the hands of EU governments to correct this situation. This is because the directive does not explicitly require the introduction of specific types of sanctions, such as fines or the minimum amounts of fines, for typically national infringements. Such obligations are only envisaged for infringements that cause harm in a larger number of EU Member States (Menszig-Wiese & Wasilewski 2020).

The nature and identity of social commerce

The emergence of online commerce tools was implied in the accumulation of large numbers of Internet users in one place and their formation into virtual communities. In this way, the sale and purchase of products via social network sites became known as social commerce. Since 2005, when the term was first used (Rubel 2005), the literature has produced a number of proposals for defining this phenomenon. An overview of the most important ones is presented in Table 5.3.

Table 5.3 Selected proposals for the definition of social commerce

Author	Definition of social commerce
Leitner and Grechenig (2007)	Social commerce/social shopping is an emerging phenomenon, 'characterized by offering platforms where consumers collaborate online, get advice from trusted individuals, find the right products in a repository, and finally purchase them'
Wang (2009)	Social commerce is a new type of online commerce (e-commerce) that combines shopping and social networks via social media
Shen and Eder (2009)	The expansion of business-to-consumer e-commerce, in which the main mechanism for conducting online shopping is the interaction between consumers. This can involve discovering products, aggregating and sharing product information, and making purchasing decisions together
Stephen and Toubia (2009)	A model of Internet trading in which the sellers are connected through online social networks and in which the sellers are physical persons rather than firms
Afrasiabi Rad and Benyoucef (2010)	The term social commerce refers to both a network of sellers and a network of buyers; it represents the evolution of 'e-commerce 1.0' which, until now, has relied solely on one-to-one interaction. Social commerce offers a more social and interactive form of e-commerce

A measure of ambiguity is associated with the definition of social commerce: it can refer both to purchases made on social media platforms, such as Facebook Marketplace, and to price comparison websites, social exchange platforms (e.g. OLX, Vinted), and group purchases. The key factor that distinguishes social commerce from traditional e-commerce is interaction, which is no longer confined to the one-to-one seller-buyer model. It may be said with reference to the model of communication in a hypermedia computer environment (Hoffman & Novak 1996) that interactions happening around purchases on social media are multidirectional and bilateral. Buyers who use social media platforms can communicate both with the seller and with other buyers, of whom they can ask questions and with whom they can share shopping carts or exchange products. Figure 5.2 displays the central features that differentiate social commerce from the traditional e-commerce 1.0 model (Rad & Benyoucef 2010).

Sales made via social commerce are primarily based on a 'pull' strategy, whereby content marketing and skilful management of user-generated content makes the messages attract the attention of e-consumers and arouse their interest. Changes have occurred both in customer relations, which are no longer limited exclusively to senders and recipients, and in the way customers are served. Social commerce customers take an active approach, so that if they are dissatisfied or have questions, they contact companies directly asking for help (via Facebook, for example) or turn to the community for support by asking questions on forums and groups.

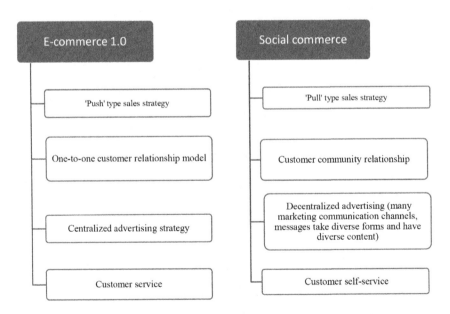

Figure 5.2 E-commerce 1.0 and social commerce: key differentiating features.

Table 5.4 The most important features of social commerce

Basic features of social commerce	Description
Social shopping	Users can chat with other users or sellers and make purchases via social media or on social exchange platforms
Reviews and ratings	Users read product ratings before making a purchase, and, after selecting a product, then become reviewers themselves by sharing their rating with others
Referrals and recommendations	Users can recommend both products and sellers to other Internet users. This applies not only to firms, but also to other users
Forums and communities	Users can sell products to other Internet users and communicate with them on customer-to-customer (C2C) platforms
Social media	Aided by brand affiliate pages on social media, firms can interact and communicate with users
Social advertising	Firms have various forms of advertising at their disposal on social media, including cost-per-click (CPC) advertising, sponsored posts, and cooperation with influencers and celebrities who recommend products

Efraim Turban et al. (2016) identified six key features of social commerce, which are described in Table 5.4.

At almost every stage of consumer decision-making, messages based on social proof are of vital importance to online purchases. The classic theoretical description of this process is the five-phase EKB model (Engel et al. 1968):

1   Identifying the need for a specific product or service.
2   Searching for information.
3   Evaluating alternatives.
4   Making a purchase.
5   Assessing the purchase.

Identifying the need for a particular product or service is the first stage in the process whereby customers decide to make purchases. Recommendations from friends and sponsored posts on influencer profiles represent common ways of generating or inducing a need to buy in e-consumers. Recommendation systems based on customer relationship management can also help firms predict users' future needs based on their past activities. The connections users establish on social networks such as Facebook or Instagram usually represent common interests or needs (Schwartz & Wood,

1993; Wellman, 1999). Analysing them makes it possible to identify potential needs, which makes it easier to target advertising based on social proof, whose aim is to arouse desire for a product.

In the second, informational phase, network users search for information and evaluate it critically. This process is described in detail in Chapter 2. Social networks enhance and accelerate information searches by:

–   Featuring trusted reviews and hosting networks of friends – social proof is thus expressed through comments, reviews, recommendations, and ratings.
–   Enabling synchronized purchases; enabling users in different locations to shop simultaneously.

Web 2.0 makes it possible to embed websites in chat tools so that groups of people can browse the web together while communicating about product profiles (Turban et al. 2016), which preserves the pleasure of shopping together and allows us to benefit from other people's ideas. What this method in fact does is to mirror the offline shopping experience, which involves groups of shoppers visiting shopping centres and, as potential purchasers, helping each other by discussing products and brands.

Product comparison platforms play an important role in the third phase, when evaluating alternatives, and in the fourth, when actually making a purchase. As well as price, it is important to take the opinions of other Internet users as a criterion of comparison. These are usually expressed using a points system that also takes the number of opinions added into consideration.

In the fifth phase, that of evaluation, e-consumers are encouraged to share their experience of the purchase, which allows firms to gather feedback and provides other Internet users with information that will help them make future purchasing decisions.

Summary of Part I

The first part of the book, which consists of five chapters, attempts to identify the phenomenon of social proof and its role in the process whereby e-consumers make purchasing decisions. To analyse this phenomenon properly required the adoption of an appropriate theoretical framework, which is developed in the individual theoretical chapters.

Chapter 1, the introduction, offers an outline of the problem that the book addresses, states the research objectives, and signals ways in which they can be achieved.

Chapter 2 considers the assumptions and characteristics of online marketing communication and places special emphasis on social media marketing. In keeping with the book's overall purpose, the focus is on the issues of persuasion and manipulation.

Chapter 3, which presents selected marketing communication strategies implemented in the virtual environment and pays particular attention to influencer marketing, viral marketing, and word-of-mouth marketing, develops the themes of Chapter 1. Furthermore, it attempts to organize these concepts and to provide an in-depth account of the uses to which they are put.

The review of selected models of social influence in Chapter 4 serves as a starting point for examining social influence on social media and the ways in which it is made manifest there. The question to which the book's title alludes, social proof, is a form of persuasion based on the mechanisms of social influence occurring in the social media environment. It is within this context that the factors determining susceptibility to social proof are investigated.

Chapter 5 sets out the forms and types of messages based on social proof that are present in the digital environment. Due to their substance and importance, particular attention is paid to the reviews written by firms and sellers and to systems for managing recommendations and reviews. Where this concerns the role of reviews and recommendations in marketing and sales and ways of managing social proof, consideration is also given to the perspective of firms. The chapter concludes with a discussion of social commerce, which is a form of online shopping conducted in the social media environment.

Attention turns in Part II to the results of an original study of social proof, which – following a chapter setting out its aims, methods, and organization – are analysed, evaluated, and discussed.

References

Deng, X., & Chen, R. (2014). Sentiment analysis based online restaurants fake reviews hype detection. In W. Han, Z. Huang, C. Hu, H. Zhang, & L. Guo (Eds.), *Web technologies and applications. APWeb 2014. Lecture notes in computer* science, *vol. 8710*.Cham: Springer. https://doi.org/10.1007/978-3-319-11119-3_1

Dobrilova, T. (2020). What percentage of amazon reviews are fake? *Review 24* (accessed online: 10.01.2021) https://review42.com/what-percentage-of-amazon-reviews-are-fake/#:~:text=Only%20just%203%25%20to%2010,Amazon%20as%20of%20March%202019

Directive (EU) 2019/2161 of the European Parliament and of the Council of 27 November 2019 amending Council Directive 93/13/EEC and Directives 98/6/EC, 2005/29/EC and 2011/83/EU of the European Parliament and of the Council as regards the better enforcement and modernization of Union consumer protection rules (accessed online: 10.01.2021) https://eur-lex.europa.eu/eli/dir/2019/2161/oj

Engel, J. F., Kollat, D. T., & Blackwell, R. D. (1968). *Consumer behaviour.* New York: Holt, Reinhart & Winston.

Hoffman, D., & Novak, T. (1996), Marketing in hypermedia computer-mediated environments: Conceptual foundations. *Journal of Marketing, 60*(3), pp. 50–68. doi:10.2307/1251841

Jindal, N., & Liu, B., (2007). Analyzing and detecting review spam. *Proceedings of the IEEE International Conference of Data Mining*, pp. 547–552. doi:10.1109/ICDM.2007.68.

Kamerer, D. (2014) Understanding the Yelp review filter: An exploratory study. *First Monday, 19.*

Lee, J. (2013). What makes people read an online review? The relative effects of posting time and helpfulness on review readership. *Cyberpsychology, Behavior, and Social Networking, 16*(7), pp. 529–535.

Lee, J. (2020). Amazon deletes 20,000 reviews after evidence of profits for posts, *Financial Times* (accessed online: 10.01.2021) https://www.ft.com/content/bb03ba1c-add3-4440-9bf2-2a65566aef4a

Leitner, P., & Grechenig, T. (2007). Community driven commerce: Design of an integrated framework for social shopping. *IADIS International Conference e-Commerce,* Algarve, Portugal, p. 4.

Li, Y. Q., & Fu, H. G. (2014). Fake comments recognition based on social network graph model. *Journal of Computer Applications, 34*(2), pp. 151–153.

Maslowska, E., Malthouse E. C., & Viswanathan, V. (2017). Do customer reviews drive purchase decisions? The moderating roles of review exposure and price. *Decision Support Systems, 98*, pp. 1–9.

Menszig-Wiese, W. (2020). Unia walczy z fałszywymi opiniami o produktach w internecine. *Prawo.pl* (accessed online: 10.01.2021) https://www.prawo.pl/biznes/falszywe-opinie-w-internecie-nowe-unijne-przepisy, 497695.html

Mukherjee, S., & Bala, P. (2017). Sarcasm detection in microblogs using Naïve Bayes and fuzzy clustering. *Technology in Society, 48*, pp. 19–27.

Mukherjee, A., Kumar, A., Liu, B., Wang, J., Hsu, M., Castellanos, M., & Ghosh, R. (2013a). Spotting opinion spammers using behavioral footprints. In *Proceedings of the 19th ACM SIGKDD international conference on knowledge discovery and data mining* (pp. 632–640), Chicago, IL, USA, 11–14 August.

Mukherjee, A., Venkataraman, V., Liu, B., & Glance, N. (2013b). What yelp fake review filter might be doing? *Proceedings of the Seventh International AAAI Conference on Weblogs and Social Media*, Cambridge, MA, USA, 8–11 July.

Rad, A., & Benyoucef, A. M. (2010). A model for understanding social commerce. *Information Systems Journal, 4*(2), pp. 1–11.

Ripley, H. (2017). *Who's managing your online reviews?* Entrepreneur Europe (accessed online on: 10.01.2021) https://www.entrepreneur.com/article/288123

Rubel, S. (2005). 2006 Trends to watch part II: social commerce. *Micro Persuasion.* http://socialcommercetoday.com/steve-rubels-original-2005-social-commerce-post/

Schnuerch, R., & Gibbons, H. (2015), Social proof in the human brain: Electrophysiological signatures of agreement and disagreement with the majority. *Psychophysiology, 52*(10), pp. 1328–1342. https://doi.org/10.1111/psyp.12461

Schwartz, M. F., & Wood, D. M. (1993). Discovering shared interests using graph analysis. *Communications of the ACM, 36*(8), pp. 78–89. https://doi.org/10.1145/163381.163402

Shen, J., & Eder, L. (2009). Determining factors in the acceptance of social shopping websites. *15th Americas Conference on Information Systems* (AMCIS), San Francisco, CA, p. 10.

Stephen, A. T., & Toubia, O. (2009). Explaining the power–law degree distribution in a social commerce network. *Social Networks, 31*(4), pp. 262–270.

Turban, E., Strauss, J., & Lai, L. (2016). *Social commerce. Marketing, technology and management,* Berlin: Springer.

Wang, C. (2009). Linking shopping and social networking: Approaches to social shopping. *15th Americas Conference on Information Systems* (AMCIS), San Diego, CA.

Wang, X., Liu, K., & Zhao, J. (2017). Detecting deceptive review spam via attention-based neural networks. *National CCF Conference on Natural Language Processing & Chinese Computing,* pp. 866–876.

Weinberg, B. D., & Pehlivan, E. (2011). Social spending: Managing the social media mix. *Business Horizons, 54*(3), pp. 275–282.

Wellman, C. H. (1999). Gratitude as a virtue. *Pacific Philosophical Quarterly,* 80, pp. 284–300. https://doi.org/10.1111/1468-0114.00085

Zhang, D., Zhou, L., Kehoe, J. L., & Kilic, I. Y. (2016). What online reviewer behaviors really matter? Effects of verbal and nonverbal behaviors on detection of fake online reviews. *Journal of. Managerial Information Systems, 33,* pp. 456–481.

Zhao, Y., Yang, S., Narayan, V., & Zhao, Y. (2013). Modelling consumer learning from online product reviews. *Marketing Science, 32*(1), pp. 153–169.

Part II

Social proof in marketing

Effectiveness and impact awareness

6 Research model, objectives, and hypotheses

Introduction

Chapter 6 presents a theoretical research model describing e-consumers' susceptibility to social proof. It attempts to synthesize the variables determining the occurrence and degree of susceptibility to social proof. Due to the multidimensional interactions that occur in virtual reality, the adopted model is likewise complex. It tries to reflect the subtle, multifaceted nature of the interactions taking place between the various factors. For this reason, its empirical verification must be accomplished in stages, which are organized over the chapters that follow to reflect the framework and methodological standards of social research. The current chapter sets out the research objectives and hypotheses formulated on the basis of the adopted model. These are described and justified in detail. The research results and verification of the hypotheses are presented in Chapters 7 and 8.

The role of comments and reviews in communication between firms and e-consumers: the grounds for the construction of the research model

The literature review in Part I of this book established that, beginning in the Web 2.0 era and continuing into the era of Web 5.0, a particular type of social influence – social proof – has played a key role in marketing.

Social media, which rely on user-generated content and user interaction, offer an ideal environment for sharing opinions, sharing reviews, and encouraging purchases. When they are online searching for information about purchases, Internet users are therefore not restricted only to official marketing messages, such as advertisements or sponsored articles, but can also browse third-party posts and comments. Firms can commission their publication, but they can also be composed spontaneously by other e-consumers who have experience of the product concerned (Figure 6.1). While sponsored content includes official announcements released in collaboration with celebrities or influencers and fake, bot-generated reviews and posts published as part of word-of-mouth marketing campaigns, Internet users

DOI: 10.4324/9781003128052-8

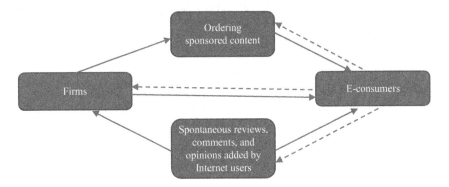

Figure 6.1 The role of comments and reviews in communication between firms and
e-consumers.

publish their spontaneous reviews and comments on their own initiative. Depending on where they are published, the latter are beyond firms' control, open to comment by firms or, in extreme cases, can be deleted by firms. Two important points should be emphasized here. First, in some cases, as indicated in Chapter 5, a proportion of the spontaneous reviews can in fact be 'supported' or 'managed' by firms promoting consumer activity. They often take the form of invitations to write a review, to recommend something to a friend, or to share something in return for a discount. Second, in the case of Web 2.0-based sites, e-consumers are able to respond directly to reviews by adding their own comments to them. Systems that allow additional review ratings, such as those for tagging helpful reviews on Booking.com or Tripadvisor, are examples of this. Many online shops take a similar approach by asking users to respond to the question: 'Was this review helpful?'

A theoretical approach to a model of susceptibility to social proof in social media

Based on the literature analysis in Part I, an attempt is now made to conceptualize a theoretical model of the impact of social proof used in research on marketing communication in the social media environment (Figure 6.2). It is important to note that the majority of existing studies in this area have focused on specific types of social proof, such as user reviews, and celebrity and influencer recommendations (cf. Dellarocas 2011; Ong & Beng 2012), as well as on identifying social media users with significant influence on other users (cf. Aral & Walker 2012). A second area of research concerns demographic and psychographic characteristics, such as trust in social networks and susceptibility to interpersonal influence (cf. Chu & Kim 2011). As the literature review demonstrates, the majority of articles concerning social proof in social media focus on mental health and the negative effects

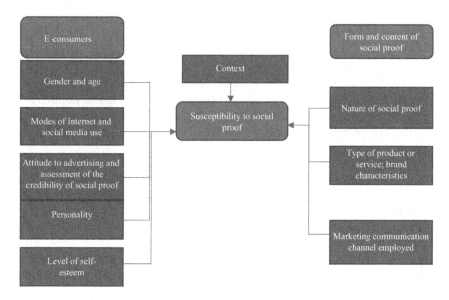

Figure 6.2 Model of susceptibility to social proof on social media.

of continuous exposure to social comparisons (cf. Keles et al. 2020). The construction of the model presented here, which is designed to reveal the essence of the problem of susceptibility to social proof, is based on the central assumption of the multidimensionality and interdependence of the various determinants.

Simply put, the determinants of susceptibility to social proof can be divided into two main categories: the characteristics of e-consumers and the characteristics of messages.

The first category is that of e-consumers. This class of determinants can be investigated at three levels:

– The demographic level, which refers to the gender and age of e-consumers.
– The behavioural level, which concerns frequency and manner of social media use, frequency of online shopping, and the degree of professionalization of the activities e-consumers pursue on the World Wide Web.
– The psychographic level, which concerns the individual characteristics of e-consumers, such as personality, self-esteem, and susceptibility to social influence, as well as overall assessment of the reliability and credibility of reviews and recommendations.

The second class of determinants pertains to the form and content of the messages that convey social proof. The extent to which e-consumers succumb to the influence of social proof depends not only on individual characteristics, but also on the attributes of the messages themselves:

- E-consumers' perception of the form, content, and authenticity (commissioned versus spontaneous reviews) of messages.
- The characteristics of the brands, products, and services communicated within a social proof context (type of product, brand popularity, frequency of brand communication in the social network environment).
- The communication channel used on social media.

Susceptibility to social proof also depends on the context in which it occurs: what activity is the e-consumer involved in? what is the relationship between the sender and recipient of a message based on social proof? what part does communication noise play in this interaction?

The model presented here assumes that susceptibility to social proof depends on two sets of factors: e-consumer characteristics and message characteristics. Although the factors that characterize e-consumers, such as personality, self-esteem, and attitude to advertising, are relatively constant, the determinants associated with the type of product that is the subject of communication, the type of brand, the communication channel, the relationship to the sender, and the stages of e-consumer decision-making vary according to the situation. This approach is the same as that proposed by Emma Williams et al. (2017).

Research hypotheses: selection and rationale

As mentioned earlier, the literature contains many examples of reports devoted to the importance of particular forms of social proof for building brand awareness and brand image or for making purchasing decisions (cf. Chu & Kim 2011; Dellarocas 2011; Ong & Beng 2012). Yet rather than attempting to comprehend the phenomenon in question from a broader perspective and from within a broader theoretical framework, these enquiries have been somewhat unsystematic in attending only to the here and now. Extensive analyses of the consequences of social media use for well-being and the role of individual differences in susceptibility to social media addiction have in turn emerged from the research literature of various social science disciplines, including sociology, psychology, and marketing. The model presented here therefore represents an interdisciplinary, and to some extent innovative, approach to social proof research in the realm of social media, which attempts to capture the phenomenon under investigation in all of its complexity. The decision to conduct the research in two independent stages was prompted by the high number of variables controlled for. The first stage involved conducting quantitative research using CAWI (computer-assisted web interviewing), while the second entailed experimental research. The research procedures are set out in detail in Chapters 7 and 8.

The central objective of the research is to determine the role and importance of social proof messages on social media for e-consumers' purchasing decisions. Formulated in this way, the central research objective comprises two specific aims:

1 To identify the determinants of e-consumers' susceptibility to social proof in social media.
2 To establish the form of social proof that is considered the most reliable or credible.

Research hypotheses were formulated in order to answer the research questions and to verify the adopted theoretical model. Along with their theoretical justifications and details of the research procedure used (quantitative research, CAWI, and experimental research), they are listed below.

Quantitative surveys of e-consumers (CAWI)

Six hypotheses, which are set out below, were formulated in the quantitative study of e-consumers (H.1.1–H.1.6).

Hypothesis 1.1: When making purchasing decisions, e-consumers are guided by the opinions of other Internet users

Studies on the role of consumer reviews in the process of making purchasing decisions have repeatedly confirmed the impact of other Internet users' opinions on consumer choices (cf. Duan et al. 2008; Masłowska et al. 2017). In fact, reviews and opinions communicated by other customers are even perceived as more interesting and trustworthy than information distributed by the brand (Blazevic et al. 2013). However, this relationship only applies to content conveying social proof added spontaneously by other users. The model, which is informed by the results of many studies of this question, assumes a positive correlation between susceptibility to social influence and believing that other Internet users' reviews are reliable and between susceptibility to social influence and the frequency of using such reviews in the purchasing process. Hypothesis H.1.1 therefore assumes that the relationship studied may vary according to the age and gender of the participants (Figure 6.3).

Hypothesis 1.2: There exist latent constructs of measurable characteristics that differentiate e-consumers in terms of their susceptibility to social proof

The complex nature of susceptibility to social proof and the internal differentiation of social proof itself mean that it is necessary for the research model to take account of the presence of latent variables. While in theory it might seem relatively straightforward to distinguish the opinions of other Internet users from reviews created on behalf of firms, in practice e-consumers are often uncertain when attempting to identify the source of an opinion (cf. Zhang et al. 2016). This demonstrated the need to include in the research an analysis of patterns of e-consumer differentiation at the

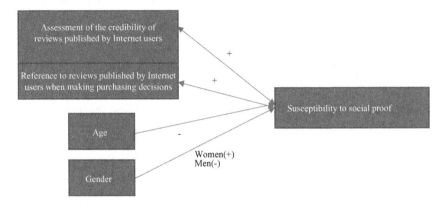

Figure 6.3 Assessment of the reliability and frequency of reference to online reviews and susceptibility to social media.

level of non-measurable characteristics so that examination of these patterns would not be limited to the traits derived from questionnaire surveys
(cf. Green et al. 1976). Variables of this kind can be measured using latent
class analysis (LCA).

*Hypothesis 1.3: There is a positive correlation between time spent on the
Internet and susceptibility to social proof*

It has been shown in a number of international studies on this topic that
there is a positive relationship between time spent online and susceptibility
to social influence. It has also been demonstrated that consumers with a
higher frequency of social media use are more susceptible to social proof
compared to those who use social media less frequently or not at all (cf.
Tussyadiah et al. 2018). It can therefore be assumed that there is a positive correlation between frequency of Internet use (including social network
sites and making online purchases) and susceptibility to social proof.

*Hypothesis 1.4: People who use the Internet for professional purposes are
less susceptible to social proof*

The types of social media and the ways in which they are used also affect
the level of susceptibility to social proof. It was posited that there are significant variations between e-consumers with regard to the professionalization of their use of the Internet and social network sites. Eric Weiser (2001),
who investigated two dimensions of web usage – Socio-Affective Regulation (SAR) and Goods-and-Information Acquisition (GIA) – performed
some interesting research in this area. In this understanding, SAR is
conceptualized as a social or affiliative orientation to Internet use, while
GIA is interpreted as a utilitarian or practical orientation to Internet use.
Weiser's research demonstrated that pursuing GIA goals benefits psychological well-being and that the negative consequences resulting from social
influence are limited.

Hypothesis 1.5: There is a relationship between positive attitudes to online advertising and the degree of susceptibility to social proof

Attitude to advertising, which has been studied intensively in the discipline of marketing (cf. Hite & Fraser 1988; Tsang et al. 2004; Wang et al. 2002), is a general research construct that reflects consumer attitudes to advertising. June Marchand, for example, addressed the relationship between attitude to advertising and social influence (2010), while Darrel Muehling (1987) demonstrated that the influence of other consumers' attitudes is a significant or very significant determinant of consumer attitudes to advertising. In light of the research results obtained, both the model and Hypothesis H.1.5 assume that people with a greater susceptibility to social proof have a positive attitude towards online advertising.

Hypothesis 1.6: People who willingly share their personal data on the Internet are more susceptible to social proof

Prospective users of social network sites must give consent to the use of their personal data. It is assumed that people who are more willing to share their personal data are more susceptible to social proof. And indeed, this relationship has been confirmed by Tamir Mendel and Eran Toch (2017) as well as by other scholars. Mendel and Toch found that the source of social influence has a significant effect on willingness to share personal information and established that individuals with high perceived behavioural control were actually much more susceptible to the influence of other users.

Experimental research

In addition to the CAWI survey, web-based experiments were used to verify the research hypotheses. They primarily focused on two key phenomena:

– The role of individual differences in susceptibility to social proof.
– Preferences for types and forms of social proof used in marketing communications on social media.

The experiments were performed in three series. The first two were conducted in Polish and the third in English.

Six research hypotheses were defined in the experimental study. The first two concern the influence of the social proof elements of marketing messages on the overall evaluation of a brand or product, while the other four investigate the significance of individual differences between e-consumers for susceptibility to social influence.

Hypothesis 2.1: Marketing messages based on social proof have a powerful influence on positive product evaluation

Hypothesis 2.2: Marketing messages based on social proof have a powerful influence on willingness to share opinions with friends

The influence of other consumers' positive and negative online reactions on purchasing behaviour (Winterbottom et al. 2008) and brand attitudes

(Vermeulen & Seegers 2009) has been demonstrated by a number of studies. Ivar Vermeulen and Daphne Seegers, for example, investigated the impact of reviews published online on attitudes towards hotels. Although both positive and negative reviews increased awareness of specific hotels, they found that exposure to positive reviews was associated with more favourable attitudes towards hotels than exposure to negative ones. Although this is quite obvious in everyday terms, their research returned concrete evidence of the influence of social proof on brand perception, which is empirically valuable. Other studies have supplied evidence of the influence of online social proof by analysing Facebook comments in contexts ranging from attitudes towards public breastfeeding (Jin et al. 2015) to the legalization of marijuana (Winter et al. 2015). Examination of the role of the impact of social proof on engagement in brand relationships and on sales is another important strand of research (Kim & Johnson 2016). Moreover, the empirical evidence of social influence online is not limited to Facebook. By investigating references to behaviour connected with smoking, among other things, studies have also demonstrated the impact of social proof in other social media, such as YouTube (Shi et al. 2014; Walther et al. 2010). A valuable contribution has also been made by Naveen Amblee and Tung Bui (2011), who studied online e-book reviews. They found that consumers primarily focused on book reviews rather than on ratings of authors, but did pay attention to the latter when the former were unavailable. This suggests that when explicit cues are lacking, consumers can turn their attention to other, more subtle elements that constitute the social proof message.

Hypothesis 2.3: The lower an e-consumer's score on the intellect scale, the higher their susceptibility to social proof

Hypothesis 2.4: The higher an e-consumer's score on the agreeableness scale, the higher their susceptibility to social proof

Hypothesis 2.5: The higher an e-consumer's score on the neuroticism scale, the higher their susceptibility to social proof

Of the comparatively few studies to have addressed the relationship between consumer personality traits and susceptibility to online social influence, that of Kiemute Oyibo and Julita Vassileva (2019) merits special attention. It demonstrated that individuals who have high levels of neuroticism are more susceptible to social influence than those with low levels of neuroticism and that individuals who score low on the intellect scale are more susceptible to social proof and social comparison than those who have high levels of openness. The study undertaken by Sabrina Stöckli and Doris Hofer (2020), which drew attention to the mediating role of personality traits, found that susceptibility to the social influence of other Facebook users depends on the extent to which the personality traits of the Big Five model, such as openness, conscientiousness, extroversion, agreeableness, and neuroticism, make it possible to predict behaviour on social network sites.

The extensive literature on the relationship between personality traits and social media use includes a paper written by David Hughes and his team

(2012), which found positive correlations between Facebook use and extroversion and intellect. Although Alev Koçak Alan and Ebru Tümer Kabadayi confirmed these results (2016), Gwendolyn Seidman (2012) found that high levels of agreeableness and neuroticism are the best predictors of using Facebook to satisfy the need to belong.

Hypothesis 2.6: The lower an e-consumer's self-esteem, the higher their susceptibility to social proof

Chapter 4 of this monograph gives a detailed account of the concept of self-esteem, which has received considerable attention in the literature in the context of social media use (cf. Jiang & Ngien 2020) or, beyond the virtual world, in the context of the relationship between levels of self-esteem and susceptibility to social influence (cf. Cohen 1959; Wilcox & Stephen 2012). Yet a careful search of the literature returns only a few items devoted to the relationship between levels of self-esteem and susceptibility to social influence in the social media environment. Of these, Elisa Bergagna and Stefano Tartaglia's paper (2018) pointed out the moderating role of the propensity for social comparison in the relationship between the low self-esteem of Internet users and some indicators of Facebook use, such as time of day, frequency of use, and turning to the site for social interaction.

The next chapters of this monograph present the analysis, evaluation, and discussion of the research results and the verification of the research hypotheses. Chapter 7 examines and discusses quantitative research conducted on a representative sample of Poles in 2019. It includes the detailed research methodology and main findings as well as the results of testing hypotheses 1.1–1.6 in quantitative research conducted using CAWI. Chapter 8 contains a detailed account of the methodological assumptions and a description of the research methodology. Verification of the second group of hypotheses is combined with a discussion and evaluation of the results of the experimental research on social proof in social media.

References

Alan, A. K., & Kabadayi, E. T. (2016). The effect of personal factors on social media usage of young consumers. *Procedia – Social and Behavioral Sciences, 235*, pp. 595–602.

Amblee, N., & Bui, T. (2011). Harnessing the influence of social proof in online shopping: The effect of electronic word of mouth on sales of digital microproducts. *International Journal of Electronic Commerce, 16*, pp. 91–114. doi:10.2753/JEC1086-4415160205.

Aral, S., & Walker, D. (2012). Identifying influential and susceptible members of social networks. *Science, 337*(41). doi:10.1126/science.1215842.

Bergagna, E., & Tartaglia, S. (2018). Self-esteem, social comparison, and Facebook use. *Europe's Journal of Psychology, 14*(4), pp. 831–845. https://doi.org/10.5964/ejop.v14i4.1592.

Blazevic, V., Hammedi, W., Garnefeld, I., Rust, R. T., Keiningham, T., Andreassen, T. W., Donthu, N., & Carl, W. (2013). Beyond traditional word-of-mouth: An expanded model of customer-driven influence. *Journal of Service Management, 24*(3), pp. 294–313.

Chu, Sh., & Kim, Y. (2011). Determinants of consumer engagement in electronic word-of-mouth (eWOM) in social networking sites. *International Journal of Advertising, 30*(1), pp. 47–75, doi:10.2501/IJA-30-1-047-075

Cohen, A. R. (1959). *Some implications of self-esteem for social influence.* In C. I. Hovland & I. L. Janis (Eds.), *Personality and persuasibility* (pp. 102–120). Yale: Yale University Press.

Dellarocas, Ch. (2011). The digitization of word-of-mouth: Promise and challenge of online feedback mechanism. *Management Science, 49.* doi:10.1287/mnsc.49.10.1407.17308.

Duan, W., Gu, B., & Whinston, A. B. (2008). The dynamics of online word-of-mouth and product sales? An empirical investigation of the movie industry. *Journal of Retail, 84*(2), pp. 233–242.

Green, P., Carmone, F., & Wachspress, D. (1976). Consumer segmentation via latent class analysis. *Journal of Consumer Research, 3*(3), pp. 170–174.

Hite, R. E., & Fraser, C. (1988). Meta-analyses of attitudes toward advertising by professionals. *Journal of Marketing, 52*(3), pp. 95–103. https://doi.org/10.1177/002224298805200309

Hughes, D. J., Rowe, M., Batey, M., & Lee, A. (2012). A tale of two sites: Twitter vs. Facebook and the personality predictors of social media usage. *Computers in Human Behavior, 28*, pp. 561–569.

Jiang, S., & Ngien, A. (2020). The effects of Instagram use, social comparison, and self-esteem on social anxiety: a survey study in Singapore. *Social Media + Society.* https://doi.org/10.1177/2056305120912488.

Jin, S. V., Phua, J., & Lee, K. M. (2015). Telling stories about breastfeeding through Facebook: The impact of user-generated content (UGC) on pro-breastfeeding attitudes. *Computer Human Behaviour, 46*, pp. 6–17. doi:10.1016/j.chb.2014.12.046.

Keles, B., McCrae, N., & Grealish, A. (2020). A systematic review: The influence of social media on depression, anxiety and psychological distress in adolescents. *International Journal of Adolescence and Youth, 25*(1), pp. 79–93. doi:10.1080/0267 3843.2019.1590851.

Kim, A. J., & Johnson, K. K. (2016). Power of consumers using social media: Examining the influences of brand-related user-generated content on Facebook. *Computer Human Behavior, 58*, pp. 98–108. doi:10.1016/j.chb.2015.12.047.

Marchand, J. (2010), Attitude toward the Ad: Its Influence in a Social Marketing Context. *Social Marketing Quarterly, 16*(2), pp. 104–126. https://doi.org/10.1080/15245001003746782.

Masłowska, E., Malthouse, E., & Bernritter, S. (2017). Too good to be true: The role of online reviews' features in probability to buy. *International Journal of Advertising, 36*, pp. 142–163. doi:10.1080/02650487.2016.1195622.

Mendel, T., & Toch, E. (2017). Susceptibility to social influence of privacy behaviors: Peer versus authoritative sources. pp. 581–593. doi:10.1145/2998181.2998323.

Muehling, D. D. (1987). An investigation of factors underlying attitude-toward-advertising-in-general. *Journal of Advertising, 16* (1), pp. 32–40. doi: 10.1080/00913367.1987.10673058.

Ong, B. (2012). The perceived influence of user-reviews in the hospitality industry. *Journal of Hospitality Marketing & Management, 21*(5), pp. 463–485.

Oyibo, K., & Vassileva, J. (2019). The relationship between personality traits and susceptibility to social influence. *Computers in Human Behavior, 98*, pp. 174–188.

Seidman, G. (2012). Self-presentation and belonging on Facebook: How personality influences social media use and motivations. *Personality and Individual Differences, 54*, pp. 402–407.

Stöckli, S., & Hofer, D. (2020). Susceptibility to social influence predicts behavior on Facebook. *PloS one, 15*(3), e0229337. https://doi.org/10.1371/journal.pone.0229337.

Tsang, M. M., Ho, S.-C. & Liang, T.-P. (2004) Consumer attitudes toward mobile advertising: An empirical study. *International Journal of Electronic Commerce, 8*(3), pp. 65–78, doi:10.1080/10864415.2004.11044301.

Tussyadiah, S. P., Kausar, D. R., & Soesilo, P. K. M. (2018). The effect of engagement in online social network on susceptibility to influence. *Journal of Hospitality & Tourism Research, 42*(2), pp. 201–223. https://doi.org/10.1177/1096348015584441.

Vermeulen, I. E., & Seegers, D. (2009). Tried and tested: The impact of online hotel reviews on consumer consideration. *Tourism Management, 30*, pp. 123–127. doi:10.1016/j.tourman.2008.04.008.

Walther, J. B., DeAndrea, D., Kim, J., & Anthony, J. C. (2010). The influence of online comments on perceptions of antimarijuana public service announcements on YouTube. *Human Communication Research*, 36, pp. 469–492. doi:10.1111/j.1468-2958.2010.01384.

Wang, Ch. Zhang, P., Risook Ch., & D'Eredita, M. (2002). Understanding consumers attitude toward advertising, *AMCIS 2002 Proceedings*. 158. https://aisel.aisnet.org/amcis2002/158.

Weiser, E. (2001). The functions of Internet use and their social and psychological consequences. *Cyberpsychology & Behavior, 4*, pp. 723–743. doi:10.1089/109493101753376678.

Wilcox, K., & Stephen, A. T. (2012). Are close friends the enemy? Online social networks, self-esteem, and self-control. *Journal of Consumer Research, 40*, pp. 90–103.

Williams, E. J., Beardmore, A., & Joinson, A. N. (2017). Individual differences in susceptibility to online influence: A theoretical review. *Computers in Human Behavior, 72,* pp. 412–421.

Winter, S., Brückner, C., & Krämer, N. C. (2015). They came, they liked, they commented: Social influence on Facebook news channels. *Cyberpsychology, Behavior and Social Networking, 18*, pp. 431–436. doi:10.1089/cyber.2015.0005.

Winterbottom, A., Bekker, H. L., Conner, M., & Mooney, A. (2008). Does narrative information bias individual's decision making? A systematic review. *Social Science & Medicine, 67*, pp. 2079–2088. doi:10.1016/j.socscimed.2008.09.037.

Zhang, D., Zhou, L., Kehoe, J. L., & Kilic, I. Y. (2016), What online reviewer behaviors really matter? Effects of verbal and nonverbal behaviors on detection of fake online reviews. *Journal of Management Information Systems, 33*(2), pp. 456–481. doi:10.1080/07421222.2016.1205907.

7 Confidence in social proof and its impact on buying decisions

Introduction

Chapter 7 presents the results of quantitative research, which was conducted using a computer-assisted web interviewing (CAWI) survey of a group of Polish respondents ($N = 1,004$), into the role of social proof in e-consumers' purchasing decisions. The analysis of the results begins with a description of the research participants and the research method. The principal aim of the chapter is to analyse and evaluate the main research problems, which are: (1) the role of social proof in the search for product information and in making purchasing decisions; (2) identifying e-consumer variation in susceptibility to social influence based on latent class analysis (LCA). The chapter then presents and discusses the results of hypothesis verification. It is determined on the basis of statistical analysis that the e-consumers in the study are often guided by the opinions of other Internet users when making purchasing decisions, which demonstrates that social proof is highly effective and important in shaping e-consumer behaviour. The LCA allowed for a deeper characterization of the impact of reviews and opinions on the e-consumers in the study and their differentiation in terms of their susceptibility to social proof, while post hoc analyses made it possible to examine the independent variables that significantly differentiate the representatives of particular classes. Through extraction by LCA, these analyses resulted in an original classification of e-consumers according to their susceptibility to social proof.

The e-consumers in the study

Susceptibility to social influence is probably a beneficial, hereditary trait that evolution has inscribed in human DNA (Sundie et al. 2012). That people possess different levels of resistance to the influence of others is determined by individual differences (and therefore by personality traits, temperament, and self-esteem), by past experiences, such as frequency of previous interactions, and by the characteristics – the form and content – of the messages themselves. It is methodologically very demanding, if not impossible,

DOI: 10.4324/9781003128052-9

to capture all of these variables simultaneously and to measure all of their variations, which is why the scope of this monograph is limited to a specific type of social influence – social proof – and to a particular situation: marketing communication in a hypermedia computer-mediated environment, including social media.

An analysis of the results obtained from quantitative studies of a representative group of Poles (N = 1,004) was conducted in order to answer questions concerning the role and importance of other Internet users' opinions in purchasing decisions and the variations in contemporary e-consumers' susceptibility to social proof. The research proper was preceded by a series of pilot studies. The first, which was conducted in Poland, was carried out to verify the research tool (N = 444), while the second, which was performed in English on an international group of foreign students, made it possible to identify culturally specific elements (N = 511). The pilot study in English included students from the following countries: Belgium, Croatia, China, the Czech Republic, Finland, Georgia, Japan, Moldova, Romania, Slovakia, Turkey, and Ukraine. The results of the international pilot studies, which will serve as a prelude to further research conducted in international settings, permitted preliminary analysis of the role and importance of the respondents' cultural differences.

The quantitative research, whose results are presented here, was conducted by PMR Consulting – in continuous consultation with the author – in November and December 2019 using quota-based sample selection. Working with a research company made it possible to recruit a specific number of people whose demographic features reflected the characteristics of the sample of Polish Internet users as accurately as possible. The research included people who had made at least one purchase in a virtual environment during the six months preceding the research. The detailed characteristics of the research sample are presented in Table 7.1.

Table 7.1 Characteristics of the Polish e-consumers included in the study (N = 1,004)

Variable	Values adopted for the variables	Proportion of sample (%)
Gender	Men	48
	Women	52
Age	18–24 years	10
	25–34 years	27
	35–44 years	28
	45–54 years	17
	55–64 years	12
	65 years and over	6
Place of residence	Countryside and small towns (population <50,000)	39
	Larger towns and cities (population >50,000)	61

(Continued)

Variable	Values adopted for the variables	Proportion of sample (%)
Education	Primary or lower secondary education	1
	Vocational secondary education	6
	Secondary education	34
	Post-secondary education	9
	Higher education	50
Household size	One-person	9
	Two-person	23
	Three-person	29
	Four-person	26
	Five-person and above	13

The participants were therefore Internet users who regularly use the World Wide Web and shop online. More than half of the respondents were young people aged 25–44, which corresponds with the age structure of Internet users in Poland (CSO 2020).

Research methodology and scope

A research procedure involving CAWI was adopted. Participation in the research was voluntary and anonymous, and it took approximately 15 minutes to complete.

The first part of the questionnaire concerned the ways respondents use Internet resources and their experiences of doing so. The responses revealed the following use of social network sites by Polish e-consumers: 68% of those surveyed use Facebook, 46% have a YouTube account, and 27% have an Instagram account. Half of the respondents (51%) use smartphones to surf the Internet and 31% use laptops to do so. Interestingly, one in four respondents (26%) declared use of a tablet, but only 1% said it was their main device. The vast majority of respondents (89%) agreed with the statement that 'Shopping online enables you to find cheaper products than in brick-and-mortar shops', while a little over half (55%) stated that they had 'full confidence in online shopping'. From the perspective of the book's research objectives, it is worth emphasizing that 73% of respondents believe that 'the opinions of other Internet users are a valuable source of product information' and that 85% look for product information online. The picture that emerges from these responses is one of active social media users who are aware of the benefits of online shopping.

An important aspect of the survey was to elicit respondents' attitudes to particular forms of online advertising – and especially to their credibility and effectiveness. According to the respondents, the opinions friends publish on social media are the most dependable source of information on the Internet (70%). Equally trusted were reviews of other Internet users (68%). It can be concluded that social proof confirmed by reviews and opinions of both friends and strangers published on social media is an important source of information about brands. Consumers trust other Internet users, who they assume to be disinterested and objective, more than they trust firms. Websites containing information about products were also rated high on the reliability scale (64%). Every second respondent (53%) also trusted sponsored articles published online. Contrary to expectations, the opinions of bloggers and influencers (36%), as well as those of celebrities and the faces of advertising campaigns (14%), enjoyed a comparatively lower level of trust. The respondents regarded information from these sources as unreliable and biased.

Respondents were also asked to share their opinions on the role of online advertising in the online purchasing process. Almost half of the respondents (48%) stated that advertising speeds up the process of looking for information connected with purchases. For 42% of those surveyed it also makes selecting products and making purchases easier, and for 37% of respondents it speeds up the purchasing process. Yet in the respondents' declarations this was as far as the advantages of online advertising went. Almost half of the participants (42%) disagreed with the statement that advertising facilitates the final purchase decision. The breakdown of responses to the statements revealed just how differently advertising is perceived among respondents.

The role of social proof in product information searches and purchasing decisions

The statistical data obtained in the quantitative research and presented in this chapter were analysed using SPSS software. The starting point for further considerations was an attempt to identify the role of social proof in purchasing decisions. This problem is expressed in Hypothesis H.1.1.

Hypothesis 1.1: When making purchasing decisions, e-consumers are guided by the opinions of other Internet users

A research construct (an index of the influence of other Internet users), assembled using factor analysis, was devised to verify the hypothesis related to purchasing decisions made under the influence of the opinions of other Internet users. Hypothesis H.1.1 was verified in four stages:

1 Selection of questionnaire indicators to form an index of the influence of other Internet users on purchasing decisions made online.
2 Verification of the reliability of the proposed research construct.
3 Verification of research Hypothesis H.1.1.
4 Assessment of the variation in responses according to demographic factors.

In the first stage, questionnaire indicators relating to the influence of others on purchasing decisions were purposively selected. Table 7.2 displays the questionnaire indicators and the responses to them that were taken into account in the construction of the index of the influence of other Internet users.

Table 7.2 Construction of an index of the influence of other Internet users

Index of the influence of other Internet users	Structure of responses (%)		
Questionnaire indicator	Negative	Neutral	Positive
The opinions of other Internet users are a valuable source of information	12%	16%	72%
Please assess the credibility of these sources of information about purchased products — Opinions of other Internet users	9%	23%	68%
Opinions of friends published on social media	8%	22%	70%
Opinions of bloggers and influencers	33%	31%	36%

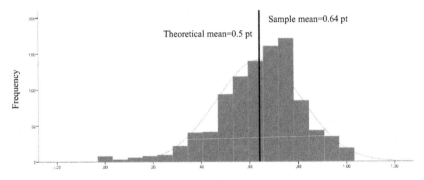

←Others' opinions exert a **lesser influence** | Others' opinions exert a **greater** influence→

Figure 7.1 Student's *t*-test for the index of the influence of other Internet users ($p < 0.01$).

The second stage involved verifying the reliability of the construct based on the four tested questionnaire indicators (Table 7.2). The Cronbach's alpha value was 0.717, which signals that the adopted index is highly reliable.

A one-sample student's *t*-test was conducted in the third stage to verify the research hypothesis. The mean of the index from the sample was 64% (the maximum possible value was 100%, and a confidence interval of 99% was assumed), which is significantly different from the theoretical mean of 50% ($p < 0.01$). The detailed distribution of the variables is shown in Figure 7.1.

In the fourth stage of data analysis, the variation in responses to the questions included in the index was assessed according to the respondents' gender, age, and place of residence.

The general conclusion from an analysis of the data in Figure 7.2 is that there is relatively little variation in the influence of other Internet users across all of the demographic variables used to describe the respondents. A greater proportion of women (67%) than men (61%) are guided by the

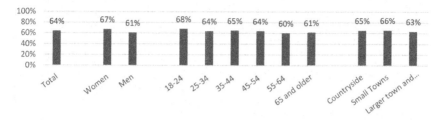

Figure 7.2 The values of the index broken down according to demographic variables.

opinions of other Internet users. The index was above average for those aged 25 and under (68%), but below average (64%) for men (61%) and those aged 55 and above (60–61%). The value of the index also varied according to the respondents' place of residence: the smaller the town, the higher the value of the adopted construct (Figure 7.2).

In finding that the opinions of other Internet users have a significant impact on purchasing decisions, the analysis confirmed the research hypothesis being tested (H.1.1). This conclusion was supported by the one-sample *t*-test. Women and those aged 25 and under are guided by the opinions of other Internet users most often. It should be stressed, however, that the role of demographic factors retains a degree of ambiguity because the variable under examination – 'susceptibility to the opinions of other Internet users' – is a complex construct that is difficult to observe. The remainder of this chapter attempts to identify subtypes – latent classes – that enable the precise identification of hidden but significant constructs.

Differentiation in e-consumers' susceptibility to social influence

LCA: description and grounds for use

Descriptive statistical methods are often employed in social science disciplines such as sociology, economics, and psychology to study relationships between variables – especially where the variables are observable and measurable characteristics. It should be stressed, however, that these methods are inadequate in the case of hidden features that cannot be directly measured or objectively assessed, such as the variables studied in the research model set out here.

LCA is a statistical method for discovering subtypes of related cases from multivariate categorical data (Lazarsfeld 1950). A latent class defines a particular abstract feature – for example, a preference for forms of advertising or a characteristic that cannot be observed directly. Thus, if the hidden construct has a step structure, i.e. a feature is qualitative and has some variants within a variable, each feature can be treated as a latent class.

LCA serves to investigate a set of multiple qualitative variables or categorical quantitative variables. In opinion polls, individual-level voting data, and surveys of inter-rater reliability or consumer behaviour, the observed data often take the form of a series of categorical responses. The technique can be employed to explore sources of variation in observed variables, to identify and characterize clusters of similar cases, and to approximate the distribution of observations across the multiple variables of interest (Linzer & Lewis 2011).

The theoretical basis of this method was formulated by Paul Lazarsfeld, who discussed the concept of this multivariate data analysis technique in detail (Lazarsfeld 1950) before refining it a few years later (Lazarsfeld 1959) – as did many other statisticians, such as Theodore Anderson (1959). Of particular importance, however, was the work of Leo Goodman (1970), who developed the method of maximum likelihood for estimating model parameters in LCA (Goodman 1974). Contemporary studies that address the issue of LCA in depth include the work of Linda Collins and Stephanie Lanza (2010). Figure 7.3 depicts the different stages of analysis of the data obtained in the quantitative research.

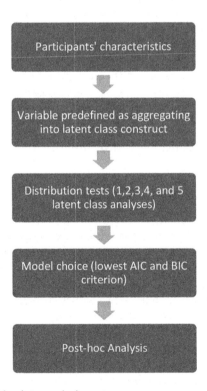

Figure 7.3 Stages in the data analysis.

Given the complexity of the construct under investigation, it may be appropriate to deploy LCA as an entry point to further detailed analysis before proceeding to study individual differences in susceptibility to social proof in advertising. LCA makes it possible to identify hidden subgroups of respondents in the survey and to simplify the structure of their heterogeneity. Examples of the application of LCA in the field of social influence can be found in research into modelling the influence of social networks using multiple-group LCA (Dey et al. 2020) and into awareness of manipulation in online advertising (Sanak-Kosmowska & Wiktor 2020).

Differentiation in e-consumers' susceptibility to social influence: verifying the research model using LCA

The next step in analysing the data obtained in the quantitative research was to verify the assumption relating to the differentiation in e-consumers' susceptibility to social proof.

Hypothesis 1.2: There exist latent constructs of measurable characteristics that differentiate e-consumers in their susceptibility to social proof

To verify the research hypothesis assuming the existence of hidden characteristics differentiating e-consumers' susceptibility to social influence (H.1.2), it was necessary to build a statistical model to identify them. To this end, the following steps were taken:

1   Selection of dependent variables and the construction of a model.
2   Verification of the distribution of latent classes.
3   Selection of class distribution based on model fit indicators.

The model studied was built on the basis of selected dependent variables relating to susceptibility to social proof, of which eight emerged from the literature analysis. These are presented in Table 7.3.

Due to the nature of the data analysed (expressed on a scale of 1–5), it was decided to conduct the analysis in the Polytomous Variable Latent Class Analysis package by Drew Linzer and Jeffrey Lewis (Linzer & Lewis 2011, 2013). The starting point for the results analysis was to verify the distribution of latent classes. LCA for ordinal coded data was used for the statistical analysis, which was conducted using version 3.4 of the R software to investigate the allocation of respondents to the various classes based on the assumed number of classes. As required by methodological rigour, distributions of the variables for one, two, three, four, and five classes were tested (Table 7.4).

On the basis of an analysis of two indicators of the fit of latent class models, the Akaike Information Criterion (AIC) and the Bayesian Information Criterion (BIC), it was decided to select a model with four latent classes. It should be emphasized that the analysis was repeated several times due to

Table 7.3 Dependent variables referring to social proof

Variable	Characteristics of variable
A (Q1_8_4)	When making purchasing decisions I look for product information online
B (Q1_8_5)	The opinions of other Internet users are a valuable source of product information
C (Q1_8_8)	I have full confidence in online shopping
D (Q1_8_9)	Purchasing on the Internet gives me pleasure
E (Q2_1_2)	The opinions friends publish on social media (reviews, comments) are the most dependable
F(Q2_1_6)	The opinions of other Internet users are the most dependable
G(Q2_1_7)	The opinions of bloggers and celebrities are the most dependable
H(Q2_1_8)	The opinions of brand ambassadors (the faces of advertising campaigns) are the most dependable

Table 7.4 Models (segmentations) of the LCA adapted to the variables referring to social proof

Dimensions of models	AIC	BIC
One-cluster model	18353.54	18491.07
Two-cluster model	17460.01	17739.98
Three-cluster model	16869.44	17291.85
Four-cluster model	**16602.71**	**17167.56**
Five-cluster model	16475.58	17182.87

Note: AIC = Akaike Information Criterion; BIC = Bayesian Information Criterion.

the risk of local maxima, and the lowest values of the AIC and BIC criteria were used for comparison.

Figure 7.4 shows the fit of a model of four latent classes along with their proportion in the population studied. The statistical significance of the variation occurring between the four latent groups studied ($p < 0.05$) was determined by non-parametric tests of one-way analysis of variance (Kruskal-Wallis) and these differences were confirmed in post hoc analysis by the Dwass-Steel-Critchlow-Fligner test. Hypothesis 1.2 was therefore confirmed: the analysis established the existence of latent variables that clearly differentiate the e-consumers studied.

It is possible on the basis of the obtained results and the analysis of the distribution of dependent variables in the classes studied to offer a preliminary description of the probability of the occurrence of particular variables among the representatives of the various latent classes. The detailed results are shown in Table 7.5.

The following section presents the results of the analyses and statistical inference aimed at verifying the four remaining research hypotheses:

Hypothesis 1.3: There is a positive correlation between time spent on the Internet and susceptibility to social proof

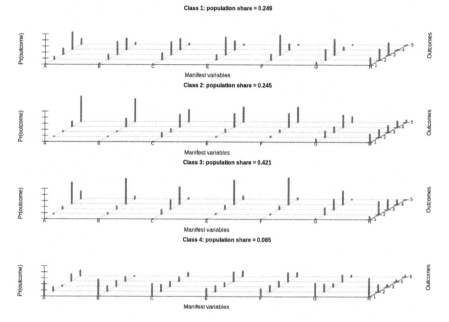

Figure 7.4 Graphical illustration of a model of four latent classes.

Table 7.5 Characteristics of the latent classes

Latent class	Proposed name	Characteristics of probability
1	Indifferent $N = 243$ (24%)	When making purchases they search for product information online, yet have limited confidence in the opinions they find there or have no view on them. They have a neutral attitude towards making online purchases and do not believe in the recommendations of bloggers or celebrities
2	Susceptible and trusting $N = 248$ (25%)	They enjoy making online purchases and have full confidence in shopping in this way. They value the opinions of other Internet users and regard friends' opinions published on social media and other Internet users' recommendations as very reliable. They also trust the views of bloggers and celebrities. For them, the recommendations of brand ambassadors are the least credible

(Continued)

Latent class	Proposed name	Characteristics of probability
3	Susceptible and cautious $N = 432$ (43%)	They like to make online purchases and trust the opinions and recommendations of other Internet users published online – but to a lesser degree than the members of Latent Class 2 (susceptible and trusting). They have little regard for the credibility of the opinions and reviews of bloggers, celebrities, and brand ambassadors
4	Resistant $N = 81$ (8%)	They dislike making purchases online, have very little confidence in shopping in this way, and very little trust in the recommendations and reviews published on the Internet. They do not look for product information online

Hypothesis 1.4: People who use the Internet for professional purposes are less susceptible to social proof

Hypothesis 1.5: There is a relationship between positive attitudes to online advertising and the degree of susceptibility to social proof

Hypothesis 1.6: People who willingly share their personal data on the Internet are more susceptible to social proof

To verify research Hypotheses H.1.3–H.1.6, the participants' responses were analysed using the Dwass-Steel-Critchlow-Fligner test and assigned to one of four latent classes. In this way, the statistically significant variables that make it possible to predict features that correlate with membership of the proposed class were identified. They can be assigned to the following categories describing respondents:

1   Demographic characteristics (gender and age).
2   Frequency of use of social network sites.
3   Frequency and degree of professionalization of Internet use.
4   Attitudes to online advertising and online purchases.
5   Degree of willingness to share personal data online.

Demographic description of respondents and their membership of latent classes

Two variables, which are presented in Figure 7.5, proved statistically significant in the case of questions describing respondents' demographic features. In the case of age, no statistical significance was detected ($p = 0.733$) only in the differences between the representatives of Latent Class 1 (indifferent)

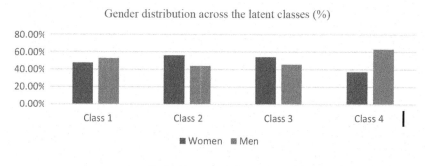

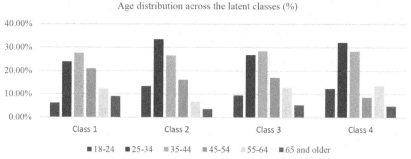

Figure 7.5 Distribution of participants' gender and age across the four latent classes.

and Latent Class 2 (susceptible and trusting). The significance of the variation of the remaining intergroup differences was $p < 0.05$.

Analysis of the distribution of the studied variables led to the following conclusions. The predominance of women is significant in Latent Class 2 (susceptible and trusting) and Latent Class 3 (susceptible and cautious), which confirms the greater susceptibility of women to social proof. It is worth noting that men predominate in Latent Class 4 (resistant), which is the least numerous. In this instance, the intergroup variations are statistically significant in all cases ($p < 0.05$).

Although respondents aged 25–55 predominated in all of the latent classes, the results of the post hoc analysis confirmed the statistical significance of the variation of all of the groups studied ($p < 0.05$). It is worth noting the intra-group variations in age distribution. The differences in the number of people aged 18–24 and 25–34 were not significant in Latent Class 1 (indifferent), but this was not the case in Latent Class 2 (susceptible and trusting) or Latent Class 3 (susceptible and cautious), in which younger people predominated. Age therefore plays a significant moderating role in the case of susceptibility to social proof: those in Latent Class 2 (susceptible and trusting) were also the youngest participants in the study.

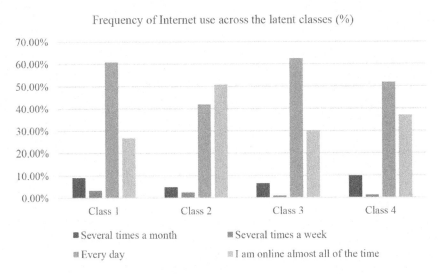

Figure 7.6 Frequency of Internet use across the four latent classes.

Frequency of Internet use and use of social network sites

To verify Hypothesis H.1.3, a check was performed to determine whether there were significant differences in Internet use between members of the latent classes (Figure 7.6). Post hoc analysis confirmed significant intergroup variations between the various classes: the majority of those in Latent Class 2 (susceptible and trusting) were online almost all of the time (51%). The most often selected answer in the remaining classes was 'every day', yet in Latent Class 1 (indifferent) and Latent Class 4 (resistant), the proportion of 'several times a month' answers was also apparent – 9% for the former and 10% for the latter. These findings demonstrate that frequency of Internet use correlates significantly with susceptibility to social proof, which confirms Hypothesis H.1.3.

Frequency of Internet use and use of social network sites

Next, a test was performed to detect significant intergroup differences in frequency of use of social network sites, including Facebook (Figure 7.7) and Instagram (Figure 7.8). Post hoc analysis confirmed a statistically significant intergroup variation ($p < 0.05$). The answers most often selected for the most popular site, Facebook, were 'almost all of the time' and 'several times a day'. It is worth comparing Latent Class 2 (susceptible and trusting), in which 49% of respondents said they used Facebook almost all of the time, with Latent Class 4 (resistant), in which, paradoxically, respondents also said they used social media frequently – especially in the case of Facebook. Immunity to social proof may therefore be a consequence of frequent

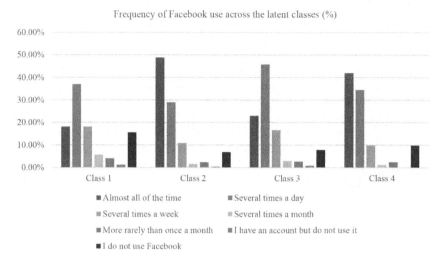

Figure 7.7 Frequency of Facebook use across the four latent classes.

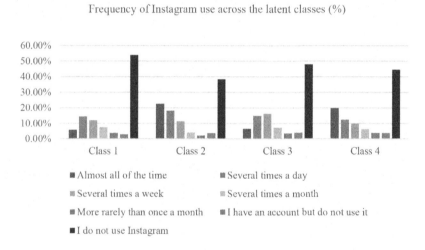

Figure 7.8 Frequency of Instagram use across the four latent classes.

exposure, but as the sample size of Latent Class 4 is small ($N = 81$), this can be asserted only cautiously.

The research revealed that Instagram was much less popular than Facebook among respondents in Poland. The dominance of the reply 'I do not use Instagram' in all of the latent classes was therefore unsurprising. Respondents in Latent Class 2 (susceptible and trusting) and Latent Class 4 (resistant) used Instagram most often, as was the case with Facebook.

Frequency and degree of professionalization of Internet use

To assess the importance of the Internet in accomplishing professional tasks was the third of the research issues in the LCA. Further post hoc tests were run on variables related to the degree of professionalization of Internet use. The statistical significance of intergroup differences and the distribution of responses given by their members were examined to enable the verification of Hypothesis H.1.4. This involved addressing two issues.

The first was the frequency of Internet use for professional purposes. Post hoc tests confirmed the statistical significance of the intergroup variation for the variable identifying the degree of Internet use for professional purposes. A visualization of the distribution of the variable across the four latent classes is shown in Figure 7.9.

The second was linked to the statement 'Internet access makes my work easier'. Here again, the intergroup differences proved statistically significant. The distribution of responses is set out in Figure 7.10.

A correlation between Internet use for professional purposes and low susceptibility to social proof was posited, which describes Latent Class 4 (resistant). Yet very nearly half of the people in this class (48%) did not use the Internet for work purposes (48%) and the same proportion disagreed with the statement 'Internet access makes my work easier'. This therefore means that Hypothesis H.1.4 cannot be confirmed. Indeed, it was the respondents in Latent Class 2 (susceptible and trusting) that used the Internet for professional purposes most often.

In light of the results, a decision was made to also check the distribution of the second variable describing e-consumers' online shopping behaviour: frequency of online shopping. The post hoc analysis revealed that the differences in the distribution of online shopping frequency in the latent classes studied were statistically significant ($p < 0.05$). The distribution of the variables is shown in Figure 7.11. The obtained results indicate that a similar proportion of people from both Latent Class 2 (susceptible and trusting) and

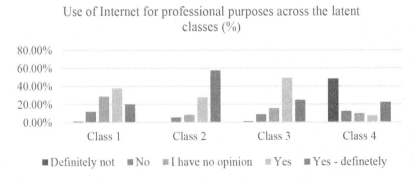

Figure 7.9 Use of Internet for professional purposes across the four latent classes.

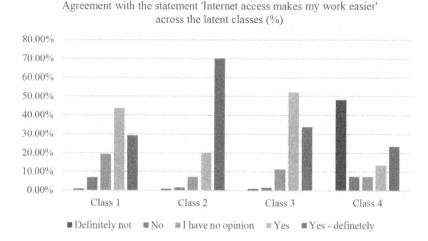

Figure 7.10 Agreement with the statement 'Internet access makes my work easier' across the four latent classes.

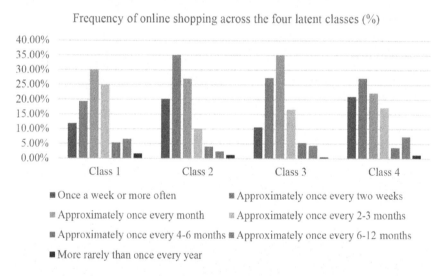

Figure 7.11 Frequency of online shopping across the four latent classes.

Latent Class 4 (resistant) shop online frequently. In the former group 55% of respondents shopped online at least once every two weeks, and in the latter 48% did so. It is difficult to draw firm conclusions from this observation owing to the differences in the size of the two classes, but this relationship merits further investigation – especially in the era of the coronavirus pandemic when access to brick-and-mortar shops is limited.

Attitudes to online advertising and online purchases

The relationship between respondents' susceptibility to social proof and attitudes to online advertising was investigated in a series of post hoc tests to determine variation in responses to the questions asked on this issue. It was assumed that agreeing with the following statements would signal a positive attitude to advertising:

–   'Advertising makes it easier to select products and make a purchase' (Figure 7.12), 'Advertising speeds up the purchasing process' (Figure 7.13).
–   Advertising makes it easier to decide (Figure 7.14).
–   Advertising is conducive to positive product evaluation (Figure 7.15).

The differences between the responses given by the members of the various classes to all of the tested questions proved to be statistically significant ($p <$ 0.05). The distribution of responses with respect to membership in the latent classes is shown in Figure 7.12.

Members of Latent Class 2 (susceptible and trusting) agreed with the statement 'Advertising makes it easier to select products and make a purchase' much more often than those in other classes. By contrast, it is worth noting the distribution of responses to this question in Latent Class 4 (resistant), over half of which were negative (53%). Of the responses in Latent Class 1 (indifferent), almost one-half (45%) were negative and 30% of the members had no opinion on the subject, which represents a situation somewhat similar to that in Latent Class 4 (resistant).

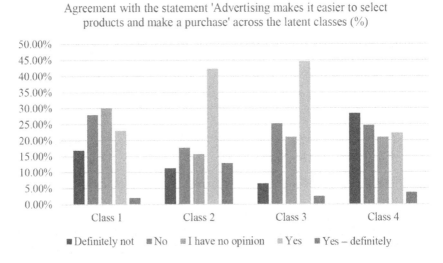

Figure 7.12 Agreement with the statement 'Advertising makes it easier to select products and make a purchase' across the four latent classes.

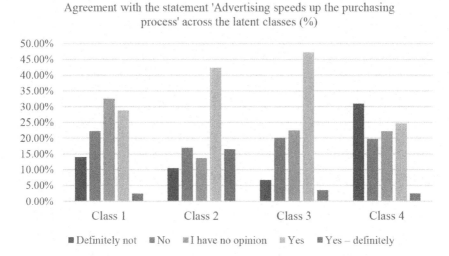

Figure 7.13 Agreement with the statement 'Advertising speeds up the purchasing process' across the four latent classes.

The distribution of responses to the statement 'Advertising speeds up the purchasing process' was fairly even. The greatest proportion of 'yes – definitely' answers was given by Latent Class 2 (susceptible and trusting; yes – definitely 16.5%; yes 42%) and Latent Class 3 (susceptible and cautious; yes – definitely 3.5%; yes 47%). Latent Class 1 (indifferent) was the most sceptical (yes – definitely 2.5%; yes 29%) along with Latent Class 4 (resistant; yes – definitely 2.5%; yes 25%).

The distribution across the classes of responses to the statement 'Advertising makes it easier to decide' led to slightly different conclusions. Those in Latent Class 2 (susceptible and trusting) and Latent Class 3 (susceptible and cautious) gave affirmative answers most often, but the proportion of negative responses was comparatively high across all classes (Figure 7.14). It was highest in Latent Class 4 (resistant), where 59% of members did not agree with the statement.

Analysis of agreement with the statement 'Advertising is conducive to positive product evaluation' led to important and interesting conclusions. Nearly half of those in Latent Class 2 (susceptible and trusting) answered 'yes' or 'yes – definitely' (49.5%). Although the proportion of negative answers in Latent Class 4 (resistant) was significant (53%), the positive answers in that class, where the total number of 'yes' and 'yes – definitely' statements amounted to 27.5%, are worth noting. It is possible that this distribution of responses is connected with a certain ambiguity in the statement tested: people who are aware of the manipulative nature of advertising and who dislike online shopping are aware of its influence not only on purchasing decisions, but also on product and brand evaluation.

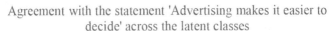

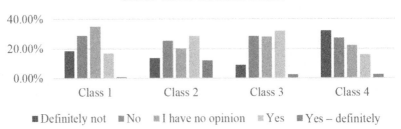

Figure 7.14 Agreement with the statement 'Advertising makes it easier to decide' across the four latent classes.

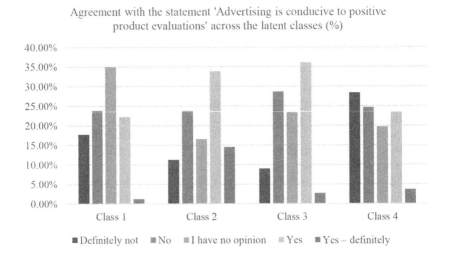

Figure 7.15 Agreement with the statement 'Advertising is conducive to positive product evaluations' across the four latent classes.

Hypothesis 1.5 can be confirmed based on the obtained results. There is a significant, empirically confirmed relationship between a positive attitude to online advertising and the degree of susceptibility to social proof. When compared to representatives of other latent classes, the respondents in Latent Class 2 (susceptible and trusting) answered in the affirmative to all of the questions analysed, which expressed their positive attitude towards advertising and its role in the decision-making process. It is also worth noting that the dominant response of the members of Latent Class 1 (indifferent) to all of the statements tested was 'I have no opinion'.

Willingness to share personal data online

The final hypothesis tested, Hypothesis H.1.6, concerned the relationship between sharing personal data online and susceptibility to social proof. A decision was made to test whether the representatives of the latent classes were differentiated by their willingness to participate in online contests or quizzes, to accept tracking cookies, to participate in loyalty programmes, and to disclose personal data when signing up for newsletters. Post hoc analysis confirmed the statistical significance of the verified intergroup differences for:

–   Subscribing to a newsletter in exchange for a discount (Figure 7.16).
–   Sharing data when participating in online competitions (Figure 7.17).
–   Setting up user accounts in online shops (Figure 7.18).

For the other controlled-for variables, the statistical differences were not significant ($p > 0.05$).

The majority of members of all of the latent classes did not share their data when signing up for newsletters. The smallest difference between 'yes' and 'no' responses was found in Latent Class 2 (susceptible and trusting; no 60%; yes 40%). In the case of disclosure of personal data when taking part in Internet competitions and promotions, it was only in Latent Class 2 (susceptible and trusting) that more people gave affirmative answers (56%) than negative answers. The differences across the classes, which were in the 10–20% range, were, however, comparatively slight.

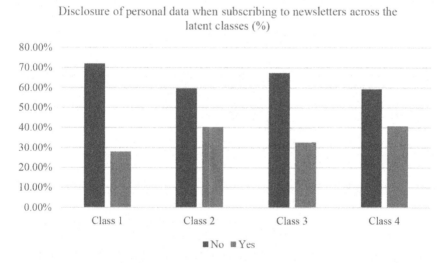

Figure 7.16 Disclosure of personal data when subscribing to newsletters across the four latent classes.

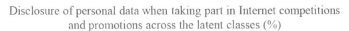
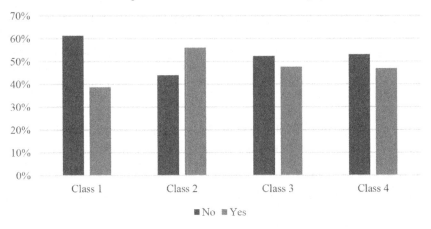

Figure 7.17 Disclosure of personal data when taking part in Internet competitions and promotions across the four latent classes.

Figure 7.18 Disclosure of personal data when creating user accounts in online shops across the four latent classes.

Although the intergroup differences were statistically significant, the distribution of responses to the question about willingness to share personal data when creating user accounts in online shops was similar and in the range 7–19%. Although the biggest differences were observed in Latent Class 2 (susceptible and trusting; yes 82%; no 18%), a proportion greater than 60% of respondents across all of the classes were willing to share their personal data when establishing accounts in online shops and were aware of doing so.

On the basis of the results, it was not possible to confirm Hypothesis H 1.6: *People who willingly share their personal data on the Internet are more susceptible to social proof.* The people most susceptible to social proof, those in Latent Class 2 (susceptible and trusting), displayed the greatest willingness to share their personal data, but the differences observed were small.

There is an important methodological observation to add to the substantive conclusions set out in the above discussion, which is that the very interpretation of the data obtained from survey responses may raise some doubts. They arise because, with reference to the specific situations the questionnaire asked about, we do not know whether respondents were consciously deciding to share their data or whether the data were in fact being 'intercepted'. Notwithstanding this reflection, though, the results of the LCA led to two important, empirically justified conclusions. First, the market behaviour of e-consumers is to a significant degree conditioned by social influence and especially by social proof. Second, e-consumers do not constitute a single, fully homogeneous segment, but do constitute a clearly differentiated group with regard to their susceptibility to social influence.

Summary

As a result of the statistical analysis, the adopted research hypotheses were verified. The results of the hypothesis testing are set out in Table 7.6.

The opinions of other Internet users have an incontrovertible impact on purchasing decisions. The respondents trust the recommendations of other Internet users and value their reliability highly. However, this is a complex phenomenon – not all e-consumers have the same level of susceptibility to social proof. To establish the determinants of these differences, we employed

Table 7.6 Summary of hypotheses tested in the CAWI survey ($N = 1,004$)

Hypothesis	Result of verification	Remarks
Hypothesis H.1.1: When making purchasing decisions, e-consumers are guided by the opinions of other Internet users	The hypothesis was confirmed	The opinions of other Internet users have a significant influence on purchasing decision, which was confirmed by a one-sample student's *t*-test. Women and those aged 25 and below are guided most by the opinions of other Internet users

(Continued)

Hypothesis	Result of verification	Remarks
Hypothesis H.1.2: There exist latent constructs of measurable characteristics that differentiate e-consumers in their susceptibility to social proof	The hypothesis was confirmed	Non-parametric tests of one-way analysis of variance (Kruskal-Wallis tests) showed the statistical significance of the differences between the four latent classes studied ($p < 0.5$)
Hypothesis H.1.3: There is a positive correlation between time spent on the Internet and susceptibility to social proof	The hypothesis was confirmed	Frequency of Internet use significantly differentiates respondents in terms of their susceptibility to social proof
Hypothesis H.1.4: People who use the Internet for professional purposes are less susceptible to social proof	The hypothesis was not confirmed	In fact, respondents in Latent Class 2 (susceptible and trusting) were the most frequent users of the Internet for professional purposes. It should be stressed, though, that the respondents' actual jobs or professions were not controlled for and the survey relied only upon a general declaration of Internet use for professional purposes
Hypothesis H.1.5: There is a relationship between positive attitudes to online advertising and the degree of susceptibility to social proof	The hypothesis was confirmed	There is a distinct relationship between positive attitudes to online advertising and the degree of susceptibility to social proof
Hypothesis H.1.6: People who willingly share their personal data on the Internet are more susceptible to social proof	The hypothesis was not confirmed	It is impossible to verify Hypothesis H.1.6 conclusively based on the results obtained. The people most susceptible to social proof, those in Latent Class 2 (susceptible and trusting), display the greatest willingness to share their personal data, but the observed differences are small

LCA, which allowed us to separate four groups of respondents with different levels of susceptibility or 'sensitivity' to social proof. A series of post hoc tests found that there were significant variations between the representatives of the four latent classes in terms of age, gender, frequency of Internet and social media use, and attitudes to advertising.

References

Anderson, T. W. (1959). *Some scaling methods and estimation procedures in the Latent Class Model, Probability and Statistics.* New York: John Wiley & Sons.

Collins, L., & Lanza, S. (2010). *Latent class and latent transition analysis: With applications in the social, behavioral, and health sciences.* Hoboken, NJ: John Wiley & Sons.

Dey, A., Mukherjee, D., & Roy, S. S. (2020). Modelling the influence of social network with a multiple group latent class analysis. *The Journal of Mathematical Sociology.* doi:10.1080/0022250X.2020.1821199.

Goodman, L. A. (1974). Exploratory latent structure analysis using both identifiable and unidentifiable models. *Biometrika, 61*(2), pp. 215–231.

Lazarsfeld, P. F. (1950). *The interpretation and mathematical foundation of Latent Class Structure Analysis, Measurement and Prediction.* Princeton, NJ: Princeton University Press.

Lazarsfeld, P. F. (1959). *Latent structure analysis. Psychology: A Study of a Science.* New York: McGraw-Hill.

Linzer, D. A., and Lewis, J. B. (2011). poLCA: An R package for polytomous variable latent class analysis. *Journal of Statistical Software, 41*, pp. 10–29.

Linzer, D. A., & Lewis, J. (2013). *poLCA: Polytomous variable latent class analysis. R package version 1.4* (accessed on: 10.02.2021) http://dlinzer.github.com/poLCA.

Sanak-Kosmowska, K., & Wiktor, J. W. (2020). Empirical identification of latent classes in the assessment of information asymmetry and manipulation in online advertising. *Sustainability, 12*(20), p. 8693. https://doi.org/10.3390/su12208693.

Sundie, J., Cialdini, R., Griskevicius, V., & Kenrick, D. (2012). The world's (truly) oldest profession: Social influence in evolutionary perspective. *Social Influence, 7*, pp. 134–153. doi:10.1080/15534510.2011.649890.

8 Characteristics of indicators of social proof based on experimental research

Introduction

Chapter 8 presents the results of research into social proof conducted on the basis of experiments carried out in the Internet environment in January 2021. Their objective was to verify research hypotheses relating to two categories of variables: the participants' individual differences and features of marketing messages that use social proof. Three experiments were performed: two in Polish and a third in English on an international research sample. The first part of this chapter describes their methodological assumptions and procedures, while the second contains a discussion of the findings and the results of testing the research hypotheses.

Experimental studies were chosen as the second of the two main research methods on substantive and technical grounds. They are useful when randomization is necessary and the purpose of the study is to understand cause-effect relationships (cf. Martin & Sell 1979; Karpińska-Krakowiak 2018). Conducting experiments online makes it possible to recruit a comparatively large group of participants, while retaining the capacity to monitor their behaviour. Moreover, it is the most favoured approach in the field of communication studies, where 65% of the research projects published in 2011–2015 in the four marketing journals with the highest impact factor (*Journal of Advertising, International Journal of Advertising, Journal of Advertising Research, Journal of Current Issues and Research in Advertising*) were based on experimental methods (Chang 2017).

The results of the survey research, which appear in Chapter 7, made it possible to capture the essence of the phenomenon of susceptibility to social proof and to comprehend the role of other Internet users' reviews and recommendations in the process of making purchasing decisions. By applying latent class analysis, it was possible to describe the e-consumers most susceptible to social proof at the level of their behaviour, that is, at the level of their Internet preferences, attitudes to the Internet, ways in which they use the Internet, and their susceptibility to social proof. The experimental research described in this chapter builds on this by making it possible to

DOI: 10.4324/9781003128052-10

analyse the determinants of the effects of social proof also at the level of individual differences.

Methodology and participants

A series of three online experiments were carried out – two in Polish and one in English – in order to verify Hypotheses H.2.1–H.2.6 (see Chapter 6). They were conducted on the basis of a classic one-factor experimental design, in which the experimental group was exposed to graphical material about a product or service that contained elements of social proof. The control group was exposed to graphical material about the same product or service, but with the elements of social proof removed. Evaluation of the product or service, willingness to test it, and willingness to recommend it to friends were the dependent variables, while personality traits, level of self-esteem, and susceptibility to social influence were treated as moderating variables. The experiments differed in terms of the materials manipulated in each of them. The materials related to different products and services and were published on a variety of social media (Instagram, Tripadvisor, Facebook).

The pilot studies and the materials manipulated in them

The experiments proper were conducted in January 2021. They were preceded by two pilot studies:

1 Pilot study one, which was conducted in order to verify the research tool used ($N = 50$; research conducted in December 2020 on a purposively selected group of e-consumers).
2 Pilot study two, which tested the visual materials to be manipulated in the experiments ($N = 80$; research conducted in December 2020 on a purposively selected group of fourth- and fifth-year students at the Faculty of Marketing and Communication of the Cracow University of Economics).

The pairs of visual materials that scored highest on the social proof visualization scale in pilot study two were used in the experiments proper. The participants' responses in pilot study one and pilot study two were taken into account when preparing the final version of the questionnaire that accompanied the experiment.

Selection of the product categories, which began with an analysis of an IAB (Interactive Advertising Bureau) report on the best-selling product categories on social media (Cyberclick 2019), was an important part of the preparation for the experiments proper. The products were selected, and the questionnaire designed, by the author.

The research proper was conducted using SurveyMonkey software, which makes it possible to conduct randomized surveys. In the question variant of its A/B test, participants are randomly assigned to a control group or to an experimental group.

The participants' demographic characteristics

Participants were recruited through social networks sites and purposive sampling was employed to select samples for Experiments I, II, and III. This method of recruitment was preferred because people aged 18–35 were overrepresented in the group. However, as people aged 18–35 are overrepresented in the overall, worldwide population of social media users, this was an intentional manipulation.

The participants' demographic characteristics are displayed in Table 8.1.

The course of the experiments

The invitation to take part in the research was posted on Facebook. It gave a neutral statement about the general aims of the research and its academic nature, while also offering basic information about procedure and duration. Prospective participants were also assured that they would remain anonymous and that the results would be used for academic purposes only. The participants were not warned that they would be taking part in an experiment and did not know whether they would be assigned to the experimental or control group. They were also unaware that they would be exposed to experimental manipulations.

Those recruited for the experiments were first asked to complete a two-part questionnaire. In the first part, respondents were asked how they use social media, how often they shop online, and how credible and reliable they

Table 8.1 The demographic characteristics of the participants in the experimental research

Experiment	Gender of participants	Age of participants
Experiment I (N = 102) Language of experiment: Polish	77 women (76%) 24 men (24%)	18–25 years – 52 people (51%) 26–35 years – 11 people (11%) 36–45 years – 22 people (21%) 46–55 years – 5 people (5%) 56–65 years –11 people (11%) Above 66 years – 1 person (1%)
Experiment II (N = 95) Language of experiment: Polish	30 women (32%) 65 men (24%)	18–25 years – 66 people (69%) 26–35 years – 16 people (17%) 36–45 years – 11 people (12%) 46–55 years – 2 people (2%)
Experiment III (N = 104) Language of experiment: English	55 women (53%) 46 men (44%) 3 people chose not to disclose their gender	18–25 years – 78 people (75%) 26–35 years – 26 people (25%)

find online opinions. In the second part, they answered ten questions from the Ten-Item Personality Inventory (TIPI) before being randomly assigned to one of the test groups. The experimental group was asked to look at graphical material – a screenshot of a post in a typical social media format – containing elements of social proof. The control group read the same post – but with the elements of social proof removed. All of the respondents then completed a questionnaire related to the product they had been exposed to. They were asked to assess the quality of the product and its perceived popularity and to state whether they were willing to try it out and recommend it to friends. They were also asked to rate it on a scale of 1–5. A series of questions drawn from Morris Rosenberg's Self-Esteem Scale (SES) and the Social Influence Susceptibility Scale made up the questionnaire's final element. Masking questions, which were used to camouflage the study's actual purpose, and questions for monitoring manipulation quality and detecting confounding variables were also included in the questionnaire. It should be stressed that only the responses of those participants with no previous experience of using the brand were analysed. The average time taken to complete the questionnaire was ten minutes.

Manipulated variables and dependent variables

The experimental procedure employed three types of manipulated (independent) variables, which are described in Table 8.2. The manipulation in Experiment I was a message devised by the author about cosmetics and published on Instagram (Figure 8.1); in Experiment II it was a recommendation of an anonymous restaurant from Tripadvisor (Figure 8.2); and in Experiment III it was a day trip to the Wieliczka Salt Mine offered by the firm MrShuttle from Facebook (Figure 8.3). MrShuttle gave permission for the image to be used in the study. To control the manipulation quality and variables, all of the posts were created by the author and designed in Photoshop for the purposes of the experiments. None of the materials used revealed the brand names or their distinguishing characteristics. Nevertheless, participants who said that they had prior knowledge of a brand were excluded from the sample. As stated above, the content seen by the control and experimental groups related to the same products, but only the experimental groups saw content containing elements of social proof. The posts shown to the experimental groups presented a higher number of reviews, higher ratings, a greater number of shares, a greater number of comments, and features such as the best-seller badge/logo and excerpts from reviews.

The average exposure time to the manipulated variables was approximately five seconds in all of the experiments. However, the research procedure did not assume any limits to exposure time, which meant that the duration of exposure depended solely on the participants. After selecting the 'next page' option, participants were shown a questionnaire measuring the dependent variables. In it, they were asked to make a global assessment

A

B

Figure 8.1 Variables manipulated in Experiment I: A – control group; B – experimental group.

A

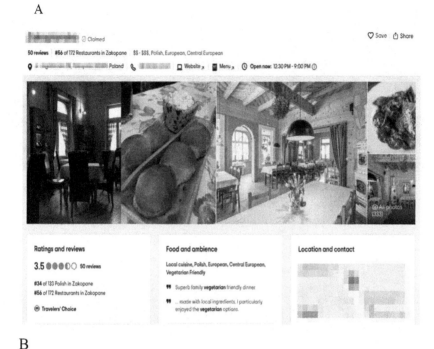

B

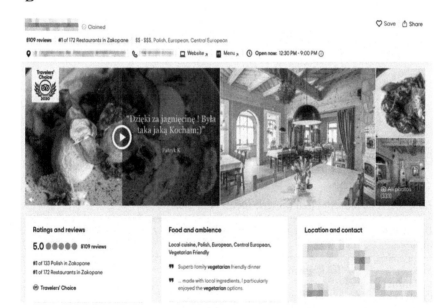

Figure 8.2 Variables manipulated in Experiment II: **A** – control group; **B** – experimental group.

A   B

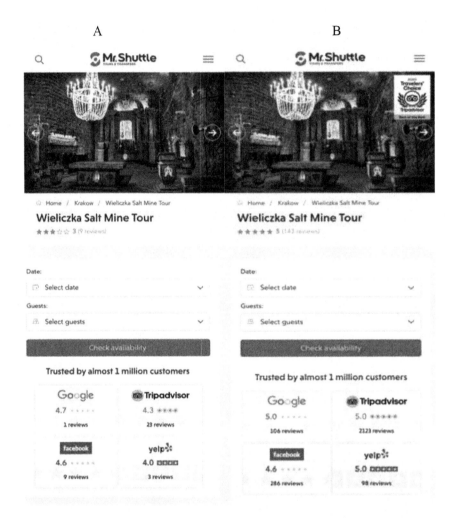

Figure 8.3 Variables manipulated in Experiment III: A – control group; B – experimental group.

Table 8.2 The manipulated (independent) variables

Description of variables	Experiment I	Experiment II	Experiment III
Message channel	Instagram	Tripadvisor	Facebook
Product category	Cosmetics	Restaurant	Day trip
Form of social proof	– Number of comments – Number of recommendations – 'Best-seller' badge/ logo	– Number of stars – Number of reviews – Use of extract from user review	– Number of ratings – Number of stars – Number of shares

of the product presented and to rate it in specific categories. Having reached this page, none of the respondents decided to return to the previous page of the survey and look again at the content associated with the product.

Measurement of moderating variables

The theoretical model assumed that it would also be possible to distinguish variables related to the psychological characteristics of the respondents among the determinants of susceptibility to social proof. Therefore, this series of experiments controlled for variables related to personality, self-esteem, and generalized susceptibility to social influence. The following subsection describes the research tools used to measure them. They were as follows:

- The abbreviated TIPI.
- Rosenberg's SES.
- The Social Influence Susceptibility Scale.

The Ten-Item Personality Inventory

Of the concise methods for measuring the Big Five personality traits (neuroticism versus emotional stability, extroversion, conscientiousness, openness to experience, and agreeableness; Costa & McCrae 1992), the TIPI (Gosling et al. 2003) is the most popular. It was selected for use in the study for its hypothetical, relatively high accuracy and reliability, and on the practical grounds of its brevity: it takes approximately two minutes to complete. Each of its ten statements begins with the words, 'I see myself as' and is completed by a pair of adjectives. For example, 'I see myself as: extroverted, enthusiastic'. The participants were asked to respond to each of these self-descriptions on a seven-point Likert scale, where one means strongly disagree and seven means strongly agree. The terms used in the test were derived from existing methods of measuring the Big Five factors. The Polish adaptation of TIPI by Agnieszka Sorokowska and her team (Sorokowska et al. 2014) was used for Experiments I and II, while Experiment III used an English version (Gosling et al. 2003).

Table 8.3 sets out the dimensions for the measurement of personality constructs along with their corresponding questionnaire indicators.

Rosenberg's SES

A standardized measurement tool, Morris Rosenberg's SES (1965), was employed to investigate the participants' levels of self-esteem. The SES is a single-item instrument that assesses the global level of self-esteem, which is a relatively stable disposition understood as a conscious positive or negative attitude towards the self. The SES, which consists of ten diagnostic statements, asks respondents to indicate the extent to which they agree with

Table 8.3 Measurement of personality constructs based on TIPI (Gosling et al. 2003)

Dimension (factor)	Questionnaire indicator
Extroversion	1 Extroverted, enthusiastic
	2 Reserved, quiet
Agreeableness	1 Sympathetic, warm
	2 Critical, quarrelsome
Conscientiousness	1 Dependable, self-disciplined
	2 Disorganized, careless
Neuroticism*	1 Anxious, easily upset
	2 Calm, emotionally stable
Intellect (openness)	1 Open to new experiences, complex
	2 Conventional, uncreative

* This is a reverse-scored item, so that a high score on the neuroticism scale denotes emotional stability

each of them on a four-point scale. It is highly reliable (the Cronbach's alpha coefficients for the various age groups are in the 0.81–0.83 range). Assessed by the test-retest method, its long-term stability index is 0.50 for measurements taken with a one-year interval, while for measurements taken with a one-week interval it is 0.83. In the course of the Polish adaptation, numerous data were collected on the theoretical accuracy of the tool, such as the results of exploratory and confirmatory factor analysis and correlations of SES with questionnaires measuring various constructs, such as narcissistic personality, temperament, locus of control, optimism, basic hope, social competence, and shyness (Łaguna et al. 2008). The Polish adaptation of the test by Mariola Dzwonkowska et al. (2008) was employed for Experiments I and II, while Experiment III, which was conducted on an international group, employed the English language version by Morris Rosenberg (1965).

Social Influence Susceptibility Scale

Of the research tools for measuring susceptibility to social influence introduced in Chapter 4, the research documented in the present chapter employs the Persuadability Inventory (PI) elaborated by Marc Busch et al. (2013) and the Susceptibility to Persuasive Strategies scale (STPS) devised by Maurits Kaptein and his colleagues (2012). Measurement of susceptibility to social influence was achieved with the aid of ten questionnaire indicators assembled as a construct that corresponds with susceptibility to social influence. In this instance, the participants in the experiments were asked to indicate the extent to which they concurred with statements about social influence on a five-point Likert scale. The instruments used to measure susceptibility to social influence are presented in Table 8.4.

Table 8.4 Instruments measuring susceptibility to social influence (Busch et al. 2013; Kaptein et al. 2012)

Instruments measuring susceptibility to social influence	*Questionnaire indicators*
Construct 1: Social learning	I often adapt my way of thinking to that of other people
	I ask for other people's opinions before taking a decision
	I quickly adapt my behaviour to that of other people
Construct 2: Social proof	I often rely on other people's opinions
	To align myself with others is important to me
	Being like other people is important to me
Construct 3: Social comparison	It is important to know what other people think of me
	I dress in the same way as my friends
	It is important to know what other people are doing
	I like to compare myself with others

Discussion of the results

In the first part of the study, participants in all of the experiments were asked to complete a brief questionnaire. It was made up of diagnostic questions to enable analysis of the following areas:

– Frequency of use of social network sites.
– The reliability of opinions published on the Internet.
– The influence of reviews and recommendations on purchasing decisions.

Modes and frequency of social media use

The first question, which was a screening question, asked participants whether they used social media and, if so, how often. Those who indicated that they did not use social media at all were disqualified from taking part in the experiments. The detailed distribution of responses is shown in Table 8.5.

In all three experiments, participants who logged on to social network sites almost all of the time (Experiments I and II) and several times a day (Experiment III) predominated, which demonstrates that they are overwhelmingly people who use social media sites regularly and intensively. Across all three samples, only one person said that they use social network sites only once a week. It should be noted that the responses of the three individuals in Experiment I who stated that they did not use social network sites at all were excluded from further analysis.

Table 8.5 Frequency of social media use: distribution of responses

Response to the question 'How often do you use the Internet?'	Experiment I	Experiment II	Experiment III
I am online almost all of the time	6 (65%)	58 (61%)	37 (35%)
Several times a day	29 (28%)	33 (35%)	59 (57%)
Once every day	1 (1 %)	2 (2%)	8 (8%)
Several times a week	1 (1%)	2 (2%)	0 (0%)
Once a week	5 (5%)	0 (0%)	0 (0%)
Several times a month	0 (0%)	0 (0%)	0 (0%)
I do not use sites or services of this kind	0 (0%)	0 (0%)	0 (0%)
Population of group	N = 102	N = 95	N = 104

The reliability and credibility of opinions published on the Internet

From the point of view of the aims of this monograph, it was important to learn about the factors that influence e-consumers' purchasing decisions. In all three experiments, price and opinions about products published on the Internet, including those of influencers, were the most frequently indicated criteria (Figure 8.4). There was no difference here in the responses of the participants in the international experiment and the participants of the experiments conducted in Polish.

Participants were also asked to identify the most reliable sources of opinions and reviews found on the Internet. Their responses were again consistent across all three experiments.

Opinions from price comparison sites were regarded as the least credible (the mean score across all three experiments was 3 on a scale of 1–7), while the opinions of other Internet users (mean score of 5) and of friends published on social media (mean score of 4.5) were seen as the most credible. Lower scores on the credibility scale were given to celebrity reviews in the international sample (mean score of 4) when compared with the two Polish ones (mean score of 5).

The influence of reviews and recommendations on purchasing decisions

The third research problem was to identify the importance of reviews in the purchasing process. In this connection, participants were asked to state whether they had ever made a purchase under the influence of the reviews and recommendations of other Internet users. The distribution of responses for the three experiments is presented in Figure 8.5. Although 'rarely' or 'very rarely' were the dominant responses across all three samples, it is worth noting that every fifth person surveyed in Experiment I said that they made purchases influenced by reviews or recommendations 'often' or 'very often'.

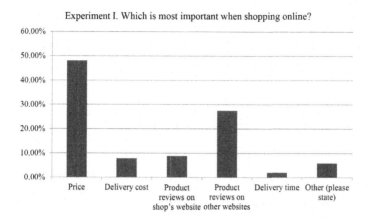

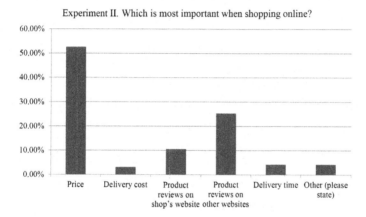

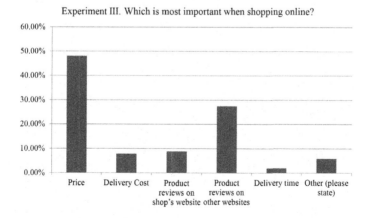

Figure 8.4 Factors influencing e-consumers' purchasing decisions (Experiments I–III).

Summarizing the above considerations, it can be stated that the participants use social media with a similar frequency and that they are primarily guided by price in their online purchasing. Nevertheless, opinions published on the Internet, of which those of other Internet users and friends are considered the most reliable, are also an important selection criterion. With the

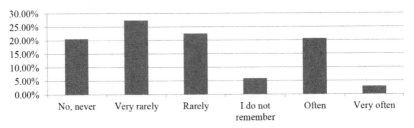

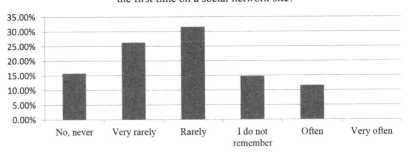

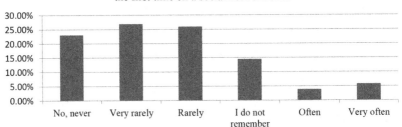

Figure 8.5 Purchases made under the influence of online reviews and recommendations (Experiments I–III).

exception of those in Experiment I, the majority of participants are rarely influenced in their purchases by online recommendations. In cognitive terms, and in terms of the overall research objectives of this book, these are important results.

Social proof as an aspect of marketing communication for brands: the e-consumer perspective

The remainder of this chapter sets out the results of the verification of the research hypotheses, which are covered in detail in Chapter 6. The results obtained in each individual experiment (Experiments I, II, and III) are presented for each of the hypotheses verified.

Hypothesis 2.1: Marketing messages based on social proof have a powerful influence on positive product evaluation

Beginning with the responses given by the participants in Experiment I (Figure 8.6), which reflected subjective evaluations of cosmetics presented in a manipulated marketing message on Instagram, product assessments expressed by study participants were analysed to verify research Hypothesis H.2.1. The distribution of responses for the control group ($N = 51$) and the experimental group ($N = 51$) is shown in the figure. The participants in the experimental group rated the product more highly than those randomly assigned to the control group. The statistical significance of the variation observed was confirmed using the non-parametric, two-sample Mann-Whitney test ($p < 0.01$).

In Experiment I, participants randomly assigned to the experimental group rated the attractiveness of the cosmetics presented in the manipulated variable higher (ratings of 4 or 5) than those in the control group. Here, the differences between the responses of the two groups were statistically significant (Mann-Whitney test: $p < 0.05$). The participants in the experimental

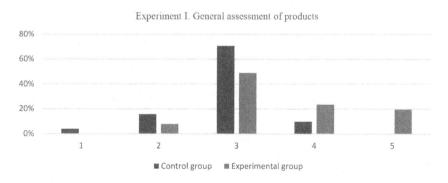

Figure 8.6 General assessment of products in Experiment I (control group vs experimental group). The assessments are expressed on a scale of 1–5, where 1 is the lowest and 5 is the highest.

group declared a greater willingness to try the product when compared to those in the control group (Mann-Whitney test: $p < 0.05$) and rated more highly the quality and perceived popularity of the cosmetics amongst the general public ($p < 0.05$).

In Experiment II, in which the manipulated variable was a restaurant review published on Tripadvisor, the overall ratings of the product expressed by participants assigned to the control group ($N = 46$) and the experimental ($N = 49$) group also varied. The distribution of responses is shown in Figure 8.7. The statistical significance of the variation observed was confirmed using the non-parametric, two-sample Mann-Whitney test ($p < 0.05$).

In Experiment II, the participants randomly assigned to the experimental group rated the attractiveness of the restaurant offer, which included elements of social proof (Table 8.2), significantly higher than did the control group. The variations in the responses of the two groups were once more statistically significant (Mann-Whitney test: $p < 0.05$). Compared to those in the control group, participants from the experimental group also reported a greater desire to visit the restaurant (Mann-Whitney test: $p < 0.05$) and rated the quality of the restaurant higher ($p < 0.05$).

The manipulated variable in Experiment III was an advertisement for a day trip published on Facebook. As in Experiments I and II, the participants randomly assigned to the experimental group ($N = 60$) rated the offer that highlighted the reviews and opinions of other Internet users higher. The Mann-Whitney test ($p < 0.02$) confirmed the statistical significance of the observed variation. The distribution of responses is displayed in Figure 8.8. Where the day trip was concerned, those in the experimental group were more willing to take advantage of the offer and rated more highly its quality and the perceived number of customers of the firm organizing it (Mann-Whitney test: $p < 0.05$).

The results support research Hypothesis H.2.1, which is fully confirmed: marketing messages containing elements of social proof, such as positive opinions, ratings, or reviews, have a highly positive influence on global

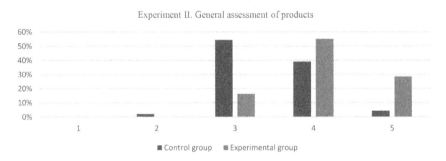

Figure 8.7 General assessment of products in Experiment II (control group vs experimental group). The assessments are expressed on a scale of 1–5, where 1 is the lowest and 5 is the highest.

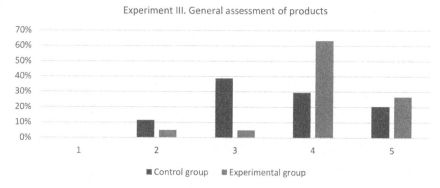

Figure 8.8 General assessment of products in Experiment III (control group vs experimental group). The assessments are expressed on a scale of 1–5, where 1 is the lowest and 5 is the highest.

product evaluation and the effect applies to all of the investigated product categories: cosmetics, restaurants, and day trips. It should be noted that none of the participants declared any prior knowledge of the products and services presented. Their global evaluation of the product was therefore based solely on a few seconds of exposure to the stimulus. The presence in the message of elements presenting other Internet users' opinions thus had a significant influence on the initial impression of, and general feeling about, the displayed offer. With the research objectives in mind, this clear confirmation of the examined hypothesis demonstrates the importance of aspects of social proof in marketing communication conducted in the social media environment.

Hypothesis 2.2: Marketing messages based on social proof have a powerful influence on willingness to share opinions with friends

To verify research Hypothesis H.2.2, which concerns the willingness to share opinions about products or services with friends, we examined how the participants in the experimental groups and control groups answered this question and whether the variations in their answers were statistically significant (Table 8.6).

For Experiment I, in which cosmetics were the manipulated variable, intergroup variations were found to be statistically significant (Mann-Whitney test: $p < 0.05$).

The same relationship was observed for the results obtained in Experiment II and Experiment III. Here, the social proof effect was present for both the restaurant profile on Tripadvisor and the offer of a day trip on Facebook, which those in the experimental groups were more willing to recommend to their friends compared to those in the control groups, who saw

Table 8.6 Willingness to share opinions on products or services with other Internet users (Experiments I–III)

Experiment	Distribution of responses	Control group	Experimental group	Statistical significance (Mann-Whitney test)
I	Definitely no	10 (8.9%)	8 (7.8%)	p = 0.001
	No	28 (27.5%)	13 (12.7%)	
	I do not know	12 (11.8%)	13 (12.7%)	
	Yes	1 (1%)	8 (8.8%)	
	Definitely yes	0 (0%)	8 (8.8%)	
II	Definitely no	2 (2.1%)	1 (1%)	p = 0.005
	No	15 (15.8%)	3 (3.2%)	
	I do not know	21 (22.1%)	24 (25.3%)	
	Yes	7 (7.4%)	15 (15.8%)	
	Definitely yes	1(1%)	6 (6.3%)	
III	Definitely no	0 (0%)	0 (0%)	p = 0.002
	No	8 (7.7%)	0 (0%)	
	I do not know	19 (18.3%)	34 (32.7%)	
	Yes	8 (7.7%)	39 (37.5%)	
	Definitely yes	9 (8.7%)	23 (22.1%)	

neutral messages, that is, messages without reviews, ratings, and recommendations. The statistical significance of the observed variation was confirmed by Mann-Whitney tests ($p < 0.05$ for both Experiment I and Experiment II).

The results of this analysis confirmed Hypothesis H.2.2, which posits that exposure to marketing messages based on social proof has a positive influence on willingness to share opinions about them with other Internet users. This relationship was detected for all of the products investigated.

The role of moderating variables, which in this case were personality traits and self-esteem, was tested in an extension to the verification of research Hypothesis H.2.2. It was assumed that individuals displaying higher levels of extroversion, intellect, and agreeableness would be more likely to recommend products to friends than those with lower levels of these traits (Figure 8.9). In the case of self-esteem, it was postulated that the correlation might be negative. Given the variation in the types of products functioning as the manipulated variable, a decision was made to test the examined relationship across all three experiments.

To this end, the correlations between the moderating variables and willingness to recommend a product or service to other users were tested in all three experimental groups. Spearman's rank correlation coefficient test was employed for the analysis. The results are displayed in Table 8.7. It was only in Experiment I – for extroversion ($R = -0.51$), agreeableness (-0.51), and self-esteem (-0.43) – that any of the moderating variables proved significant. Contrary to expectations, participants with higher levels of extroversion and agreeableness shown a marketing message based on social proof were less likely to recommend it to friends than those who scored lower on these scales. This effect was observed only for the manipulation involving

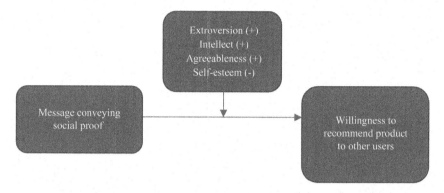

Figure 8.9 Theoretical model of the role of moderating variables in the relationship between exposure to a message conveying social proof and willingness to share product opinions with other users.

Table 8.7 Spearman's rank correlation coefficient values for the variable specifying willingness to recommend products to friends

Experiment	Extroversion	Intellect	Agreeableness	Self-esteem
Experiment I	−0.51	−0.27	−0.51	−0.43
Experiment II	0.14	−0.04	0.02	0.12
Experiment III	−0.01	0.17	0.18	−0.03

cosmetics on Instagram. The result obtained for self-esteem confirmed the research thesis: the higher the level of self-esteem, the lower the willingness to recommend products to others. Figure 8.10 presents the distribution of median scores for the responses relating to the moderating variables for the results obtained in Experiment I (experimental group).

It can be concluded from the data presented in Figure 8.10 that personality traits and self-esteem influenced willingness to recommend products to other users in the case of a marketing message about cosmetics published on Instagram. The investigated relationships proved statistically insignificant for the services investigated in Experiment II and Experiment III. This might lead us to think that the product category – and cosmetics belong to a specific one – is of particular importance. If so, there are two implications. First, cosmetic brands make frequent and intense use of social media for their marketing communications. Second, cosmetics advertisements are closely associated with appearance and self-presentation, so that the motivation for sharing information about them might be slightly different than in the case of services. Moreover, given that 76% of the participants in

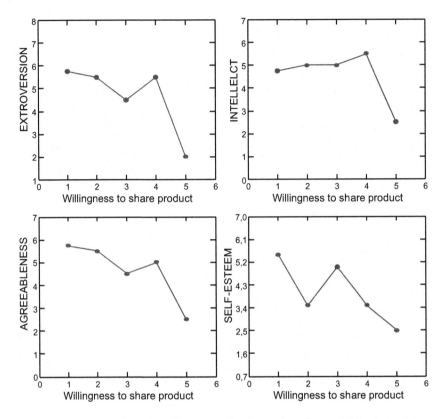

Figure 8.10 Distribution of median scores for the moderating variables (experimental group, Experiment I).

Experiment I were women, the results should also be interpreted with reference to the sample's demographic characteristics.

Personality, self-esteem, and susceptibility to social proof

Hypotheses H.2.3–H.2.5, which assume the existence of relationships between various personality traits and susceptibility to social proof, were verified in the next stage of the research.

Hypothesis 2.3: The lower an e-consumer's score on the intellect scale, the higher their susceptibility to social proof

Hypothesis 2.4: The higher an e-consumer's score on the agreeableness scale, the higher their susceptibility to social proof

Hypothesis 2.5: The higher an e-consumer's score on the neuroticism scale, the higher their susceptibility to social proof

Correlations between individual personality traits and overall product evaluations were investigated to verify the research hypotheses assuming the interdependence of personality traits and susceptibility to social proof. For participants randomly assigned to experimental groups, it was posited that overall product ratings communicated on social media using social proof would correlate significantly with the personality traits studied. The investigations were performed with the aid of the Kruskal-Wallis test, which is a non-parametric alternative to one-way analysis of variance. The statistical significance of the relationships tested are displayed in Table 8.8.

Only in Experiment I did the tested relationships prove significant; they were statistically insignificant in the other two. In Experiment I, the examined relationships proved statistically significant for all of the personality traits controlled for: intellect, neuroticism, agreeableness, and extroversion ($p < 0.1$). Though statistical trends were detected in Experiment III for agreeableness and extroversion ($p > 0.1$), the remaining relationships between variables proved statistically insignificant. Spearman's rank correlation coefficient test was then applied to the variables showing statistical significance. This procedure made it possible to determine the following directions of correlation:

Experiment I

- For intellect, the correlation coefficient was (−0.29).
- For agreeableness (−0.44).
- For neuroticism (−0.34; not statistically significant).
- For extroversion (−0.49).

Experiment III

- For agreeableness, the correlation coefficient was (0.3).
- For extroversion (0.1).

The most powerful correlation in Experiment I was thus between the extroversion and agreeableness of a participant and susceptibility to social proof. Contrary to expectations, the observed correlations were negative, that is, individuals with lower levels of agreeableness and extroversion rated the product as more attractive (Figure 8.11).

Table 8.8 Statistical significance of relationships between personality traits and susceptibility to social proof (Kruskal-Wallis test)

Experiment	Intellect	Agreeableness	Neuroticism	Extroversion
Experiment I	0.01	0.02	0.07	0.001
Experiment II	$p > 0.1$	$p > 0.1$	$p > 0.1$	$p > 0.1$
Experiment III	$p > 0.1$	0.07	$p > 0.1$	0.06

Spearman's rank correlation coefficient test did not confirm the statistical significance of the correlations tested in Experiment III.

The results of the analyses indicate a clear rejection of Hypotheses H.2.3–H.2.5: other than in Experiment I, where the manipulated variable concerned cosmetics, no effect of personality traits on susceptibility to social proof was detected. It should be noted, however, that the observed relationship was the opposite of what had been assumed – all the examined correlations turned out to be negative. Introverts, that is, those with lower scores on the extroversion scale, rated the cosmetics they were shown more highly than those with higher scores on that scale. Similarly, those with lower scores on the agreeableness scale gave the tested product higher ratings.

Hypothesis 2.6: The lower an e-consumer's self-esteem, the lower their susceptibility to social proof

A statistical analysis based on the Kruskal-Wallis test was conducted to verify research Hypothesis H.2.6, which posits a negative correlation between the level of self-esteem and susceptibility to social proof – as the latter

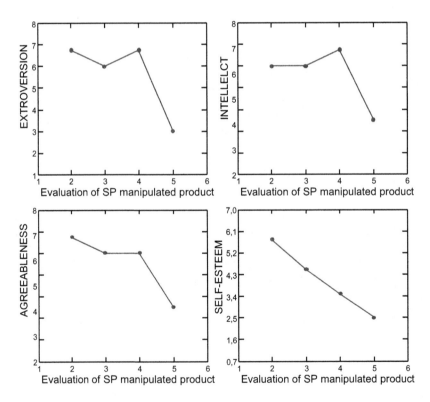

Figure 8.11 Personality traits versus overall product assessment (experimental group, Experiment I).

is expressed through evaluation of the product presented to the experimental group. The results for the three experiments are displayed in Table 8.9.

In Experiment I, the result was statistically significant and indicated a negative correlation between the level of self-esteem and susceptibility to manipulation, while for the other two experiments, the results of the test detected no statistical significance for this relationship. Research Hypothesis H.2.6 therefore depends on the product context and cannot be confirmed for all of the experimental samples. Only in Experiment I was a relationship between the level of self-esteem and susceptibility to social proof confirmed. Two tentative explanations are possible for this result. First, it is a matter of the product category and, second, in Experiment I, which involved cosmetics, there was a preponderance of women, who were found to be more susceptible to social proof than men.

The next relationship tested was that between the level of self-esteem and the overall level of susceptibility to social influence, which was also controlled for in the series of experiments described here. In this case, the responses of all participants in the study were analysed without dividing them into an experimental group and a control group. Furthermore, the variables studied were not manipulated (Table 8.10).

The results only partially confirmed the existence of correlations between participants' self-esteem and the overall level of susceptibility to social influence. A powerful negative correlation was observed in the experimental group in Experiment III for the social comparison construct (-0.55). The observed correlation is negative: the lower the self-esteem, the higher the susceptibility to social learning. Where susceptibility to social proof

Table 8.9 Statistical significance of the influence of self-esteem on a variable specifying overall evaluation of a product (Kruskal-Wallis test)

Experiment	Self-esteem
Experiment I	0.03
Experiment II	0.72
Experiment III	0.19

Table 8.10 Spearman's rank correlation coefficient values for three dimensions of a relationship between the level of self-esteem and overall susceptibility to social influence

Experiment	Social learning	Susceptibility to social proof	Social comparison
Experiment I	-0.21	-0.37	-0.31
Experiment II	-0.24	-0.11	-0.37
Experiment III	-0.68	-0.15	-0.55

is concerned, the results of Experiment I confirmed a low negative correlation (−0.37). Interestingly, the negative correlation for the propensity to social comparison dimension was significant across all three experimental samples: Experiment I (−0.31), Experiment II (−0.37), and Experiment III (−0.55).

The relationship between self-esteem and susceptibility to social influence may therefore be non-specific and complex. It can be stated that people with lower self-esteem are more sensitive to social proof messages, and that their perception of messages of this kind triggers comparisons with other people, e.g. in terms of physical appearance or attractiveness.

In this stage of research and analysis of the experimental results, statistical investigation of the distribution of responses tested the overall level of social influence – as expressed by the three research constructs analysed: social learning, susceptibility to social proof, and social comparison – to discover whether it is a moderating variable in the case of exposure to a marketing message containing social proof.

First, the internal consistency of the constructs tested was established for all three experiments and was found to be high in every case, which demonstrates that the individual constructs are correlated with each other: Cronbach's alpha coefficient was 0.780 for Experiment I, 0.561 for Experiment II, and 0.748 for Experiment III. The correlations between the individual constructs were also confirmed by Spearman's rank correlation coefficient.

Using robust linear regression, a check was then performed of the correlation between the level of susceptibility to social influence (as expressed in the three investigated constructs) and the overall evaluation of the product reported by the participants in the experimental groups. The R coefficient for Experiment I was 0.805, which indicates a strong linear regression between the studied variables. The parameters of this regression are displayed in detail in Table 8.11. In the context of these results, it is worth highlighting the particularly strong correlation of the social comparison construct: people who record high scores on this subscale rated the product communicated with the aid of social proof higher than those less susceptible to this

Table 8.11 Parameters of the linear regression for constructs of susceptibility to social influence (Experiment I)

Construct	Coefficient	Standard error	95% confidence interval	
			Lower	Upper
General level of susceptibility to social influence	0.752	0.451	−0.155	1.659
Social learning	−0.037	0.053	−0.143	0.068
Social proof	0.084	0.055	−0.026	0.195
Social comparison	0.203	0.031	0.141	0.265

type of social influence. In this case, the standard error was at the relatively low level of 0.031.

The *R* coefficient for Experiment II was 0.193 and the analysed regression explained only 3% of the observed co-variation, which means that it is not statistically significant. Regression analysis of the variables obtained in Experiment III led to similar conclusions. Here the *R* coefficient was also low (0.343) and the analysed regression explained only 17% of the co-variation observed. The investigated relationships therefore lack statistical significance.

Summary

By examining the results of the experiments it was possible to verify the adopted research hypotheses, which refer to the influence of social proof on purchasing decisions and to the role of personality traits and self-esteem in this process. The results of the analyses are set out in Table 8.12.

A number of conclusions can be formulated based on the verification of the research hypotheses and the statistical analyses. The most important of these are outlined below.

First, the category of the product shown to participants turned out to be an extremely important determinant of susceptibility to social proof. The effect on product evaluation was greatest in the experiment whose manipulated variable was a marketing message about cosmetics published on Instagram. In this case, moderating variables such as personality traits and self-esteem were also significant. Although this effect was present for the other products studied, the moderating variables played no significant role.

Second, in Experiment I, where the cosmetics message was the manipulated variable, there was a strong negative correlation between the level of extroversion, and product evaluation and willingness to recommend the product. It was assumed that – as in the case of offline marketing messages – extroverts would be more likely to play the role of 'marketing mavens' and therefore be willing to share information with others. The results of the experiments – which are best interpreted in the context of studies published in the literature (cf. Mooradian 1996; Steenkamp & Maydeu-Olivares 2015), even though there are comparatively few of them and their results are inconclusive (cf. Bowden-Green et al. 2020; Clark & Calli 2014) – were not consistent with the hypotheses. There is no doubt that further study is needed on the relationship between extroversion and the evaluation of products containing elements of social proof, where the decisive factors are probably brand, product category, and the content of reviews or opinions. That more than three-quarters of the participants in Experiment I were women (76%) is also not without significance. It was this group too which – more often than the other groups – reported making purchases on the recommendations of

Table 8.12 Verification of the hypotheses adopted in the experimental research

Hypothesis	Result of verification	Remarks
Hypothesis H.2.1: Marketing messages based on social proof have a powerful influence on positive product evaluation	The hypothesis was confirmed	Participants exposed to messages containing social proof rated products higher than those shown neutral messages. This effect held for all of the manipulated variables
Hypothesis H.2.2: Marketing messages based on social proof have a powerful influence on willingness to share opinions with friends	The hypothesis was confirmed	Participants exposed to messages containing social proof were more willing to recommend products to other users than those shown neutral messages. This effect held for all of the manipulated variables
Hypothesis H.2.3: The lower an e-consumer's score on the intellect scale, the higher their susceptibility to social proof	The hypothesis was rejected	The influence of intellect on susceptibility to social proof was significant only in Experiment I, where the correlation was negative
Hypothesis H.2.4: The higher an e-consumer's score on the agreeableness scale, the higher their susceptibility to social proof	The hypothesis was rejected	The influence of agreeableness on susceptibility to social proof was significant only in Experiment I, where the correlation was negative
Hypothesis H.2.5: The higher an e-consumer's score on the neuroticism scale, the higher their susceptibility to social proof	The hypothesis was rejected	The influence of neuroticism on susceptibility to social proof was not statistically significant in any of the experiments
Hypothesis H.2.6: The lower an e-consumer's self-esteem, the higher their susceptibility to social proof	The hypothesis was partially confirmed	The investigated relationship depends on the nature of the product; a relationship was confirmed in the case of cosmetics (Experiment I). The studied relationship carried no statistical significance in the case of Experiment II (restaurant) and Experiment III (day trip) The analyses confirmed a statistically significant relationship between the general level of susceptibility to social influence (in the dimension of social comparison) and self-esteem

other Internet users: 24% of respondents in this group declared they did this frequently or very frequently.

Third, with reference to the obtained results it is possible to outline the directions of further research on the issue of social proof in social media. An important and interesting area of investigation could be e-consumers' self-esteem and their susceptibility to social influence. Another could be the relationship between susceptibility to social comparison and low self-esteem that was observed in all of the experiments. Both are of considerable scholarly interest and have the potential to contribute to the development of interdisciplinary research on social influence in psychology, sociology, management, and marketing. Significant practical value can also be derived from research into these issues. They can be considered through the prism of firms/advertisers and Internet users/e-consumers. For firms, the findings can act as a resource for shaping effective marketing communication strategies in the online environment and, especially on social media, while to Internet users they can offer a framework for developing market knowledge about advertisers' online communication mechanisms and for raising levels of education, digital competence, and social skills, so that they grow more sensitive to the concealed persuasion and manipulation of advertising messages. Finally, the importance of research into the subject this book addresses – social proof and online buyer behaviour – is closely related to the ethics of marketing and advertising.

References

Bowden-Green, T., Hinds, J., & Joinson, A. (2020). How is extraversion related to social media use? A literature review. *Personality and Individual Differences, 164*, p. 110040. doi:10.1016/j.paid.2020.110040.

Busch, M., Schrammel, J., & Tscheligi, M. (2013), Personalized persuasive technology – Development and validation of scales for measuring persuadability. *International Conference on Persuasive Technology.* Berlin: Springer.

Chang, Ch. (2017). Methodological issues in advertising research: Current status, shifts, and trends. *Journal of Advertising, 46*(1), pp. 2–20, doi:10.1080/00913367.2016.1274924

Clark, L., & Calli, L. (2014). Personality types and Facebook advertising: An exploratory study. *Journal of Direct, Data and Digital Marketing Practice, 15*(4), pp. 327–336. https://doi.org/10.1057/dddmp.2014.25

Costa, P. T. Jr., & McCrae, R. R. (1992). *Revised NEO personality inventory (NEO-PI-R) and NEO five-factor inventory (NEOFFI) professional manual.* Odessa, FL: Psychological Assessment Resources.

Cyberclick. (2019). *The 7 best selling products on social media* (accessed on: 10.01.2021) https://www.cyberclick.net/numericalblogen/the-7-best-selling-products-on-social-media

Gosling, S. D., Rentfrow, P. J., & Swann, W. B., Jr. (2003), A very brief measure of the big five personality domains. *Journal of Research in Personality, 37,* pp. 504–528.

Kaptein, M., De Ruyter, B., Markopoulos, P., & Aarts, E. (2012). Adaptive persuasive systems: A study of tailored persuasive text messages to reduce snacking. *ACM Transactions on Interactive Intelligent Systems, 2*(2), pp. 1–25. http://doi.org/10.1145/2209310.2209313.

Karpińska-Krakowiak, M. (2018). *Kapitał marki w mediach społecznościowych. Perspektywa konsumenta.* Łódź: Wydawnictwo Uniwersytetu Łódzkiego.

Łaguna, M., Lachowicz-Tabaczek, K., & Dzwonkowska, I. (2007). Skala Samooceny SES Morrisa Rosenberga – polska adaptacja metody. *Psychologia Społeczna, 2*, pp. 164–176.

Martin, M., & Sell, J. (1979). The role of the experiment in the social sciences. *The Sociological Quarterly, 20*(4), pp. 581–590.

Mooradian, T. (1996). The five factor model and market mavenism. *Advances in Consumer Research, 23*, pp. 260–263.

Rosenberg, M. (1965). *Society and the adolescent self-image.* Princeton, NJ: Princeton University Press.

Sorokowska, A., Słowińska, A, Zbieg, A., & Sorokowski, P. (2014). *Polska Adaptacja Testu Ten Item Personality Inventory (TIPI) – TIPI-PL – wersja standardowa i internetowa.* Wrocław: WrocLab Uniwersytet Wrocławski.

Steenkamp, J. E. M., & Maydeu-Olivares, A. (2015). Stability and change in consumer traits: Evidence from a 12-year longitudinal study, 2002–2013. *Journal of Marketing Research, 52*(3), pp. 287–308.

9 Discussion of findings in a global context

Introduction

The following deliberations address the implications of the research in the context of the research objectives and methodological assumptions. On the one hand, they constitute an interpretation and discussion of the research results, and on the other they provide a platform for formulating further research directions on social proof in marketing communication in the international environment. The argumentation unfolds in three interrelated sections that address the study's main findings, the limitations of the empirical research, and the global context of research on social proof.

Implications of the empirical research

The aims of this monograph are examined in three dimensions: cognitive, empirical, and practical. The main objective in the cognitive dimension was to describe and identify the role and importance of social proof for decisions made by e-consumers in the social media environment.

The theoretical framework is derived from the subject literature and concerns four spheres of interest:

1 The nature, functions, and importance of online marketing and social media marketing and the reasons for their development.
2 The functions and mechanisms of online marketing tools.
3 The rationale and determinants of social influence, with particular reference to social proof.
4 The role and importance of social proof in online marketing communications and social commerce.

It proved possible through the theoretical investigations to reveal the category of social proof in a new research context: that of examining the mechanism and determinants of susceptibility to other Internet users' opinions about advertising in the virtual environment.

DOI: 10.4324/9781003128052-11

Although the research problem essentially sits within the field of management science, including marketing, the issues addressed are of an interdisciplinary nature, which explains the numerous references to disciplines such as sociology and psychology.

The book's primary aim is described in the Introduction, while the theoretical framework of the problem is expounded in Chapters 2–5. Chapter 6 sets out the aims of the research in detail and introduces the author's original research model.

The study is based on methodological triangulation, which is an approach that combines quantitative and qualitative research. The first stage involved a quantitative computer-assisted web interviewing (CAWI) survey of a representative sample of 1,004 Polish e-consumers, while three experiments conducted in the Internet environment, of which two were conducted in Polish and one in English on an international sample, made up the second stage.

A synthetic summary of the research is presented below in the form of the following conclusions:

The quantitative CAWI surveys of Polish e-consumers

1   When making purchasing decisions, e-consumers are guided by the opinions of Internet users. The opinions of other Internet users are a valuable source of information for 72% of respondents, who rate highly both the credibility of friends' opinions published on social media (70%) and the opinions of other Internet users (68%). However, only 36% of them gave a positive response to the opinions of bloggers and influencers, which they regarded as the least credible. An index of the influence of other Internet users, which was devised using factor analysis, permitted verification of research hypothesis H.1.1 – that the opinions of other Internet users have a significant impact on purchasing decisions – and confirmed the influence of social proof on consumer behaviour. Women (67%) are more likely to be guided by the opinions of other Internet users than men (61%) and those aged 25 or below (68%).

2   The latent class analysis confirmed that the e-consumers studied were differentiated in terms of latent constructs of measurable characteristics. In the course of the analysis, a four-class model of response distribution was extracted based on an analysis of their fit indices. The latent classes were then named and described. The dominant attitude of the respondents in Latent Class 1 (indifferent) is of moderate trust in the opinions found on the Internet, which is accompanied by a neutral attitude to online shopping and little confidence in the credibility of the opinions of bloggers and celebrities. The respondents in Latent Class 2 (susceptible and trusting) are very receptive to the opinions of other Internet users, including bloggers, influencers, and celebrities, while those in Latent Class 3 (vulnerable and cautious) like to shop online, place

a high value on the credibility of opinions and recommendations, but have little trust in bloggers and celebrities. Attitudes to online shopping and online reviews and recommendations among the respondents in Latent Class 4 (resistant) are negative.

3 The results of the post hoc tests confirmed a relationship between the frequency of Internet and social media use and susceptibility to social proof. Latent Class 2 (susceptible and trusting) was dominated by respondents who are logged on almost all of the time and can be described as heavy Internet users. It is worth noting that – contrary to initial expectations – those who use the Internet for work purposes are more susceptible to social proof than those who use it exclusively for private purposes.

4 The results confirmed the thesis that attitude to advertising is a significant determinant of susceptibility to social proof. A positive attitude to advertising prevailed among respondents in Latent Class 2 (susceptible and trusting) and Latent Class 3 (susceptible and cautious), who thought that it plays an important role in the process of making purchasing decisions.

Experimental research conducted in the online environment

1 Marketing messages based on social proof have a powerful influence on positive product evaluation. In all three experiments, the participants randomly assigned to experimental groups rated the products and services they were shown more highly than the representatives of the control groups. The manipulation in the experimental groups consisted of exposure to a marketing message containing elements of social proof, such as the reviews and opinions of other Internet users. Control group participants were exposed to the same messages, but with the elements of social proof removed. The strongest social proof effect was observed for messages about cosmetics. This fact can be interpreted more broadly in the following way: the type and category of the product or brand are important for the occurrence of the social proof effect. Clearly, though, great caution must be exercised in advancing this important and interesting conclusion, which invites further in-depth research.

2 The research confirmed the hypothesis that there is a powerful relationship between exposure to marketing messages containing social proof and willingness to recommend products to other Internet users. Despite no prior awareness of the brands shown to them, participants in the experimental groups showed a greater willingness to recommend products and services to friends than did participants in the control groups. This effect occurred in all the experiments performed and constitutes an important finding.

3 The research hypotheses concerning the influence of personality traits on purchasing decisions were rejected following the statistical analyses. This finding prompts two comments. First, in Experiment I, whose

manipulated variable was a marketing message about cosmetics, a statistically significant negative correlation was observed between scores on the intellect and agreeableness scales and susceptibility to social proof. In the other two experiments, the tested correlations proved to be insignificant, which means that it is possible to advance the tentative thesis that personality traits are an important or significant determinant of susceptibility to social proof when it concerns a specific product category. Second, it is worth noting that most of the previous research in this area has been done using only one message or one product (cf. Talib et al. 2017; Vashistha et al. 2018). Its conclusions may therefore be somewhat fragmentary and narrowly focused.

4   The research proceeded to investigate the influence of self-esteem on e-consumers' susceptibility to social proof. Here, again, the relationship studied was confirmed only in Experiment I. In Experiments II and III, it showed no statistical significance. However, it should be stressed that in all of the experiments the analysis confirmed a statistically significant relationship between the overall level of susceptibility to social influence (in the dimension of social comparison) and the self-esteem of the e-consumers studied. There is therefore reason to believe that people with lower levels of self-esteem are more susceptible to social proof when the content of the message triggers the mechanism of social comparison.

The presented research on the role of social proof in e-consumers' purchasing decisions also has practical implications. In the case of e-consumers, there are three key areas in which the research results can be applied.

First, they allow us to interpret the role and importance of social proof in the process of making purchasing decisions in the social media environment.

Second, they allow us to identify the determinants of susceptibility to social proof and to reveal the complexity and interchangeability of the factors determining that effect.

Third, they can offer a platform for acquiring market knowledge of online advertisers' communication mechanisms, for raising levels of education and honing digital and social competences, and for developing an awareness that will enable e-consumers to detect hidden persuasion and manipulation in advertising messages.

The research findings, which can offer a reference point for marketing communication specialists on how and to what extent to include social proof in brand communication strategies, have important implications for firms operating in the virtual environment.

Limitations of the empirical research

In the name of academic rigour, an important element of the research is to indicate its limitations. In this spirit, the principal limitations of the present study are specified below.

1   Limitations of the research sample:

– Although it was representative, the quantitative research presented in Chapter 7 was conducted in a single country, which was the result of the particular options available and the conditions in which the study was carried out. When designing future research, an international cross-section should be taken into account. Advertising is, after all, strongly culturally conditioned, and for this reason cross-cultural research is of great cognitive value. Such research makes it possible to determine the degree of similarity or variation in the influence of online advertising on e-consumers in culturally disparate countries, where the consumption and market behaviour of e-consumers is governed by different social and economic conditions.

– Although the qualitative research reported in Chapter 8 was conducted on a national (Polish) sample and on an international sample, nationality and cultural factors were not controlled for. It would be advisable when planning future research to (a) expand the research sample while controlling for nationality, (b) consider developing different language versions of the research tool and conducting studies in a number of different countries, and (c) include cultural variables, which are of great importance in the category of social influence, in the research model.

2   Limitations of the research model:

– The research construct used to identify latent variables in the quantitative study of e-consumers was adopted arbitrarily, based on the theoretical premises set out in Part I of the book. In subsequent studies, it would be worth considering a slightly more complex methodology or attempting to replicate the results to confirm the validity of the research model's assumptions.

– Detailed studies of individual differences and general susceptibility to social influence were absent from the quantitative research. To expand it to include these constructs would undoubtedly be of high cognitive value, but the survey would take longer, and that could place an excessive cognitive load on participants. This issue should be addressed in further research projects.

3   Limitations of methodology and procedure:

– The experimental research was conducted in an online environment, which is the 'specific' setting that was the correct choice from the point of view of the research methodology. However, it would be worth replicating the study in an auditorium setting – where the duration and conditions of exposure of the manipulated stimulus are identical for all participants.

– Only three product categories were represented by the manipulated variables in the three experiments. To confirm the observed effects, it would be necessary to expand the list of manipulated variables and, rather than social proof being either present or absent, to vary the intensity of the presence of social proof in the marketing messages presented.

Attention now turns to the possibilities for taking into account the international context of the research problem.

The global context of research on social proof

One of the primary drawbacks of social science research, which is subject to a number of limitations, is that it is conducted on relatively small samples, which represent only the residents of a selected country or a specific segment of a population, such as people within a single age range. What is more, the participants are often university and college students (Ferguson et al. 2004).

The research presented here attempts to capture the global context of the analyses in two ways. First, the quantitative research was preceded by an international pilot study conducted in English. The data thus obtained, though statistically insignificant due to the relatively small size of the samples studied, will serve as a starting point for designing quantitative international studies in the future. Second, one of the experiments was conducted in English on an international research sample and, as methodological rigour requires, the variation between this group and the two Polish groups was verified. The observed intergroup variation was exclusively concerned with the effects of manipulation, while variables such as frequency of social media use, assessment of the credibility of opinions and recommendations, or the influence of recommendations and reviews were similar for all samples studied. It should be noted, though, that the majority of participants in the study were young people aged 18–25. In the longer research perspective, it would be essential to extend the research to other age groups.

Any extended research model should also consider cultural factors, whose role and importance in social influence have been studied on many occasions in the subject literature (cf. Wosinska et al. 2014). An international study conducted by Robert Cialdini and his colleagues (Cialdini et al. 1999), who compared the susceptibility to social influence of Polish and American students, is particularly noteworthy in this regard. Because the two countries differ in individualistic-collectivistic orientation, which is one of the basic dimensions of culture, the choice of nationalities was not accidental (Hofstede 1980; Kim et al. 1994). Cialdini and his associates began with the assumption that the Polish students represented an individualistic orientation, whereas the American students represented a collectivistic one. And, indeed, the results confirmed the role of cultural differences: the rule of commitment and consistency had a greater impact on American students, while the Polish students were more susceptible to social proof. Therefore, it would be justified to repeat the research in an international setting to see if cultural differences also condition susceptibility to social proof in an online environment. It should be emphasized that an important aspect of conducting research in an international setting is maintaining the methodological rigour appropriate to that context. In particular, care needs to be taken to devise a repertoire of research tools that can take into account cultural factors at the linguistic, contextual, and symbolic levels. Here, matters are simplified by the use of research tools with standardized linguistic adaptations, such as the Ten-Item Personality Inventory and Rosenberg's Self-Esteem Scale, which are used in the present research. Undertaking research from these perspectives and in these dimensions will allow us to explore the global context of research into social influence, including social proof, and make it possible to identify its specific international and cross-cultural determinants.

References

Cialdini, R. B., Wosinska, W., Barrett D. W., Butner J., & Gornik-Durose B. (1999). Compliance with a request in two cultures: The differential influence of social proof and commitment/consistency on collectivists and individualists. *Personality and Social Psychology Bulletin, 25*, pp. 1242–1253.

Ferguson, L. M., Yonge, O., & Myrick, F. (2004). Students' involvement in faculty research: Ethical and methodological issues. *International Journal of Qualitative Methods, 3*(4). http://www.ualberta.ca/~iiqm/backissues/3_4/html/ferguson.html.

Hofstede, G. (1980). Culture and organizations. *International Studies of Management & Organization, 10*(4), pp. 15–41, doi:10.1080/00208825.1980.11656300

Kim, U., Triandis, H. C., Kâğitçibaşi, Ç., Choi, S.-C., & Yoon, G. (Eds.). (1994). *Cross-cultural research and methodology series, Vol. 18. Individualism and collectivism: Theory, method, and applications.* New York: Sage Publications, Inc.

Talib, A., Yakimin, Y., & Mat Saat, R. (2017). Social proof in social media shopping: An experimental design research. *SHS Web of Conferences, 34*(2). doi:10.1051/shsconf/20173402005.

Vashistha, A., Okeke, F., Anderson, R., & Dell, N. (2018). 'You Can Always Do Better!': The Impact of Social Proof on Participant Response Bias. *CHI '18: Proceedings of the 2018 CHI Conference on Human Factors in Computing Systems*, Montréal, Canada, April 2018, Paper No. 552, pp. 1–13. doi: 10.1145/3173574.3174126.

Wosinska, W., Cialdini, R. B., Barrett, D. W., & Reykowski, J. (2014). *The practice of social influence in multiple cultures.* New York: Routledge.

10 Summary

The aim of this book has been to assess the role of social proof in the process whereby e-consumers make purchasing decisions and to understand and pinpoint the determinants of Internet users' susceptibility to social proof. The reasons for framing the aim in this way are twofold. The first concerns the sweeping advances made in the sphere of technology, which have refashioned patterns of purchasing so that the virtual environment, and in particular the Internet, has become not only a place to search for information about products, but also a place where e-consumers can buy them. The second reason refers to our knowledge of the cognitive processes underlying e-consumers' purchasing decisions, which, in scientific terms, remains slight. Nevertheless, modern consumer behaviour is no longer examined or understood solely in terms of rationality (Kahneman 2011) or the conscious mind (Mlodinov 2012), but also in terms of emotionality (Mruk 2017; Ohme 2017) and the unconscious. This monograph assumes that the importance of, and susceptibility to, the particular type of social influence that social proof is should be considered from a multi-level and interdisciplinary perspective that takes account of various levels of analysis of e-consumers' behaviour and does not omit their individual psychological characteristics.

In Part 1, the category of social proof was adopted as a key element of the book's theoretical framework, to which five chapters are devoted. The introduction sets out its objectives in detail, while Chapter 2 defines online marketing and social media marketing within the context of social proof and online buyer behaviour. Chapter 3, meanwhile, describes and analyses selected tools and strategies of online marketing. Particular attention is paid to the social influence strategies used by firms, such as e-word-of-mouth, buzz marketing, influencer marketing, and celebrity endorsement. Chapter 4 reviews selected basic concepts of social influence in psychology and sociology. Here, the primary focus is on the models of social influence and principles of persuasion proposed by Robert Cialdini. An important part of the chapter is a review of research on the determinants of susceptibility to social influence. Chapter 5 offers a characterization of the book's central idea – social proof, which constitutes a special case of social influence. A detailed

DOI: 10.4324/9781003128052-12

analysis of the forms of social proof – as they operate in the context of marketing communication in the social media environment – is undertaken.

The results of the empirical research are presented in Part II. Chapter 6 relates the construction of the research model and the theoretical justification of the hypotheses, while Chapter 7 and Chapter 8 discuss and portray the results of the research, which was conducted according to the combination of quantitative and qualitative approaches known as methodological triangulation. The quantitative research covers a representative sample of Polish e-consumers ($N = 1,004$), while the qualitative research, which was carried out in the form of three experiments, includes an international group (Polish participants $N = 197$; international participants $N = 104$). The research hypotheses are confirmed, partially confirmed, or rejected following a detailed analysis of the results. The key findings of the study, its limitations, and the prospects for further research, including within a global context, are presented in Chapter 9.

The principal findings are as follows. First, e-consumers trust opinions and recommendations expressed by other Internet users, including influencers and bloggers, and regard them as an important source of information when making purchasing decisions. The opinions of friends published on social media and those of other 'average Internet users' enjoy particular trust. The latent class analysis and the results of the experiments confirmed the hypothesized variation in e-consumers' levels of susceptibility to social influence. It was possible on the basis of the statistical analyses to formulate the two most important conclusions. First, susceptibility to social influence is conditioned by many factors that moderate each other and thus strengthen or weaken their significance. The influence of demographic, behavioural, and psychographic determinants was confirmed (Table 10.1).

In the case of demographic characteristics, it should be noted that their statistical significance was confirmed only in Experiment I, in which the manipulated variable was cosmetics. This observation led to a second important conclusion. The results establish that susceptibility to social proof depends not only on the individual characteristics of e-consumers, but also on the product category. The tentative thesis can therefore be advanced that it is the product category communicated with the aid of social proof that determines which personality traits will affect susceptibility. This phenomenon, which is known in psychology as 'priming', may be related not only to self-esteem, but also to self-image or to an emotional reaction to the stimulus exposed in the message. These relationships may be verified in further, planned research on social proof.

The research problem this book addresses is consonant with current research in the field of marketing, but also sociology and social psychology. To take an interdisciplinary view of e-consumer behaviour and susceptibility to social proof in online marketing communication has a number of benefits. First, it represents a contribution to the development of research on the category of social influence, including social proof. Second, it is conducive

Table 10.1 Determinants of susceptibility to social proof in the online environment

Category of determinant	Influence on susceptibility to social proof
Demographics	The research results indicate that women, and young people aged 18–25, are more susceptible to social proof
Behavioural traits	The following have an influence on social proof: – frequency of social media and Internet use (+) – degree of professionalization of Internet use (+) – frequency of online purchases (+) – attitudes to Internet advertising (+)
Experiment III ($N = 104$) Psychographic features	– extroversion (−) – agreeableness (−) – self-esteem (−)

to increasing the effectiveness and efficiency of marketing communication strategies in the social media environment. Third, it raises social awareness and fosters multidimensional social, educational, and normative action, including the formulation of legal regulations governing advertisers' use of social proof as a form of covert persuasion and manipulation of e-consumer behaviour.

References

Kahneman, D. (2011). *Thinking fast, thinking slow.* New York: Farrar, Straus and Giroux.
Mlodinov, L. (2012). *Subliminal: How your unconscious mind rules your behavior.* New York: Pantheon.
Mruk, H. (2017). Zachowania konsumentów w świetle ekonomii behawioralnej, *Studia Ekonomiczne. Zeszyty Naukowe Uniwersytetu Ekonomicznego w Katowicach, 317*, pp. 82–95.
Ohme, R. (2017). *Emo Sapiens. Harmonia emocji i rozumu.* Ożarów Mazowiecki: Bukowy Las.

Index

Note: **Bold** page numbers refer to tables and *italic* page numbers refer to figures.

Abbassi, Zeinab 60
Academia 35
Adjective Check List (ACL) 71
advertising: ethics and social proof 2; pull strategy of 9; push strategy of 9; and social influence 51–53; *see also* marketing
Advertising Standards Authority 39
Ajzen, Icek 20
Akerlof, George 15
Alan, Alev Koçak 109
Allport, Gordon Willard 52
Amazon 19, 37, 85, 88, 89
Amblee, Naveen 108
Amichai-Hamburger, Yair 70
Amiel, Tel 69
Anderson, Theodore 118
Aral, Sinan 60
Arrow, Sarah 38
Asch, Solomon 53–54
AT&T 9
attitudes: to online advertising 128–130; to online purchases 128–130
authority: formal 64; real 64; and social influence 63–64

Babik, Wiesław 24
Bandura, Albert 65
banner advertisement 9
Bergagna, Elisa 72, 109
Big Five model 68–69, **69**
Blackshaw, Pete 15
Bornman, Hester 9
Boyd, Danah 16
Brand24 87
brands: cosmetic 153; social proof as aspect of marketing communication for 149–154

Brandwatch 87
Brehm, Jack 64, 67
Broadcasting Act 39
Bui, Tung 108
Busch, Marc 73, 144
buying decisions and social proof 112–135
buzz marketing 34, 41–42

Cacioppo, John 21
Campbell, Jennifer 54–55
CAWI *see* computer-assisted web interviewing
celebrity endorsement 44–45
Chaiken, Shelly 22
Chen, Runyu 89
Chen, Serena 22
Cialdini, Robert 13, 51, 66, 168, 170; principle of authority 63–64; principle of commitment and consistency 62–63; principle of liking and sympathy 63; principle of reciprocity 61–62; principle of scarcity 64–65; principles of social influence 61–65
Cohen, Arthur 71
Collins, Linda 118
commitment and social influence 62–63
Committee of Advertising Practice 39
communication: goals 23; marketing 7, 15–16, 23; online marketing 9; and social media 15
computer-assisted web interviewing (CAWI) 3, 104–105, 109, 114; quantitative CAWI surveys of Polish e-consumers 164–165; summary of hypotheses tested in **133–134**
consistency and social influence 62–63
consumer behaviour 12–13; models of **13**

Correa, Teresa 69
Costa, Paul 70
credibility of opinions on the
  Internet 146

Dann, Steven 8
Dann, Susan 8
dark psychology 19
Deng, Xiaolong 89
dependent variables 139–143; referring
  to social proof **120**
Deutsch, Morton 53–54, 66
DICE 56
differentiation: in e-consumers'
  susceptibility to social influence
  117–133; internal 105; patterns of
  e-consumer 105–106
digital environment: social proof in
  83–88; types of social proof-based
  messages in **85**
digitization 7–15; history 7–8; Internet
  marketing 8
Dobele, Angela 43–44
Dubrovsky, Vitaly 57
Durgee, Jeffrey 72
Dwass-Steel-Critchlow-Fligner test
  120, 122

e-commerce: growth of 12; importance
  of 8; traditional 92
e-commerce 1.0 and social commerce *92*
e-consumers 112–114; attitudes to online
  advertising 128–130; attitudes to
  online purchases 128–130; behaviour
  2; communication between firms and
  101–102; demographic description of
  respondents 122–124; differentiation
  in susceptibility to social influence
  119–122; frequency of Internet
  use 124–125; and LCA 117–119;
  personality and susceptibility to social
  influence 68–71; Polish 33–34, 164–
  165; professionalization of Internet
  use 126–127; purchasing-decision
  path *14*; selected tools for managing
  reviews and feedback **87**; use of social
  network sites 124–125; willingness to
  share personal data online 131–133
elaboration likelihood model (ELM)
  20, 21
electronic word-of-mouth (eWOM)
  marketing 34, 35, 39–41; role in
  building customer relationships 45–46,
  46; types of reviews 40–41

Ellison, Nicole 16
e-marketing: techniques 31; tools 3, 31;
  see also online marketing
emo sapiens 1
empirical research: experimental
  research conducted in online
  environment 165–166; implications
  of 163–166; limitations of 166–168;
  limitations of methodology and
  procedure 167–168; limitations of
  research model 167; limitations of
  research sample 167; quantitative
  CAWI surveys of Polish e-consumers
  164–165
European Parliament 89
European Union (EU): Member States
  91; New Deal for Consumers 89
experimental research 107–109;
  characteristics of indicators of social
  proof based on 136–161; conducted
  in online environment 165–166;
  verification of hypotheses adopted in
  160

Facebook 60, 68, 72, 84, 93, 108,
  114, 137
Facebook Marketplace 92
Fairey, Patricia 54–55
fake reviews as unfair business practice
  88–91
Festinger, Leon 54, 67
Financial Times 89
firms: comments in communication
  between e-consumers and 101–102;
  reviews in communication between
  e-consumers and 101–102
Fishbein, Martin 20
Floyd, Kristopher 40

Gerard, Harold 53–54, 66
Gibbons, Henning 83
Gladwell, Malcolm 36–37
global context of research on social
  proof 168–169
Goodman, Leo 118
Goods-and-Information Acquisition
  (GIA) 106
Google 12, 38
Gregory, Larry 62

Haenlein, Michael 16–17
heuristic processing 22
heuristic-systematic model (HSM) 20,
  21–23

Hofer, Doris 108
Hoffman, Donna 9
Hollingshead, Andrea 57
homo oeconomicus 1
Hootsuite 87
Hughes, David 108
hypermedia 9–10; communication model
  10, 10–11

IAB (Interactive Advertising Bureau)
  report 137
identity of social commerce 91–94
indicators of social proof:
  characteristics based on experimental
  research 136–161; course of the
  experiments 138–145; credibility of
  opinions published on Internet 146;
  manipulated variables and dependent
  variables 139–143; measurement
  of moderating variables 143;
  methodology and participants 137–
  138; modes and frequency of social
  media use 145–146; participants'
  demographic characteristics 138;
  personality 154–159; pilot studies
  and materials manipulated 137–138;
  purchasing decisions 146–149;
  reliability of opinions published on
  Internet 146; reviews and purchasing
  decisions 146–149; Rosenberg's
  SES 144; self-esteem 154–159;
  Social Influence Susceptibility Scale
  144–145; social proof as marketing
  communication for brands 149–154;
  susceptibility to social proof 154–159;
  Ten-Item Personality Inventory
  143, **144**
influence marketing 30, 33, 35
influencer(s): classification criteria
  and key characteristics of **36**;
  communication with e-consumers *37*;
  defined **35**; macro 38–39; micro 38;
  referent 38; types of 36
information: manipulation 24; overload
  24–25
Instagram 68, 93, 137
International Conference on Data
  Mining 88
International Journal of Advertising 136
Internet: credibility of opinions
  published on 146; reliability of
  opinions published on 146
Internet marketing 8; *see also* online
  marketing

Internet use: frequency and degree
  of professionalization of 126–127;
  frequency of 124–125
Internet users: active 38; average 38, 46;
  behaviour of 52; construction of an
  index of influence of **116**; ordinary 37;
  Polish 113–114; skills of 11

Jindal, Nitin 88
Journal of Advertising 136
Journal of Advertising Research 136
*Journal of Current Issues and Research in
  Advertising* 136

Kabadayi, Ebru Tümer 109
Kaplan, Andreas 16–17
Kaptein, Maurits 66, 73, 144
Karpinska-Krakowiak, Malgorzata 18
Kennedy, Patricia 73
Kotler, Philip 44
Kruskal-Wallis test 155, 156, 157

Lanza, Stephanie 118
Latané, Bibb 55
latent class analysis (LCA) 112;
  description and grounds for use
  117–119; verifying research model
  using 119–122
latent classes: characteristics of **121–122**;
  distribution of participants' gender
  and age across four *123*; frequency
  of Facebook use across the four *125*;
  frequency of Instagram use across
  the four *125*; frequency of Internet
  use across the four *124*; graphical
  illustration of a model of *121*
Lazarsfeld, Paul 118
Lewis, Jeffrey 119
liking and social influence 63
Linzer, Drew 119
Liu, Bing 88

macro-influencers 38–39
manipulated variables 139–143, **142**
manipulation: forms of 23–24;
  information 24; at linguistic level 24;
  perpetrators of 23; *vs.* persuasion 25;
  in physical field 24; in social media
  19–25
Mann-Whitney tests 149–152
manus pellere 23
Marchand, June 107
marketing: buzz 34, 41–42; evolution
  of *14*; eWOM 34, 35, 39–41, 45–46;

old *vs.* new principles of 11, **12**; recommendation 34; social influence 34–39; social media 15–19; T-shape 30–31, *31*; viral 42–44; word-of-mouth marketing 16; *see also* advertising
Marketing 2.0 14
Marketing 5.0 14
marketing-centred research 2
marketing communication 7, 15–16, 23; strategies **32**
Martin, Mary 73
Marx, Gary 57
Matzler, Kurt 69
Mayzlin, Dina 41
McCracken, Grant 44
McCrae, Robert 70
McElroy, James 70
McKinsey 12
McQuail, Denis 17, 18, **18**
Mendel, Tamir 107
'messy middle' model 40
micro-influencers 38
Milgram, Stanley 64
moderating variables 143
modes of social media use 145–146
Modic, David 73
Mooradian, Todd A. 69
Moore, Kelly 70
Moussaid, Mehdi 65
Muehling, Darrel 107
Mullen, Brian 56
Munzel, Andreas 41

nature of social commerce 91–94
Nazzaro, Mike 15
NEO Five-Factor Inventory (NEO-FFI 2004) 70
'new media': *vs.* traditional content publishing **11**
Nitzschner, Marco 70
normative conformity 54
Novak, Thomas 9

Office of Competition and Consumer Protection (UOKiK) 91
online advertising: attitudes to 128–130; and online purchasing process 115
online environment: determinants of susceptibility to social proof in **172**; development of 52; experimental research conducted in 165–166
online marketing 7–25; communication 9; defined 8; digitization 7–15; methods, taxonomy of 30–34; overview 7; tools **9, 32,** *33,* 33–34; *see also* marketing

online purchases, attitudes to 128–130
online reviews, categories of *86*
online social influence 56–61
Other-Total Ratio (OTR) model 51, 56
Oyibo, Kiemute 65, 108

Penrod, Steven 51, 56
personality 154–159
personality traits 70
Persuadability Inventory (PI) 73, 144
persuasion: *vs.* manipulation 25; models of 20–23; in social media 19–25
Petty, Richard 21
The Picture of Dorian Gray (Wilde) 1
PMR Consulting 113
Polish e-consumers: characteristics of **113–114**; quantitative CAWI surveys of 164–165
Pool, Gregory 72
Pornsakulvanich, Vikanda 70
Pratkanis, Anthony 51
Pride, William 8
product information searches and social proof 115–117
product ratings: categories of *86*; and personality traits 155
professionalization of Internet use 126–127
psychological reactance 67
psychology: dark 19; social 52
pull strategy, of advertising 9
purchasing decisions: influence of reviews and recommendations on 146–149; and social proof 115–117
push strategy, of advertising 9

quantitative CAWI surveys 105–107; of Polish e-consumers 164–165

Rayport, Jeffrey 43
reactance theory 64
reciprocity and social influence 61–62
recommendation marketing 34
referent influencers 38
Rein, Irving 44
reliability of opinions published on Internet 146
Rennie, Alistair 12
Reputology 87
research: experimental 107–109; hypotheses 104–105
research model: grounds for construction of 101–102; and hypotheses 104–105; and objectives 101–109
Revised NEO Personality Inventory (NEO-PI-R 1992) 70

Rosen, Emanual 39
Rosenberg, Morris 71; Self-Esteem Scale (SES) 139, 143, 144, 169

Sargent, Stephanie Lee 69
scarcity, and social influence 64–65
Schnuerch, Robert 83
Schouten, Alexander 44–45
Scott, David 11
Seegers, Daphne 108
Seidman, Gwendolyn 109
self-esteem 154–159; described 71; and social influence 71–73
Shiller, Robert 15
social commerce: most important features of **93**; nature and identity of 91–94; selected proposals for definition of **91**; social proof as a key factor in 83–95
social comparison 66
social exposure, and behaviour 67–68
social impact 2–3
Social Impact Theory 55
social influence 1; Cialdini's principles of 61–65; differentiation in e-consumers' susceptibility to 119–122; e-consumer personality and susceptibility to 68–71; history of 53–55; importance, in contemporary advertising 51–53; instruments measuring susceptibility to **145**; marketing 34–39; models of 55–56; online 56–61; and self-esteem 71–73; strategies of 65–66; ways of measuring susceptibility to 73–74; *see also* influence marketing; influencer(s)
Social Influence Model (SIM) 51, 56
Social Influence Susceptibility Scale 139, 144–145
Social Influence Theory (SIT) 51, 55
social learning 65
social media (SM) 7; and communication 15; defined 16; gratifications categories 17, 18, **18**; honeycomb model *16*; marketing 15–19; model of susceptibility to social proof on *103*; persuasion and manipulation in 19–25; theoretical approach to model of susceptibility in 102–104
social media marketing 3, 34, 51, 56, 94, 163, 170
social media use: frequency of **146**; modes and frequency of 145–146
social network sites (SNS): marketing communication on 7, 15–16; use of 124–125

social proof 1; and advertising ethics 2; as aspect of marketing communication for brands 149–154; and cognitive level 1; confidence in 112–135; defined 83; dependent variables referring to **120**; determinants of susceptibility in online environment **172**; in digital environment 83–88; e-consumers 112–114; e-consumers' susceptibility to social influence 117–133; and empirical level 2; fake reviews as unfair business practice 88–91; global context of research on 168–169; impact on buying decisions 112–135; as key factor in social commerce 83–95; and marketing ethics 2; models of LCA adapted to variables referring to **120**; nature and identity of social commerce 91–94; overview 65–66; and product information searches 115–117; and purchasing decisions 115–117; research methodology and scope 114–115; and social media 102–104; as a special case of social influence 66–67; susceptibility to 154–159
social proof-based messages **85**
social psychology 52
Socio-Affective Regulation (SAR) 106
von Solms, S. H. 9
Sorokowska, Agnieszka 143
Stewart, David 30
Stöckli, Sabrina 108
Stoller, Martin 44
Structured Interview for the Five-Factor Model of Personality (SIFFM) 70
SurveyMonkey software 137
Susceptibility to Persuasion-II 73
Susceptibility to Persuasive Strategies scale (STPS) 73, 144
Swan, K. Scott 69
sympathy and social influence 63
systematic processing 22

Tanford, Sarah 51, 56
Tartaglia, Stefano 72, 109
technology acceptance model (TAM) 12
Ten-Item Personality Inventory (TIPI) 139, 143, **144**, 169; measurement of personality constructs based on **144**
terminological chaos 16
theory of reasoned action (TRA) 20
Toch, Eran 107
Tripadvisor 84, 102, 137, 150, 151
Trull, Timothy 70
T-shape marketing 30–31, *31*

Turban, Efraim 93
Twitter 17, 60

unfair business practice, fake reviews as
    88–91
United States Federal Trade
    Commission (FTC) 39
user-generated content (UGC) 14–15;
    and modern businesses 15

variables: dependent 139–143;
    manipulated 139–143; moderating 143
Vassileva, Julita 65, 108
Vermeulen, Ivar 108
Vinitzky, Gideon 70
viral marketing 42–44; communication
    model of *43*; defined 42; *see also*
    marketing
Vogel, Erin 72

Walczyk, Paulina 38
Walker, Dylan 60
Walther, Joseph 58

Web 1.0 57
Web 2.0 15, 52, 57, 58–59, **59,** 84, 94, 101
Web 2.0-based sites 102
Web 4.0 57
Web 5.0 52, 101
Wehrli, Stefan 70
Weisband, Suzanne 57
Weiser, Eric 106
Widiger, Thomas 70
Wilde, Oscar 1
Williams, Emma 104
Wood, Wendy 67
word-of-mouth marketing (WOM)
    16, 39
Word-of-Mouth Marketing Association
    (WOMMA) 42
World Wide Web 7–8, 9–10, 56–57, 103,
    114; Marketing 2.0 13; and UGC 15

YouTube 108, 114

Zhang, Dongsong 89
Zimbard, Philip 71

Printed in the United States
by Baker & Taylor Publisher Services